Book Reviews

Excerpts from letters sent by readers from all over the world

"My experiences with workshops held by self-named masters of the Toltec discipline were comical and entirely useless. I am grateful beyond words that amongst these frauds a true practitioner of the Warrior's discipline remains. Although he refuses to be known as anything other than a Warrior, I will say that I have found a teacher in don Jesus."

-Kevin Wilkinson, Civil Engineer, Vancouver, Canada

"Shockingly awakening! *Escape from Texas* provides Seekers with a roadmap to follow. Don Jesus guides and encourages us to find our own path to freedom by taking action. A Warrior's knowledge and true liberation from a hurtful past cannot be inherited or shared with anyone. We must earn freedom ourselves, and we must do it alone. Thanks to don Jesus, we now know what to do, we just have to do it!"

-Elizabeth Stafford, M.D., Palo Alto, California

"Don Jesus does it again! In this heroic autobiographical tale he demonstrates a true mastery of storytelling, while illuminating the path towards knowledge. Ancient Toltec wisdom has never before been translated in such an accurate and practical manner. Seekers need only follow his example to find the spiritual freedom he speaks of."

-Desmond Archer, Author, San Francisco, California

"As a Native Tejano whose ancestors fought alongside Davy Crockett and Jim Bowie within the walls of the Alamo, I have longed for a genuine Warrior to appear. Without apology or reservation, don Jesus strips away the shallow veneer of so-called 'race relations' in America, particularly in Texas. As a retired teacher and perpetual student of history, I have been sickened and dismayed at the blatant omissions of Tejano accomplishments to Tejas history. Thanks to don Jesus, thousands of bigots will be turning over in their graves, as a new generation learns what it means to be Tejano, while simultaneously learning how to be a Warrior."

-Gabriel Esperanza, Retired Teacher, San Antonio, Texas

"I spent eight years in prison as a member of a major white supremacist gang. For safety reasons I've chosen to not share its name. Although it's been years since I learned I was lied to and brainwashed about the myth of white supremacy, *Escape from Texas* reopened my eyes and gave me a deeper understanding. I saw the true impact this cycle of hate has on the culprit and the victim. In realizing the harm I helped perpetuate upon my fellowman, I was consumed with regret and self-loathing. If don Jesus were an average man he would have left me with my pain, but instead showed me how to live like a Warrior. Thanks to him, I too can escape from Texas, and my painful past. I may be the only Anglo person who refuses to be called White, and just wants to be known as a human being."

-Scott Freeman, Electrician, Dallas, Texas

"*Escape from Texas* demonstrates why lies repeated over generations become accepted as 'truth.' The veil of self-deceit has been removed, exposing the cost of government approved racism. Native Tejanos have found a genuine hero in don Jesus."

-Richard A. Steinberg, Ph.D., Durham, North Carolina

"Reading *Escape from Texas* was like listening to a story someone had written about my life. My childhood was very similar to that of don Jesus, and prior to finding his work I never believed it possible to find true happiness. He accurately articulated so many of the emotions and opinions I had locked up inside, but didn't know how to express, even to myself. Although I physically left home so long ago, I am just beginning my spiritual escape from Louisiana. As don Jesus says, 'We all start where we are.' Thank you, don Jesus."

-Virginia Holloway, Retired Nurse, Cleveland, Ohio

Escape from Texas
Journey Out of the Abyss

Also by don Jesus M. Ramirez

Sorcerer's Secrets, Book 1
Translated Secrets of Carlos Castaneda

Sorcerer's Secrets, Book 2
A Modern Guide to Ancient Toltec Wisdom

Escape from Texas, Book 1
Born into Darkness

Sorcerer's Disagreements, Book 1
Searching for Nirvana

Sorcerer's Disagreements, Book 2
Tearing the Thin Veneer

Sorcerer's Disagreements, Book 3
A Facade of Freedom

Sorcerer's Disagreements, Book 4
A Warrior's Greatest Challenge

Escape from Texas
Journey Out of the Abyss

Book 2
Don Jesus M. Ramirez

Edited by Christopher Kiyosaki
Cover designed by Angel Valadez

Copyright © 2013
All rights reserved

In accordance with the U.S. Copyright Act of 1976, no part of this publication may be reproduced or stored in a retrieval system, or transmitted in any form or by any means, electronic, mechanical, photocopying, recording, or otherwise, without the prior written consent of the author. For information regarding permissions, contact Toltec Institute.

Toltec Institute
PO Box 6552
San Jose, CA 95150
www.toltecinstitute.com
info@toltecinstitute.com

The author is not responsible for websites (or their content) that are not owned by the author.

ISBN 978-1-939163-10-3

Disclaimer

This work addresses highly controversial subject matter. The majority of the names, places, dates, and identifying characteristics have been changed to protect the innocent and not antagonize the guilty. In addition, many of the illustrations, examples, and events described within this work have either been altered or are fictitious. Any similarity to real persons, living or dead, is coincidental and not intended by the author. The content found within this work is the sole expression and opinion of the author, created with the intention of providing information. No warranties or guarantees are expressed or implied, and no part of this work is intended as a substitute for the medical or psychological advice of physicians. Neither the publisher nor the author offer any type of psychological, legal, or any other such professional advice, nor shall they be liable for physical, psychological, emotional, financial, or commercial damages, including, but not limited to, special, incidental, or consequential damages. This work is distributed with the understanding that the publisher and author suggest extreme caution. You are responsible for your own choices, actions, and results.

Cover Artwork
Designed by: Angel Valadez

During the crusades thousands of knights traveled to the Holy Land seeking their fortune, and a few their salvation. The few who sought a cleansing of their souls did so earnestly, swearing celibacy and devotion to Christianity. Having sworn fidelity, they contemplated upon the skulls of dead saints and religious relics, considering themselves already dead. These warrior monks swore to be fearless before their enemies, honest and upright. They spoke only truth, protected their king, and swore to safeguard the helpless, even if it meant their death. The image of the hooded monk skull symbolizes a Warrior's awareness of his death. Death then becomes his greatest motivator, ally, and adviser. The cover artwork was selected and designed to convey our awareness and sense of urgency.

Dedication

For my grandfather, Jesus M. Ramirez
A hero of the Mexican Revolution

An unforeseeable series of events led to my grandfather becoming an unwilling participant of the Mexican Revolution. While traveling to México City, the train on which he was a passenger was attacked and captured by Pancho Villa's forces. When soldiers confiscated the horses he was transporting, he protested against the injustice. His actions were interpreted as bravery, and as such opportunity found him in the form of an ultimatum. He was invited to enlist in the famous División del Norte, or face a firing squad upon his refusal. With no alternative he reluctantly joined the rebellion. As a man of action, he accepted his fate, acknowledging there was no turning back. He earnestly played out his role and via his deeds advanced to the rank of officer, becoming a recognized and trusted companion of the General.

Contents

	A Warrior's Aloneness	I
Introduction	Knowing Where You Are	1
Chapter One	The Evil One Lives	3
Chapter Two	No One Forgets Nothing	34
Chapter Three	No Tejano Football Heroes Wanted	72
Chapter Four	The Golden Gloves Champion	96
Chapter Five	California Dreaming	109
Chapter Six	Blues and the Blue Techniques	127
Chapter Seven	The Knife Fighter	163
Chapter Eight	Accidental Gunfighter	187
Chapter Nine	Fall of a Tyrant	199
Chapter Ten	Love Is Hard to Find	203
Chapter Eleven	Death of a Tyrant	217
Epilogue	Born under a Wandering Star	224
	Essential Concepts and Vocabulary	A1

A Warrior's Aloneness

"Fighting your loneliness with writing is like fighting fire with prayers. It seems just as powerful, but in the end, words are just words and not what you need."

–don Jesus M. Ramirez

Many years of solitude created a distant personality within me which I once found troubling. I have spent much time alone and have developed strategies to manage loneliness. Today I am no longer lonely, and have learned that loneliness and aloneness are not one and the same. However, it has taken years for me to arrive at this point. I now prefer to be alone, but only because average people are so toxic. I've not met anyone from Epitaph, the town in which I currently reside, whose company I enjoy. I've come to prefer my own company to the best average person I've ever known. I have several students, who aside from the few who are more advanced, I only care to tolerate intermittently. Burdened by their averageness, after several hours their energy becomes too taxing, heavy, and unpleasant. In search of a defensive weapon to combat loneliness I sought to become a writer, and have worked endlessly to develop my skills. I often found myself surrounded by crowds, yet always feeling alone. One of these times was in a college cafeteria, which was flooded with students making enough noise to wake the dead. In the midst of this madness I began to write.

The first time I heard voices as a child I knew I would not be an ordinary man. I was only nine-years-old or so and thought I was dreaming, but then the voice told me to look outside and listen to the birds. I did. The trees in our front yard were filled with sparrows singing their happy songs. I assumed the voice was God's, and it never occurred to me that it might have only been my imagination. Perhaps the brainwashing I received by the obsessive sisters of the Church was responsible. Whatever the explanation, I felt special and happily behaved as if I had a secret, which I did. However, this inner happiness was not met with curiosity by my teachers at school, but seen as a sign of concern. They assumed I was disturbed, which by today's standards I would have been. I had no idea that I was in the company of muses, madmen, and prophets, as poor Native Tejano children in Texas were not supposed to feel happy or special. The experiences of hearing voices impacted my life tremendously, but as a child I never knew how the knowledge of these occurrences would have been received by others. I never knew that some would have preferred I be burned at the stake like Joan of Arc, or be ordered to commit suicide like Socrates. Today, after all these years I've accepted that the voice I heard belonged to power. It is then no wonder I never fit in. I would not have fit in even amongst others who did not fit in. I was never a rebel seeking to burn down society or free political prisoners, but I am in a constant state of revolution. I am more of an extremist than the enraptured religious zealots who attack their enemies with bombs strapped to their chests. I find there is an ocean of distance between myself and the average man. The ability to *see* has haunted me throughout my life. As ordinary people chat around me, I've learned to carry a book to read or a notepad to write in. I used to envy their commonality and simple, uncomplicated lives. I don't have a best friend, nor do I belong to a group. Not for the lack of wanting, but because I know none worthy of receiving or capable of giving true friendship. My oldest and most trustworthy companions have always been words, and even they only serve to distract me. In the past I admired men whose words appeared to hold truth — those who allegedly loved their principles and raged valiantly against evil. Now, after so many years on the Warrior's path, the words that matter most, those that move and stir my blood, are my own. I am by definition an author, philosopher, thinker, and a loner. This is no passing fancy, but an extreme affliction, an illness of the heart that is incurable by modern standards. There is no ancient ritual or alchemy which can remove the memory of the voice that spoke to me as a child. I suffer from a self-imposed punishment, driven by a hunger for understanding. Whether by habit or affliction, I write when I am happy and while I am sad. Mostly, I write to keep myself company. Like many other writers, I am surrounded by a self-made fortress of solitude which no one can penetrate. My words imprison and protect me, while at the same time confuse and liberate me. In those rare and precious moments when I am able to put together a poignant phrase, words also free me beyond the bonds that restrain average men. It is in these instances that time stops, and if only for one moment, I catch a glimpse and can almost grasp understanding of the power that can only be called God. I find myself soaring, lifted by the beauty and mastery of words, while at other times I think myself an egotistical fool.

I have been alone many years and have grown accustomed to my isolation, as I feel a part of something bigger than myself. I belong to the millions of unknown and unheralded fellowship of Seekers, who sought understanding via the power of words. I belong to a fellowship that has no membership, no roll, and does not exist. I've found efforts to belong to my fellowman below standard and unworthy of association. These men and women cannot be the best mankind can produce. Instead of friends to offer advice, or a comforting touch, these average people seek to soil my spirit and contaminate me with their greed and vanity. These are not friends to share secrets with, so I share mine with my journal, and even then, only in code, in the event unwanted eyes should uncover my secrets. Untrusting of casual friendships, I hide myself from the unworthy and claim no peers. Daring to say so, yet truth, I am no stranger to myself. It is impossible to discover who we are unless we are alone, as growth can only be measured in solitude. Seekers of the past offer solace, but only superficially. As I roam the halls of academia I find only confused children wearing adult masks. I have to believe this must be a joke, as this just cannot be. Can these really be the best professors and allegedly learned professionals society has to offer? There must be more. Somewhere out there amongst the millions of supposedly educated people, there must be a group which holds themselves to a higher standard. These cannot be the people who I was brainwashed to believe could guide me. It is devastating to discover they cannot teach what they've never learned, no more than the ghosts of the dead.

I've learned that the ramblings of professors seeking tenure could not guide or assist me. Instead of a Warrior's dedication to a challenge, they exchanged their quest for money and prestige. They are mere self-serving hypocrites calling themselves teachers, and their arrogance smells like dung. Their presence is repulsive and their pomposity ridiculous. In all their years of living they have yet to discover that time is fleeting, and as their faces will wrinkle, so death will expect them. These fools believe they are important and immortal, not recognizing that their place would be filled in an instant. In their hunger for accolades they forget that we will all die alone. These self-deceiving frauds fail to inspire and betray the trust bestowed upon them by knowledge hungry students. I once moved like a phantom on the periphery of these academic hallways, seeking passage through the barriers blocking my entry. I struggled to fit in and unravel the mystery, like a modern-day Doctor Frankenstein. I often felt exiled into purgatory, where I could not hear, feel, or be touched.

Throughout the years of searching I found not only my own failings and self-indulgence, but those of whom I came to for answers. I discovered that these learned individuals had not obtained knowledge. Instead they had gathered information which had been passed down from others like themselves, seeking a position of respect in false society, made up of lies and liars. These men are frauds, liars, and thieves, and are not worthy of respect or dedication. My discovery was revolting, and yet social obligations forced me to continue on my quest for an academic degree. A Warrior's quest is a learned habit of solitude. It is not a self-imposed sentence, but a journey for freedom. I willingly adopt it and once more sit in a crowded room, surrounded by people, yet still alone, but not lonely. There are other silent Seekers who long to feel a part of the Universe, yet like myself are unable to bridge the gap. The riddle of how much to surrender to the average man's world in exchange for membership is not worth entertaining. Like broken tree limbs lying upon the ground, I have been beguiled with compromises and hypocrisy. My memories of broken promises have faded. All that remains is the bitterness of betrayal and isolation, as well as the knowledge that the magical passage which will release me from myself is... silence. It is the same silence in which I first heard the voice that spoke to me as a child, telling me of birds singing in the trees outside my window.

I've asked myself a hundred times where I learned this and who or what terrible event caused it. For many years I lived as a stranger to myself, surrounded by the sounds of the living, while moving like a spirit through the crowd. Like one of the souls of the charging Light Brigade I was just following orders, never replying or reasoning why, riding into the Valley of Death. I longed for a band of brothers to shed blood with me, and I found a battle worthy of sacrifice; my quest for freedom. Something no fool dressed in academic robes or religious ceremonial gowns can provide.

I am unwilling to surrender my independence for membership in cliques, gangs, clubs, frats, or groups of any kind. I no longer seek to believe or belong. I suffer the common affliction amongst modern-day Seekers and live like a Rōnin Samurai without a master, teacher, or Shogun lord. A faithful apostle without a savior, I struggle beneath the cross of this knowledge and journey through the Valley of Death. Like an ancient knight lost among his obligations while still trying to solve the riddle of life. I no longer seek a quest worthy of my mettle, and accept that outside of myself there are no causes worth fighting for. Although I sharpen my sword daily, read and write unceasingly, I acknowledge that life amongst average men is folly.

Texas escapee,

-don Jesus M. Ramirez

Introduction
Knowing Where You Are

"Life is getting up every day, knowing you'll have to face your victories and defeats anew. It's knowing you have to face the same opposition you fought against yesterday, and doing so anyway."

-don Jesus M. Ramirez

The story of my escape from Texas has been broken into two parts: *Escape from Texas, Book 1: Born into Darkness*, and *Escape from Texas, Book 2: Journey out of the Abyss*. The second installment of this work is a direct continuation of the first. As such, characters, themes, and experiences relating to the storyline will not be reintroduced, but rather continue in a fluid manner. Those wishing to obtain the most from their reading experience in terms of storyline and entertainment value are recommended to read this series in sequence. However, Seekers and Warriors should note that this recommendation only pertains to the storyline. Beneficial information concerning the Toltec discipline is present and accessible throughout both works, regardless of the order in which they are studied. As a deliberate act of war made by a Warrior in the course of his development, this series has been written and examined from a *detached* perspective. Great effort has been made to describe experiences precisely as they occurred, without exaggeration or indulgence. To accurately portray the environment, characters, and mood, as well as convey the desired message, the occasional use of vocabulary which may be deemed inappropriate or vulgar is essential. Readers who have not read my book, *Sor-*

cerer's Secrets, Book 1: Translated Secrets of Carlos Castaneda are directed to *Essential Concepts and Vocabulary*, located at the back of this book. This section will provide the essential introduction for concepts, themes, and vocabulary used throughout this work.

Texas escapee,

-don Jesus M. Ramirez

Chapter One
The Evil One Lives

"Demons exist amongst the poor, oppressed, and hungry. They are easily seen in their suffering, envy, and longing. Possession is as easy as abandoning yourself to despair. It's not difficult to find any time and everywhere."
—don Jesus M. Ramirez

I loved going into the woods which stood across the cotton field near our house on Main Drive. I was just a kid the first time I took my father's 22. cal rifle and shot my first of many rabbits. I felt like I'd crossed some tremendous invisible boundary into the land of hunters, warriors, and kings. It was a memorable time. I'd come home from school and do my chores, then sneak into my dad's closet, where he kept his rifle. I had several 22. cal bullets which I'd gotten from my brother Bumper. He was the one who first exposed me to the woods and helped me discover the wonderful feeling of the wild. He also showed me how to cut up potatoes and cook them in a pan over an open fire. I can still remember the smell of fried potatoes, and feeling like a pioneer in one of the old Westerns I'd watched on TV. Bumper was also the person who helped me find my first sense of freedom. I don't believe he felt the same way about being in the woods, but I loved it. The freedom of being surrounded by wild things awoke my primal senses and spoke to me. The wooded area I frequented was small, although it seemed enormous at the time. The woods were on land that had been dug up by prospectors searching for oil, and was covered with old, large mesquite trees, coyote weed, cactus, and everything with thorns. There were a lot of rattlesnakes, cotton tails, and large jack rabbits. I recognize how insignificant these woods might seem today, but at the time they represented freedom. I made them my hunting grounds.

I adopted an old WWI Army backpack which Bumper found somewhere, and salvaged some of my mother's old kitchen utensils from the trash; an old frying pan without a handle, a knife, fork, spoon, and an old army canteen. I felt like I was ready for combat. I remember feeling very prepared, proud, and self-sufficient. Just like how I imagined a soldier would be. Thanks to the stories my mother told me about my grandfather, who fought with Pancho Villa during the Mexican Revolution, I daydreamed of someday being a real soldier. I pictured myself riding a horse, wearing a gun and a huge Mexican sombrero, smiling ear to ear. I went to the nearby woods every day, and soon began displaying the traits of a hunter. I developed the inner peace and serenity of a hunter. I learned patience, persistence, *focus*, and courage. Strangely, I discovered courage had more to do with knowing what to do, than some secret magic some people had and others didn't. I found that while alone in the woods, I was everything I needed to be. My stuttering didn't matter, neither did how small and skinny I was. In the woods I was self-sufficient. I trusted my aim, my knife, and my rifle. I was the happiest I'd ever been.

I was also very proud of my army surplus gear. In my imagination I was a soldier going out into enemy territory on patrol. I already knew how to move as quietly as a shadow from living around my father. I'd already developed a sixth sense and felt whenever someone was around or watching me. I'd always felt alone, and could not depend on anyone if I'd gotten into trouble. Transferring these attitudes into behaviors which mattered in the woods came naturally.

I discovered I already knew how to act, think, and respond, as if I'd been doing so all my life. I don't know how I knew, but I knew when I should hide and be silent. It was the beginning of many new experiences and great adventures. As usual I was alone and never had anyone to share those experiences with, but it didn't matter. I loved being in the woods. It was exciting. Especially after the sun set and I hiked alone through the semi-darkness. Looking back, it's hard to believe I had the courage to be out there all alone. With the exception of characters from books I read, I never had a role model. I have no idea how or why I became this person, as I never knew anyone who loved wild places as much. Other kids spent their afternoons indoors, watching television, or doing God knows what. Not me. I'd be in the woods hunting, skinning rabbits and raccoons, and searching for bird's nests.

I moved throughout the woods without making a sound, and got very good at it. I recall one time in particular, while walking beneath a giant mesquite tree I felt something watching me. It wasn't the first time I'd perceived something watching me, without knowing how I knew. I'd been able to do this all my life and it has saved me countless times. This was a tremendously important trait, as I became sensitive to everything around me. I could sense energy around me even at a very young age, which scared the hell out of me. No one could tell me I didn't see what I saw, or felt what I felt. I knew there were things living out there in the darkness, and knew they knew me as well. I turned and looked up in the direction I sensed the energy was coming from, and was met by a pair of giant yellow eyes staring down at me. The eyes belonged to a huge white owl. We stared into each other for a magical moment. Then suddenly, as I stood mesmerized by its gaze, the great owl spread its massive wings and flew away in a whisper. I was stunned and remained silent, knowing I had just witnessed a miracle and received a gift from the Universe. The power that moves through all things allowed me to witness one of its magnificent creatures in its natural environment. I can still see it clearly in my mind. I know it was magic, because on that day hope was born within me. The seeds of *forbearance* had been planted and the knowledge that I could make things better began to blossom. I knew if I stayed *focused* on my objectives and learned I would be successful. I knew if I stalked my enemies with patience and discipline, I'd find each of them and make them pay. I knew I'd seen something no one else had, and realized the Universe, which allowed me to view this majestic creature, also connected our spirits. I felt privileged and knew I was better, more connected, and more aware of my surroundings. The thought that being sensitive to my environment was better and preferable, had never entered my mind until that day. I'd never given the idea of being different any consideration. I changed after seeing that beautiful, magnificent creature. The experience cut all ties to the world of average men. The perception of an unseen power made me desire to return to the woods and reconnect with the great white owl again. I had always felt different, but never in a positive manner. I'd been singled out by my family and peers as an inferior. On that day, I discovered the ability to quiet myself enough to connect with something more powerful than the animals in the woods. I began a quest to connect with the depths of my inner knowledge, and via doing so, connect to my surroundings. This quest has continued over all these years, and is something I've always treasured and never regretted.

My connection to these unseen powers has grown. In those woods, for the first time as a child, I felt alive and connected to everything. Strangely, even though I felt connected to the energy I found in the woods, I never expected anything other than what I could claim via my efforts. Out there I wasn't dependent on or subordinate to anyone. Yet at home, I was nobody, made fun of incessantly. Even my mother would call me, "Sad Eyes," as if it were my fault I was so sad. Looking back today, I realize I was a reflection of all her misery. I was proof of her desperate isolation and despair, and a manifestation of her pain. My parents saw truth in my sadness and lashed out at their own inadequacies. This was why they were ashamed of who they were and how they lived. The sadness in my eyes was a reflection of their misery and self-condemnation. In typical average person fashion, which should serve as a warning, instead of changing their reality, they hated me for reflecting it. My existence challenged them, and made them feel inferior. My father's dysfunctional character would not acknowledge that the pain my eyes reflected was due to his cruelty. Seeing genuine sadness in an innocent child was biblical condemnation.

Unbelievable as it may sound, this was also why Beelzebub felt superior to me, which says a lot about his lack of quality as a human being. I would not have stood aside as someone inflicted suffering upon a child. Yet he reveled in it. Instead of protecting his younger brother, he saw it as proof of his superiority. Beelzebub imitated our father's behavior, which gave him pleasure. He sought opportunities to torment me without any apparent reason or logic. For example, I'd be playing quietly alone in the sandbox, or somewhere else in our backyard with my plastic toy soldiers, minding my own business, when he'd randomly decide to pick on me. He'd hold one of my arms locked behind my back, and then poke me in the butt with a broomstick. I realize now that he was acting out sexual perversions, demonstrating the effects of being sexualized via forcible exposure by our father's lack of concern for privacy. Our father insisted on having sex with our mother within hearing distance from the rest of our family. It's no wonder Beelzebub's cruel nature never caused him to question his own behavior. After having worked with sexually molested, abused, and neglected children, I understand how disturbed his behavior truly was. At that point of my life, being a child of only six-years-old or so, I did not understand that his behavior was disturbed. Like a dog seeking dominance over the rest of the pack, he was exerting his position. It was only after years of self-examination and being far away from such dysfunctional behavior, that I was able to examine those experiences and understand how deeply disturbed he is. He is still the same person he always was. Such fundamental character flaws aren't washed away with the oceans of time. The world is filled with sociopaths hiding behind riches and success. The next time you meet an allegedly successful person, look into their eyes and search for compassion. In many instances you will instead find an absence of humanity and the abyss where such creatures dwell.

I grew up in a closed culture of poverty, which is the perfect breeding ground for sexual perversion. The racial hierarchy, along with absolute power over another's autonomy is the perfect formula for sexual abuse. Add alcohol, a lack of boundaries, no moral barometer, and you have the answer as to why so many older children molest their siblings. You have the answer as to why most incidents of sexual abuse by older siblings upon their younger and weaker siblings never come to light. Millions of parents are unknowingly sexualizing their children via their inappropriate behavior. Single mothers who bring home boyfriends, and single fathers who move in with their girlfriends who have daughters, are creating a perfect storm of sexual transgressions. In my father's case, he never considered anyone other than himself. To him, no one else mattered. He never cared that there was no privacy in our very small house. Add into this horrible setting a man whose sexual deviance and absence of boundaries permitted him to view his daughters as sexual objects. This will give you a glimpse of the dysfunctional environment where I lived. As a result we were all sexualized at a very early age. I could plainly hear my parents having sex, as could everyone else in the house. There was no way to avoid it and my father never cared, or worse, he was using it to groom my sisters for future use. Via this behavior he imposed himself upon us sexually, which is a very troubling childhood memory. Today, as a former Child Protective Services (CPS) social worker, I cannot comprehend why or how my father insisted on having sex with my mother, when he knew we could all hear everything. The only answer I've been able to come up with is that he was grooming his daughters as sexual objects to be used at his discretion. There may be a word to describe this in academic terms, but I can only think of the word, "monster."

At one time I used to wonder how my parents were able to nurture each other during their love making, or if they had to rush through it in order to avoid waking everyone. Then one day it hit me. It was not love making. I'd have to pretend I was asleep while they were having intercourse. It was a very awkward, troubling, and conflicting experience, which forced me to have sexual thoughts of my own mother. It was more than my child's mind could manage. My childhood and innocence was stolen by their indifference. In response to their inappropriate conduct, I'd get up and make noises so they would hear someone was awake, and hopefully quiet down. It only worked some of the time. I have no idea what a reasonable alternative might have been, even if my father had considered it. I could have never approached such a topic, even if I were able to gather the courage to do so.

I've since recognized how ignorance and poverty brutalizes children in ways that would make a stone cry. As far as my father was concerned, sex was a biological event, and like his father before him, he believed he had a right to indulge as he pleased. As the only income earning adult in the house, he saw sex as a privilege. He did not have to excuse, explain, or apologize if his actions interrupted his children's sleep and resulted in them being sexually aroused. After working all day as a mason in the humid Texas heat, enduring racism and poverty, sex was his reward. He never saw his behavior as being traumatizing, abusive, or irresponsible. Like millions of poverty stricken people around the world, he was raised in an overcrowded environment, and never experienced privacy or a carefree moment. Thus, the presence of children during his sexual acts did not matter. My mother's behavior troubled me until I realized she had been raised the same way. Their ignorance was passed on to another generation of unplanned, unwanted children. It sexualized all of us. It also stripped away any notions of my wanting to be a parent. Looking back, I wonder if all sociopaths weren't at some point exposed to unwanted sexual events. The question that remains is why did I respond one way, while Beelzebub another? Did the Universe withhold the quality of compassion from him for unexplained reasons? Was his behavior a learned response or a quirk in his nature? Was his innocence stripped away by what he'd witnessed as a child? If so, what could that have been? Why after enduring similar experiences did I seek to help people I saw as being unfortunate, weak, afraid, or different, while he used those reasons as an excuse to oppress? My observations of Beelzebub's development have dark beginnings. To me, the sickest and most troubling was that because I was quiet, he believed I was also weak. Misinterpreting quiet behavior for fearfulness or cowardice has cost many would-be bullies a beating. Beelzebub, like our father, was a bully. It's because of them I have always hated bullies. Instead of feelings of protection towards his younger brother, he sought to subjugate me. Without anyone to protect me, I appeared to be the perfect victim. Being the disturbed individual he was, he thought I'd go along with his abnormal advances.

Imagine how you would feel if these were the memories you had of your older brother. Even though many years have passed, it angers me that anyone would victimize a child. He is the reason why I learned how to fight and later started boxing. All of his attacks were met with a fight. It would be impossible to count all the times we fought. His solution, like my father's, was to beat the hell out of anyone who was weaker than him. I fought back with all the fury and strength of a smaller and wrongly treated individual. He beat me too many times to count, but I never surrendered. As I've said before, no one ever forgets being fucked over. Even though I took hundreds of beatings, they were not as hollow a victories as they may appear. All were momentous and represented how I faced the world. Every fight enhanced my ability to manage my fear and anger. I learned to think while under attack and utilize my limitations, replacing speed and multiple attacks for size and physical strength. I learned to be furious and unrelenting while attempting to injure, disable, or kill my opponent. Being forced to fight while injured taught me that the secret of survival is to never surrender and continue to fight, even if winning is unlikely. Once you're engaged, the fight won't end until one of you is disabled, unconscious, or dead. I would have never adopted such drastic measures had I not been under constant attack by a larger, stronger adversary.

Today, after having worked as a social worker, counselor, and therapist, I have come to grasp the depth of how deeply troubled he must be. Add to this, the knowledge that he tortured small animals. I have to wonder if he's not a secret serial murderer. I would not be surprised if a grisly discovery is made, and horribly mutilated bodies are found buried under his multimillion dollar home. I would also not be surprised to discover that every time he and his wife return home after traveling abroad, he leaves behind multiple murder victims. Knowing him, they would be random, innocent, and weaker people who had the great misfortune of coming across him. The best indicator of future behavior is past behavior, and his seems to have dark clouds looming in the horizon.

The fights against his tyranny continued throughout high school and lasted until the day he left for the Army. I was always fighting. I fought thugs at school and Beelzebub at home at least three times a week for years. I avoided him as much as possible and endured him only when I had no alternative. Beelzebub is the most cowardly and persistent bully I've ever faced in my life. He provided me with the incentive to fight and hate bullies. To this day I hate bullies and consider them cowards. I believe they are all hiding darker secrets, just like his. I learned many valuable lessons. One is, once the first blow is thrown, or the first gun is fired, it doesn't matter who started it, or what you're fighting about. A fight is about survival, and things get real ugly real fast. As a result of his torment, I vowed never to take abuse from anyone, anywhere. I squared up against anyone, any time, and anywhere. I must have had over a hundred street fights before I left Corpus, not counting boxing and sparring matches. I have hunted down gang members who tormented me across the country, and have no regrets or remorse for having done so. The most recent was a bully who I'd been hunting for over twenty years and finally found. It was easy. He never expected me, and forgot that no one ever forgets being fucked over. Those who impose themselves upon others do not recognize their conduct has caused irreparable damage. As a result of their actions the lives of their victims have taken a turn away from a happier path, which is why they should not be excused or forgiven. Living like a Warrior, gathering and storing energy, will direct you towards a means by which to balance the scales. Religious leaders who preach the concept of turning the other cheek do not live amongst these tyrants. Average people should be aware, Warriors only turn away to get betting footing. Rolling with a blow prior to responding, whether literal or figurative, is the only way to manage 96ers. I can attest to the healing effects of knowing those who bullied me felt what it's like to be hunted, ambushed, and haunted. This is another reason to remain anonymous. There are many lessons a Seeker must learn before taking action. There are no shortcuts. As a result of living this discipline I may not be allowed into Christian heaven, but thanks to Norse mythology, I will enter Valhalla, where only the brave my go.

    There were many other bullies I had to confront during my life on Main Drive, but I hated Beelzebub the most. I learned that the only way to handle a bully is to fight him as often as you see him. You have to fight them every time, any time, and anywhere you find them. You have to fight them with all the intensity of all the injustice you've suffered. You cannot back down, even if you are beaten every time you stand up for yourself. It's also all right to stalk them until the time and place is right. I guarantee there will be an opportunity to balance the scales. I also learned there are far worse things than getting an ass kicking. Those who fight back don't have to live with the humiliation of backing down in front of peers. Those who fight back don't end up hating themselves for the rest of their lives. The bruises, bloody noses, and black eyes are a small price compared to the murder of your spirit. You don't have to go far to find victims of bullies. The papers are full of suicides, shootings, and murders at high schools across the country. Research indicates that 77 percent of all students report having been bullied during school. Bullies, and those who tolerate them, are a far greater danger than sexually transmitted diseases.

As an adult I've helped put many child molesters in prison via my role as a CPS social worker. As a therapist I have helped dozens of sexual assault victims work their way past the horror of their childhood memories. I've learned that life is a linear experience, as one act is connected to the next, with ongoing consequences. Millions of lives are ruined by bullies like Beelzebub, who is now a millionaire and married with children. In studying sexual predators, I've learned that there is no such thing as a onetime violator, and no such thing as a cured sexual molester. With this being true, he must have attacked dozens of weaker, smaller people along the way. I hope his victims had the courage to spit in his face, fight back, and never surrender.

I have never thought Beelzebub to be anything other than what he was when he tormented me with a broomstick and laughed at my displeasure. His riches mean nothing. I have repeatedly rejected his offers of airline tickets and a place to stay. I've learned that you cannot excuse or forgive a tyrant, no matter what they offer. A tyrant will never simply believe that you are just being a nice person. They will believe you are as weak as you were before and want something other than what you're saying. Average people believe everyone is as corrupt as they are. Many of my saddest and most profound realizations have included my brother Beelzebub. Looking back, I honestly cannot say I ever felt close to him. Although as a child I often wished I could, I cannot recall ever feeling safe or glad he was my brother. I feel sorry for anyone who becomes involved with him and comes to know the cruelty of which he is capable. He is deeply disturbed. Though he has now changed his last name in an effort to appear more Anglicized, to me he's still the same bully who took pleasure in beating me, laughing while doing so. He's the same cruel, sadistic individual who laughed while he forced wire through the mouths of frogs, until it ripped through their bodies, exposing their entrails. For years his sarcastic laughter rang in my ears and was the subject of horrible nightmares. Seekers should note that developing the strength to protect yourself while sleeping requires tremendous work. Defeating the demons that haunt your dreams requires ruthlessness. As a Seeker, you must stop wishing things had been different and accept that you are shaped by your experiences. This is why when a Warrior speaks of the past he must reframe unpleasant events. Erasing your past removes the weight of your experiences, freeing you to become whomever you wish. This begins by refusing to be bitter about your past, as bitterness is repugnant and self-destructive.

As a result of my father's tyranny and of having to fight Beelzebub daily, I spent most of my time alone. I thank the Universe for directing me towards the woods, which gave me solace. I remember wanting to get away from Beelzebub, who was our father's favorite. I believe all average parents pick favorites, but have no idea how badly this impacts the rest of their children. I believe Beelzebub saw himself as more deserving because of our parent's attention. He saw attention from them as a sign of his worthiness, while I saw it as injustice. Via my parents conduct, I learned that no one will play a game they are not allowed to win. My parents kept changing the rules. They had one set of standards for Beelzebub and another for me. No matter what I did, it was never good enough. After years of trying to gain their approval, at the tender age of fourteen, I stopped trying. It was the only possible alternative, but they never understood it. By that time Beelzebub no longer cared about them, or anyone for that matter, except of course himself. Our parents convinced him he no longer needed their approval. He withdrew into his own make-believe world in which he was a misunderstood teenager seeking his righteous freedom, like James Dean in *Rebel Without A Cause*. He saw himself as the star and hero in a Hollywood movie. His narcissism had grown into a full-blown state of dysfunctional delusion, and of course included drama and romance. By the time he left for the Army, he'd burned every bridge in Corpus. Our parents would have never believed what a cruel, disturbed, and sadistic bastard he really was. He repaid their attention by rejecting them and the rest of our family, refusing to let anyone meet his children. He did not want his DOEI in-laws to meet his Genghis Khan like father, or his siblings. The phony family he created, which connected him to English royalty, did not allow for Tejano and Mexican roots. He cut ties to everyone who knew him in the past and possessed tidbits of his history which might be exposed. He saw himself as some kind of great man, who'd built an empire on his own, without the help of anyone, like in the movies. Contrary to his delusions, I never saw him as a leader or a brave person. I never saw him as anyone other than who he is. Beelzebub, like so many other self-loathing average people of color, pretends to be a DOEI, and lives the life of an "insurance executive" in San Antonio, Texas. He calls himself a self-made millionaire, good

Christian, great husband and father, and a pillar of the community. In my eyes he's just another self-serving, money hungry, distorted 96er with grandiose and dysfunctional deviances.

After a while I got used to my father's indifference. Yet, what really hurt me was my mother's. I relived those moments during my self-analysis. In truth, I would have preferred not to live through those days again. I understood my father and Beelzebub's cruelty, but I've never been able to understand her cruel jokes or indifference. If there was ever a loving child, it was me. Like all innocent children, I had nothing but love for her and cannot find the limits of my affection. Via her neglect, it's no wonder I felt like such a wretched creature. As a young boy, before my sadness turned to rage, it is no wonder there was so much sorrow in my eyes. Perhaps this is why I felt her loss so deeply. If the Christian god called Jesus stood before me today and asked my one deepest desire, besides being able to fly, I would ask to feel loved by my mother. I would ask to have been nurtured, protected, and loved. During my in-depth self-examination sadness utterly overwhelmed me when I realized I never felt she loved me. I would have loved to have felt her affection as a child. The unfairness of it ripped me apart, as I foolishly believed for years that had she lived I might have still been able to win her love.

Taking a Warrior's inventory taught me very harsh, yet useful lessons. One you may not be ready to consider is that every time someone important in your life dies, a part of you dies with them. It is so valuable and such a treasure you must take care to protect it with all your energies. In the case of a parent or loved one who you knew as a child, you must accept that you'll never be able to consummate unresolved childhood issues. The hope of ever feeling affection, nurturing, or protection, dies with them, so a part of you dies as well.

Not only does your innocence die, but all the parts of your childhood that never experienced that affection. I'll admit that I did not have this knowledge the first time I took an in-depth Warrior's inventory. It was only after five years later that I was able to share this insight without tearful self-absorption. This also serves to validate that such a challenge is not a single event, in which a Warrior clears the slate once and forever.

It's a miracle I did not act out more as I grew up. I believe the Universe noticed me. I cannot explain how despite a lack of nurturing and protection I somehow managed to survive. My accomplishments amaze me. Looking back, I realize I must have been a very powerful child. Even though I stuttered, stammered, and suffered, I survived and excelled. Beelzebub will not thank me for exposing his behavior, nor will he ever admit to it. I am certain he'd deny every word, and to the best of his ability hide this from the world. However, as I said earlier, we are not punished for our sins, but by our sins. I have no idea what today's society would call his actions, nor do I care. I do not forgive or forget cruelty, and I suggest you don't either. I've explained that I am a product of all those experiences. I draw the analogy of a tree who has had one of its limbs tied down, forcing it to grow in an unnatural and unhealthy manner. Even after that limb is freed it must then fight to regain its balance, restore its natural state, and grow straight and strong. Such efforts distract and demand much attention away from what would have otherwise been a normal growth. Much could have been accomplished if its limbs had not been tied down in the first place. I have had to overcome the negative aftereffects of those years of torment before I could continue my growth. I have had to battle against unhealthy tendencies created by those years of abuse. It has cost me years of struggle, merciless self-analysis, and discipline to find the roots of my behavior and make corrections. It is bad enough that Beelzebub abused, tormented, and attempted to assault me, but now to pretend as if it never happened is more than I will consider. A Warrior does not indulge by placing emphasis on one experience over another, as he knows all things are equal. Yet, I've learned it is best not to pretend certain experiences did not impact you more than others. Forgiving someone also requires they be worthy of forgiveness, acknowledge their wrongs, ask for forgiveness, make amends, and vow never to do so again. None of this has happened with Beelzebub. I do not believe I could forgive him, even if he begged me to do so. It has been too long and my experiences with him have shaped the course of my life. If it were not for those experiences I would have never become a fighter, soldier, police officer, hunter, cowboy, tracker, surfer, and etc. I would have preferred to have been a poet, painter, farmer, or a priest.

      My experiences living with the devil also taught me that tyrants never change. You must never forgive or forget someone who deliberately harms you. Deliberate maliciousness deserves retribution, not understanding. Those who disagree because of alleged Christian beliefs are reminded of the "Cleansing of the Temple," when Jesus Christ cast out the money changers, spoken of in all four Canonical gospels of the New Testament. Now that my mother is dead, her spirit knows all. She knows she failed to protect me and my sisters by not taking appropriate action. It must be very painful for her to acknowledge her failures, even more that she favored the evil one. Today, as a mentor to my students, I am puzzled by how wrong parents are about their children. I am perplexed by the distorted images they have of them, and at how little they actually know about them. My parents favored the devil, and helped him grow as a positive symbol of their self-image, while neither had any idea who he really was. Their example made me realize that I was not willing to bring a child into this world and risk hurting them as badly. There should be a required testing prior to being allowed to have children. I would have preferred not to have been born to such unqualified individuals. Their ignorance exaggerated my helplessness and distorted my world view. All three of them stole my innocence and devastated my childhood. It left me unprepared and poorly qualified to deal with life. As a consequence, I've made many mistakes based on my need to belong, feel loved, and to be a part of something bigger than myself. Life under their tyranny was the beginning of a horrible downward spiral of self-destructive choices and behaviors. Once again the question of character troubles me. I have accepted that people are who they are. However, I've yet to understand why. The puzzle of man's cruelty is as troubling and absurd as delusional ideals of innate superiority. The power which man calls "God" is indifferent to suffering and sacrifice, and only responds to energy. I arrived at this conclusion via my experiences traveling the world. I've sought out shamans and gurus of many cultures, and much to my disappointment, never found anyone who understood the concept of energy, or how to channel and use it. As a Seeker on this path, you may not know how lucky you are to have gotten this far in your development. Unfortunately, most of you will go no further.

One of the many wrongs my parents conveyed to me was the concept of a Catholic Christian god. I was wrongly indoctrinated to believe in a god of miracles, and brainwashed to expect spontaneous changes within people. Like millions of naïve, helpless children before me, I was taught to believe in the power of good over evil, and that in the end good would always triumph. I was taught to believe all the nonsense found in all the parables repeated untold times during mass and catechism. It was harmful beyond description, requiring years of discipline to remove. As I mentioned before, the struggle to disconnect from the baggage of your past is never-ending, and mine continues today. After all the brainwashing I endured it is a miracle I believe in anything at all. I certainly do not believe in the Catholic Church, nor do I believe that Jesus Christ is God. I also do not believe the Bible is the word of God. I do however believe in an indifferent powerful force, which others call God. Yet, this force does not deliberately work for or against anyone, nor does it make one human better or worse than another. This indifferent force only recognizes stored energy, personal power, and what Warriors refer to as *intent*. It does not care whether you're a thief, liar, whore, or a playboy. If you act in an impeccable manner as per the discipline of a Warrior, you will succeed. Other people's interpretation of right or wrong, morality, religion, and etc., means nothing. Therefore, if you have been robbed, beaten, betrayed, or etc., do not expect divine justice, because it doesn't exist. Keep in mind that revenge is not justice. It is just revenge. Also, remember that you are risking your freedom to get it.

    As in all sensitive areas of human nature there are many contradictions. For example, as I stated before, I do not agree that it's correct or necessary to forgive your transgressors. I do not agree nor do I believe that someone who has deliberately harmed, humiliated, or betrayed you with malicious intent should be pardoned or given another chance. I believe doing so goes against the laws of the Universe. To excuse someone who has deliberately harmed you is to cosign their behavior and validate your inferiority. Here is where it gets touchy, and everyone who reads this is warned against taking my words out of context. If you break the law, you will face consequences. I do not give you or anyone else permission to use these words as justification for doing so. The first rule of starting the Warrior's path is accepting responsibility for all your actions, and lack of them. Therefore, if you elect to extract personal justice, you do so at your own peril. It gets more confusing, as I don't believe punishing your oppressor is a sin, rather it's a balancing of the scales and a cleansing of the spirit. However, and this is of paramount significance, only a Warrior is capable of "balancing the scales." For an average man to commit the very same acts, it would be revenge. This is so because a Warrior acts from a point of complete *detachment*, never rationalizing his behavior or allowing for his emotions to distort his objectives. Indignation and pride cannot be involved. Those who indulge are feeding their self-importance, which will destroy them. When a Warrior seeks to balance the scales, they do so for the following reason. Those who have deliberately harmed you have caused your life to change course. Their malicious acts have interrupted your natural growth, keeping you from becoming who you would have been had they never crossed your path. You've had to overcome not only their initial attack, but carry the pain of that experience and restore yourself via years of struggle, merely to regain your footing. The effects of their behavior altered who you were then, and who you are today. These experiences denied, prevented, and distorted every relationship you have had since. Bear in mind, Germany is still searching for Nazis who participated in the murder of millions during World War II. Why, you ask? There is no statute of limitations on those who harm the innocent. Anyone considering such action must remember that society does not approve, nor tolerate what they interpret as revenge. Unless of course it is extracted through the legal system, at which point it will be called justice. You will be guilty of a crime and subject to criminal prosecution.

This cannot be trivialized, as your freedom is too high a price to pay. If you decide to act, you must first complete the following checklist.

- Establish a detailed plan and clear objectives for your efforts.
- Establish a fail proof plan for disguising your involvement.
- Decide on a beginning and ending to your attempt.
- Determine the degree, boundaries, and possible consequences your plan will reflect.
- Establish a method of monitoring effects of your efforts as you go about them.
- Determine the long-term effect your efforts will have upon your target.
- Recognize your limitations and consider all the alternatives.
- Acknowledge that you cannot recover the lost innocence of your childhood and adolescence.
- Accept that you will never, ever be able to reveal this effort to anyone.

The act of balancing the scales is an extremely difficult challenge that only a Warrior would consider. Remember, prison is full of people who could not keep their mouths shut. The developmental prerequisites for such an act are silencing of the *internal dialogue*, recapitulation, and *seeing*. If you have not met these requirements, you are not ready. Only a Warrior who has been dedicated to following this path, under the guidance of a genuine teacher, for at least five to ten years is capable of balancing the scales. This does not include years spent as a Pathfinder and Seeker. Keep in mind that I am not at a point in my development where "making the final leap" is my primary objective. I do not have an ally that guides me, speaks to me, or helps me make decisions. I am one hundred percent human and still live on this plane. I do not have a mentor, and have learned all these lessons via personal experience. I am still subject to the same restrictions and hardships as you. The only difference is I have been practicing this discipline most of my adult life. Therefore, bear in mind that seeking personal justice in this society has consequences. The Warrior's path has taught me many lessons, and few, if any, reflect the claims made by countless self-named Toltec masters. Ultimately, these are my observations after many years of having lived this discipline. I am not seeking your endorsement or that of anyone else. I don't need anyone's energy to accomplish my objectives or make the final leap. I know that as an average person you'll take the fragments of my words which match your reality, and ignore the rest. It's what I did when I first started this journey. In doing so, you are as alone and as subject to the whims of the Universe as I was. Unless you can set your ego and idea of reality aside, you're as big a loser as all those people you point your finger at. You're the average person I warned you about. You are the same person your mother warned you about. If you haven't already, you'll soon discover there is no solace, no safe haven. Everyone has to earn their freedom alone. The lucky few whose personal power has led them to find this book may have a slight advantage, but only as far as they are able to set their ego aside and follow directions, without changing them. Unless you learn to take all the emotion out of your dealings with average people, you have absolutely no chance of living like a Warrior.

I've learned that if I store my energy and live like a Warrior, the Universe will align itself on my behalf. I believe power will give me an opportunity to meet my oppressors under different circumstances. I believe if I am patient and practice *forbearance*, and *focus* my life towards storing energy, this will come to pass. I have learned to *focus* on the tasks at hand. I believe we are punished by our sins, not for our sins. The seemingly insurmountable challenge is removing all of your pent up emotions, emptying your baggage, and viewing your life as if it happened to someone else. It's only through the horrible hardships of examining your past that you can store energy. Do not waste time demanding to know why. There is no why. All that matters is acceptance of the events and what you determine to do about them. A Warrior's response is only possible if you remove the emotion, otherwise it will only be the reactions of an average person. Unless you develop *detachment*, you'll never become merciless with yourself. You'll never stop indulging in self-pity, and you'll never defeat the demons that haunt your dreams, refusing to let you live life in the present. Unless you adopt *detachment* as a strategy you'll never balance the scales against those who've harmed you. If you think you'll gain pleasure in watching them suffer, you're indulging in an average man's concept of vengeance, which is empty and has horrible consequences. You should keep in mind that you can never, ever, share your ideas or actions with anyone for as long as you live. This literally means no one, ever. Once you do, your life is completely at their whims. Prison is filled with people who could still be free if they'd just kept their secrets, secret.

I teach my students a required technique I call *grounding*. This is a difficult concept to grasp and is best conveyed in person, as describing it is nearly impossible. I demonstrate that via *grounding* we connect ourselves to every living creature around us, proving that no one is better than anyone else. This technique is the first step towards learning how to *see*, which is described incorrectly by a myriad of self-proclaimed masters of the Toltec discipline. *Grounding* teaches us the foolishness of comparing ourselves to others. The only thing that can be compared as better or worse is our behavior. It is only via behavior that anyone can claim to be better, and this is purely subjective. I now understand how even as a child I always knew perception made my behavior better, simply because it gave me more options. I now understand why I never thought of Beelzebub as anything other than what he's always been. I am proud to say I've never accepted any of his manipulations, riches, or gifts. I am also proud to be the only one of my father's sons who did not accept his gifts of money, which he randomly decided to bestow. I consider my father's rejection and omission as a badge of honor and the highest status I could aspire to. Not to be claimed as one of his children conveys the message that I never relented, compromised, or negotiated for his approval. I am proud that I've never called Beelzebub or my father during the many times I've visited Corpus Christi and San Antonio. I once believed that perhaps upon their deathbeds I might desire to visit them, if only to be a reminder that no one forgets being fucked over. However, upon hearing my father was close to his end, I discovered that my lack of interest in seeing him persisted. I did not wish any contact with him in life, nor do I wish any connection with his spirit after his death, and the same goes for Beelzebub.

  In truth, this analysis of my childhood memories has taught me that everything matters. We are all connected to everything and everyone. I've learned that only by knowing myself as well as I do, am

I able to better understand average people. It's only via discipline that a Warrior gains insight into 96ers, who will undoubtedly be a challenge worthy of a Warrior's best effort.

The storing and pushing of energy is sorcery, and an example of our perception. I was able to perceive power as a child. The problem was I had no one to explain it to me, or help me understand what I perceived. I was knowledgeable beyond my years, but ill-prepared to manage what I perceived. One of the many challenges I faced growing up as a sickly child was that being able to *see* led me into a state of sadness, which always accompanies knowledge. It became a destructive habit and loomed over me like a storm cloud, even under the sunniest skies. My ability to perceive left me unprepared for the reality of existence, as I perceived my mother's indifference and my father's disdain. I only managed to survive because I escaped into an imaginary world. I can relate to stories of children having imaginary friends. Too bad the entities I perceived were not imaginary, or friendly. An imaginary friend would have been a great companion.

I have made a deliberate and conscious effort to delve into my past, so as to finally be rid of it. Doing so intentionally while refusing to indulge is another challenge. Like all average people, I spent years trying to bury and forget it, which is why it continued to haunt me. When I conducted my first Warrior's inventory I was still romanticizing my history. I am now attempting to store energy, which was wasted during all the times I've had to fight the same monsters. I am committed to the Warrior's quest and acknowledge that death will take me long before I've accomplished all I have to do. Therefore, I have no time to waste on romance or self-pity. I must be merciless and relentless in seeking freedom.

It has been a painful journey and every memory is a reference point, reminding me of how far I've come. One memory connects to another, and once you deliberately seek to engage them they make themselves known. I remember being attacked by a large dog and a white foghorn rooster. I remember having to shoot my dog, who had become sick with mange and every other illness connected to poverty. I remember wandering in the woods, lying on the ground, and looking up into the Texas sky, gazing at the clouds. I'd spend hours daydreaming and asking God to let me die. I didn't understand why God would let a child suffer so much and not allow him to simply die. It went against everything I'd been taught about God and how he supposedly felt about children. I expected to witness a miracle at any moment, but none occurred. Even though I went to church and prayed for hours on end, I never received respite from my unhappiness. It was horrible to pray so hard, be so good, try so hard, and have God reject and ignore my prayers. I don't know if it was worse to think that the Christian god refused my petition, or to discover he didn't exist. Average people brought up in our alleged Christian society believe they will be rewarded for their good conduct, and unknowingly establish an expectation of payment. This concept has been the cause of millions leaving the Church and turning towards evil, wherein they demand payment. This is one of many examples of how religious leaders have failed the faithful, who eventually give up standing in line waiting to be recognized and validated. It is no wonder so many 96ers turn to mass murders, political aspirations, or covert criminal activities, rather than wait for God's kindness to be demonstrated via the American dream.

      At times, while in the solitude of the woods, I wouldn't feel lonely or afraid. There were brief moments where I could forget my suffering and pretend to be someone else. At times while playing in the sandbox in our backyard I pretended I was a soldier. It was never intended to function as a playpen, just a storage my father had built for the sand he needed to make cement. In the harsh environment where I lived, everything and everyone had a purpose, provided a service, and had a job or a role, except for me. I was a sickly kid who did nothing but cause problems, and was an additional burden for my mother and sisters. I was seen as useless baggage, nothing more than deadweight. In the harsh Texan agricultural world in which I lived, this was unheard of. When an animal broke its leg or outlived its purpose, it was killed, gutted, and eaten. Nothing was wasted. In a world of survival of the fittest, I was as useful as a spent bullet. I recall an experience which demonstrates the severity of this reality. Bumper was a teenager at the time and was suffering the confrontations of a domineering father. I'd seen my father beat the hell out of him with extension cords, sticks, belts, and his fists on many occasions. I never understood why Bumper never fought back, but now I know he lacked courage. As a result of these beatings Bumper warned me not to leave my toys in the sandbox. Our parents made the older siblings responsible for the younger ones, and my father didn't like finding toys in his sand when he needed to make cement. Being a child who survived off his imagination, I was unaware of how strongly he felt about this. One day I made the mistake of forgetting to put my toys back into the milk crate I used as a storage box. My father, who worked as a mansion, arrived home that day angry or half-drunk, as usual, and saw them. He beat Bumper relentlessly because I'd left my toys in the sandbox. After the beating had finished, in one of the many cruel acts I endured as a child, I watched as Bumper gathered up my toys and carried them to a fifty gallon drum we used as a fire pit. He started a fire, and in one toss murdered a part of my innocence, stripping me of one of the few outlets I had as a child. He also broke my heart, again. Reflecting upon this event I am shocked by his cruelty. It is difficult to believe this was an act by my own sibling, who also happened to be my hero at the time. Since then I've learned that cruelty is learned via life experience, and no one is immune. A person who has been brutalized will impose the same cruelty that was inflicted upon them. Bumper burned my toys in a moment of blind anger and self-preservation, and demonstrated what mattered most was his survival, not anyone else. He reflected the same indifference and insensitivity he'd learned via our father's example. Average people always think, "me first," and the hell with everyone else. He demonstrated that the rule of survival applied to innocent children as well. After throwing my toys into the fire he walked away, leaving me standing in the darkness, staring at the fire pit as black smoke from the burning plastic toy soldiers rose into the air. My eyes filled with tears and my heart broke. I stopped loving him and never played with plastic toy soldiers again.

By assigning the responsibility of parenting me to my older siblings, my parents robbed them of their childhood and pitted us against each other. I don't blame Bumper for destroying my toy soldiers, and understand that because of my behavior, he was being punished. In his abused mind, he sought to remove the source of that punishment via the easiest route. He gathered my toy soldiers and simply burnt them, just as my father would have done. I am still stunned by the immense cruelty which abuse generates amongst those who are forced to endure it. Cruelty is transferred via such actions. My brother, who was as much a victim of our father's cruelty, joined the ranks of the cruel and indifferent.

As of the day I'd first written about this experience, I'd never reminded Bumper of his actions. However, since then, during one of our phone conversations, I asked him about it. I did not expect he would have remembered, but he did. He didn't deny it happened and remembered it completely, but felt justified in having burnt my toys. He validated what I have taught my students, and proved that it's pointless to ask an average person why they did something which you felt was wrong. He felt no remorse, did not apologize, and gave no indication of being worthy of forgiveness. He validated everything I've said. He is an average person, no better or worse than 96 percent of the population. His many marriages, divorces, and God only knows how many sexual adventures, continue as you read this book. He has learned nothing and continues to feel justified in his actions.

The destruction of my toys threw me into an even deeper depression. I must have blanked out the following events because it all seems to blur into more painful memories. I don't know how I survived, only that I did. I also don't know how I managed to maintain my sanity, or if I did. My mother bore my brother Punk only nine months after I was born, and pushed me aside, handing me off to my eldest sister Precious. My mother, who had so much anger in her after suffering years of abuse, was as volatile as my father. One minute she'd be perfectly quiet, the next she'd explode into violent outbursts, striking out with whatever she held in her hands. I wish I could say she grew kinder and more caring with age, but the truth is she grew more violent as my father's abusive behavior worsened. I recall one experience which serves as an excellent example of her violent outbursts. It involved my sister, who out of love and respect for her privacy, I will refer to her as, "Red Riding Hood." My mother had kept her home from school one day, which was something she often did when she needed extra help around the house. She was as cruel as my father at times, and I am ashamed to say, just as evil. That particular day Red Riding Hood was washing dishes next to my mother, who was pealing and slicing potatoes on the kitchen counter. My mother, who had a problem with anger, was verbally abusing Red Riding Hood, who rebutted in a disrespectful manner. My mother, who'd been beaten by my father on many occasions for doing just that, told her to shut up. However, Red Riding Hood, who'd learned from my mother not to do so, replied. My mother then lashed out at her with the kitchen knife she had been using to slice potatoes. She claims to have been trying to hit her with the flat side of the blade, and that Red Riding Hood raised her elbow, causing the knife to slice through the better part of her forearm. I remember the blood, the screaming, and the violence, which instead of subsiding after the slicing of Red Riding Hood's arm, increased. My mother knocked my sister down, who was screaming in agony and fear. She then opened the salt shaker as she held my sister down and poured it over her wound. My sister screamed in agony as the salt struck her open flesh, stopping the blood from gushing. I don't know if my mother was even aware I had witnessed the entire event, but I did, and it left a terrible scar upon my innocence. I think I went half-nuts and ran into the woods to hide. Yet where would a stuttering, sickly kid go for solace if not to his mother, who at this moment was the villain? My poor sister is still under a doctor's treatment for all the abuse she incurred at our parent's hands. She has had children of her own, and like all brutalized people has passed on the abuse to her children. For average people the effects of bad parenting go on and on, unrelenting until they die.

    I never thought of my mother as the person to go to for comfort after that. I'd seen her nearly slice my sister's arm off. I had been taught a son is supposed to love his mother and a mother is supposed to love her children. I did not see examples of this in her behavior. Maybe this is why I was devastated when my mother finally died. After years of suffering, her cruelty has been burnt into my mind like an ugly scar, down deep inside. It is one of the darkest memories of my life. I remember having dreams in which my mother was pushing me away after I had come to her in tears. I don't know if it was only a dream or if it really happened. Were it not for what I've learned upon the Warrior's path I would not be able to write about these events, much less seek to recall them. At the time of my first dedicated Warrior's inventory, I hoped I'd be done with these ugly moments of my life forever. I pulled them back to the forefront of my life, only so I could finally cut them away from me once and for all. Yet, I discovered that recapitulation is not a onetime event. The only magic found is one discovered on the other side of accepting your reality as if it happened to someone else. Peace can only be found via *detachment*, merciless self-analysis, and no longer demanding explanations or justice. I will never know if my mother loved me, or if she was just too tired, had too many children, or after years of abuse, was no longer capable of it. Either way, it changes nothing. I cannot imagine my mother is in heaven, as she claimed to be a Catholic who loved God. I cannot believe the god she claimed to believe in would love her back. If the god she believed in exists, then she must be burning in hell. Is the act of harming a child not an unforgivable sin? I acknowledge that like all abused and neglected children, my emotions towards my mother are conflicting.

Texas escapee,
don Jesus M. Ramirez

Chapter Two
No One Forgets Nothing

"Seeking balance in your life sometimes requires revisiting old enemies and reopening old wounds, thereby creating a few new ones. Graveyards are full of men with grudges."

-don Jesus M. Ramirez

Revenge is good no matter how it's served, although some say it is better served cold. I never cared how I got it, as long as I got it. In the film *The Godfather Part II* Michael Corleone said, "Keep your friends close, but your enemies closer." I was never as sophisticated and openly hated. If I'd had the wisdom of a Warrior to guide me my life would have been much easier. As a result of a lack of guidance I never knew how to handle my enemies. I simply reacted when attacked and fought blindly as if I had nothing to lose. I learned that a person who is not afraid to die is a very dangerous individual. I knew at the time, not fighting back would have been to invite more of the same. On Main Drive there was never any code of honor or boundaries. The people were too busy fighting for survival. The poverty was oppressive, as was the weather. No one cared for logical explanations, nor did they entertain notions of right or wrong. They simply wanted to survive. To the bullies it meant intimidating the brutal world they found themselves in. Looking back, I realize that had my oppressors not been such lowlife bastards, without a single redeeming quality, I wouldn't be a Warrior today. Had my father not been a complete and brutal bastard, I would have become someone else. A genuine student of this discipline would say I was lucky to have found such a perfect tyrant, as a Warrior's struggles are the keys to his freedom.

Today, years after my first recapitulation, I reflect on questions I once had regarding those who were defeated by their experiences. I am now certain that such individuals were merely average, and not Warriors. However, at the time I was also not a Warrior. A Warrior would not have confronted his enemies openly, but instead go around them. He would not have defied them openly, nor would he have indulged in self-pity or expected anything from anyone. He would have never felt outraged at the injustice. A Warrior would have gotten up after being knocked down, dusted himself off, and stepped back into the fray.

Like all average people I indulged to the point of making myself emotionally crippled. I was filled with anger, resentment, and every version of the seven deadly sins. I was defeated, and then the Universe smiled upon me. I crossed paths with other Seekers, and I learned via their association that I was not alone in being unhappy or mistreated. I learned others had suffered similar experiences and as long as I kept trying I had a chance. I discovered along the way to never surrender to my weakness, and that the battle I must win was not against those who harmed me, but against myself. I learned my greatest fear was true, and that I was alone. I suffered for many years with this knowledge, and finally came to accept it. It was a painful realization. I began to analyze my life as if it were someone else's. I have no idea how many times I was knocked down and felt like giving up. Maybe if I'd been given a chance I might have taken it, but peace was never offered.

On Main Drive, not fighting back was not a reason for your attackers to stop beating you. I decided that if I was going to take a beating, I would fight back. Maybe I could get in a few lucky shots. It was better than just lying there while those bastards beat me. Seeking revenge helped heal me, and each step I took towards vengeance added an ounce of self-esteem to my life. Each attack upon my oppressors gave me confidence in my ability to survive in their brutal world. Looking back, I would have preferred things to have been different. It may be wrong to admit that hate gave me the motivation to endure, plan, study, and learn, but it did. I cannot explain how I knew to plan my attacks like a hunter and stalk my enemies, choosing the site of engagement, and always making sure to have the edge. I have no explanation as to how I knew to plan attack routes, as well as first, second, and third escape routes. I somehow knew at this early age to always be alone, and never have an accomplice who'll hold your future in their hands via their knowledge.

I had grown up as a victim, but it did not suit me. I hated bullies, and hated being afraid even more. I hated feeling angry at myself for not fighting back. I remember the moment when it dawned on me that it was literally dog eat dog, with the biggest dog getting the most to eat. This degree of primitive behavior puzzled me, as did the evil and violence within so many people. My gentle spirit was not prepared for such fury and violence, nor was I prepared for the indifference amongst people. I was a quiet and shy child who stuttered, stammered, and had little to say. I played with my toys, read my comic books, and never bothered anyone. Had I had better parents and a different older brother who wasn't such a bastard, I would be an entirely different person today. Who knows who I might have become. I think I might have been a doctor, helping those in need, or perhaps a scientist working towards the advancement of mankind. I've also learned that indulging in what might have been is like killing for peace, or fucking for birth control. The injustice, beatings, and the disappearances went unnoticed, as did the violence inflicted upon the weak by the strong. It was an existence of sheer terror, with adults who should have been protectors, actually being the problem. It was their horrible examples that the kids followed. It was not uncommon to see drunken adults brawling in the street over insults. They numbed themselves to their miserable existence, and then surrendered to the demons they'd known all their lives. My parents behaved in the same self-destructive manner, and although my mother never drank, she surrendered to the evil inflicted by my father. Instead of being kinder, it was my mother who coined the nicknames I grew up with; Sad Eyes, Midnight, Long Face, Lazy, Jew, and others.

Ridding myself of emotional baggage requires that I be brutally honest and lose my self-pity. I would love to paint a nurturing picture of kindness and love, but that would be fiction. It was my fate to be born to my parents and raised on Main Drive, so I played the hand dealt to me, which sometimes I did badly. The clearest early memory I have of being beaten in school was in the third grade. A family of migrant workers had recently moved into Main Drive, but I never paid them any attention, as people came and went all the time. If a family didn't come to church, where everyone studied everyone else, no one ever met them. I don't recall the name of the family, but I believe the son's name was Neto, or Ernest in English. He was three years older than me, and I don't know why they stuck him in my class. He dressed in the pachuco style, and spoke the same mixture of English and Spanish usually only found along the Texas-Mexican border. I don't know why he came to school at all, as he always seemed bored, never listened, never did homework, and never spoke in class. However, he was completely different out of class, where he acted tough amongst the smaller kids and tormented me during recess. I was skinny as a stick with big ears and freckles, and I stuttered like Porky Pig, the Warner Brothers cartoon character. I was also extremely shy and never spoke because when I did everyone laughed due to my stuttering. I kept to myself and the teachers didn't care as long as I didn't cause any trouble. None of them expected me to do well, much less finish school.

Neto was a bully and not only did he steal my lunch, he'd knock my books out of my hands and trip me. Then he'd laugh about it. Once while the teacher was gone he beat me up in class because I refused to give him something. I remember him kicking me in the face. I told the teacher who took him to the principal's office, where he was paddled. The trouble was that there was no one to protect me on the way home from school, on the bus, or any time I wasn't in front of the teachers. This was the beginning of a war between myself and Neto, Juan Yanez, Tommy Trejo, Joe Flores, Joe Garza, and other thugs who were a part of their gang, and it lasted for the next ten years. None of these bastards amounted to a damn thing and their lives as adults were a reflection of their behavior as kids. Looking back, it has come to me as the ultimate truth that no one forgets nothing. Those of you who have led lives filled with misdeeds should list everyone you've harmed, bullied, humiliated, oppressed, betrayed, and etc. Living in denial of those experiences is not only foolish, but dangerous, as I guarantee they have not forgotten you. Although 96ers are not known for courage, they are known for acts of desperation and randomness. There may be someone stalking and hunting you right now.

The memory of what they did motivated me to train and grow stronger, and it fed my rage. I fed upon anger for years and dreamed of revenge. Hate fed me, giving me reason to do my pushups, sit-ups, and lift weights, because I knew someday I'd make them pay in aces. I had plenty of reason to hate those bastards. I often came home with shoe prints on my back from where they'd kicked me. My mother yelled at me for having torn my shirt and soiled my clothes, but never confronted their parents about it. My parents never made an issue of it, and the beatings and humiliation continued. Neither the teachers nor my parents took steps to protect me. Neither did any of the other kids who were also being picked on by these thugs. This might have continued indefinitely had Neto, the leader of the gang, not disappeared. I don't know if he was arrested or if his family continued on the migrant trail. All I know is that the following year in the fourth grade, he was no longer around.

    During that summer between third and fourth grade I arrived at the conclusion that if I was going to take a beating, I was going to fight back. I'd been fighting Beelzebub all my life, the problem was I didn't want to fight. I wanted to read my books, draw my pictures, and be left alone. I never wanted to become a tough guy. However, I saw no alternative but to fight back, because I was still going to take a beating whether I did or not. I started doing pushups and sit-ups like I was preparing for a championship boxing match. I had to be ready even though I had no hope of fighting off four or five opponents, who would come at me any time and anywhere. It was one of the saddest moments of my life when I realized how alone I truly was. I had no one to ask for help. I would have to face those thugs alone. At the same time I could not continue to allow them to humiliate me. I listened to my mother when she spoke of her father's mounted cavalrymen during the Mexican Revolution. She said before each battle they'd say goodbye as if they were going to die, because it was the only way they could face their fear. One night after dark I walked out into the freshly plowed fields behind our house and challenged the Devil in order to face my fear. I shouted insults at him alone in the darkness. I was terrified, but nothing happened. It was the same day I ventured into the woods and asked God to remove fear from my heart, and prayed he grant me the courage to fight back or die. I surrendered my soul and asked only that he let me die fighting, and declared that I preferred to die rather than be a coward.

School resumed shortly thereafter and I began my fourth grade year. It wasn't long before the thugs attempted to pick up where they'd left off the previous year. During recess one of the gang members made fun of my stuttering. I had always been the perfect target, only on that day I refused to be a victim any longer. I became enraged and saw a white light before my eyes, my knees shook, and I exploded into a kamikaze attack. I charged like an animal, screaming in rage, knocking him down and then pounding him as hard as I could. I must have been growling or foaming at the mouth, because all three of his fellow gang members froze. All the years of fury and pent up anger rose within me like a black cloud, and I rained blows on him. Not only did I manage to knock the shit out of him, I scared the rest of the gang as well. I frightened everyone, including a teacher who finally pulled me off of him. The punk laid on the ground beaten bloody as I was dragged to the principal's office, where Mr. Cox, the same man who would beat me years later, gave me five swats with a wooden paddle. He never asked how or why the fight started, and only cared that I was the one who threw the first punch. When I explained why I'd fought back, he replied, "Sticks and stones may break your bones, but words will never hurt you." I knew that was pure adult bullshit even then. I knew words had power and permitting someone to abuse you verbally was to agree to take abuse. I rejected everything he said and hated him for paddling me unfairly.

The paddling taught me to hate and I learned that every behavior has consequences. Mr. Cox was typical of Texan DOEIs who had been raised with the idea that Tejanos were inferior, untrustworthy, and stupid. He'd been brainwashed and was now feeding others the same lies, continuing the cycle to justify the inhumanity such people have perpetuated upon the world. This is the same thinking which allowed Hitler and the Nazis to murder six million Jews. During the Sixties and Seventies this was prevalent amongst DOEIs across America, usually with the support of the government. Next to Father Hamilton, Mr. Cox was the biggest guy I'd ever seen at the time. He was huge, balding, and had a potbelly which hung out over his belt. He had giant feet and wore shoes that looked like boats. His conduct would be called child abuse today, even in Texas. He is part of the reason why I hate bullies. He taught me that in a street fight size is important, and wrong or right won't matter if you're lying on the ground bleeding. Later, in both elementary and junior high school, he beat me regularly with his paddle, supposedly as punishment for my transgressions. He beat Tejano children much more often than DOEI kids, mostly because DOEI parents would come to the school to complain. Due to the passive nature of our parents, Native Tejano students in the Andrew Jackson School District might as well have been bound and gagged. We had no voice, no power, and no one gave a damn. It's the way things had always been. Mr. Cox, along with his administrative staff, was there to enforce DOEI privilege, perpetuate the system, and stomp on anyone who defied it. It was considered normal and for the greater good.

I returned to class a new person and wore the paddling I'd received like a badge of honor. Not only had I stood up to the bullies, I had done so with fury and scared everyone, including the teachers. I had also been paddled, which was something only done to "bad kids." I however did not fit into that category and no one could explain the bizarre change in me. The puzzled female teachers would gather and point at me, whispering softly amongst themselves. None of them realized that it was their indifference which fed the behavior of thugs and bullies. It was their racist attitudes which led them to believe we deserved what we got. Their apathy, ignorance about growing up poor, and lack of understanding of our culture fed the problem. Looking back, I feel loathing towards them for blaming the children. I was not fighting to make a point or because I was angry. I was fighting against bullies that abused me relentlessly, but none of them could understand my drastic changes. The male teachers found it amusing. As for myself, aside from noticing their stares, I didn't care. I knew none of them would intervene on my behalf. I knew I was alone and was about to take another beating on the bus ride home. I don't know why, but I refused to surrender and vowed to fight back until I died. I might have become aware of some past life experience and vowed to take vengeance when opportunity presented itself. I'd never been in such a situation and assume I arrived at those decisions because of the brutality I'd experienced. Or maybe it was a desperate act of a cornered animal that fights when forced. I am still puzzled because I'd never been told what to do when attacked by a gang, but somehow I knew.

  I decided to walk home and deliberately missed the bus. I saw the thugs looking at me from inside as it pulled out of the schoolyard. I hoped they'd just go home and forget about me, but I knew that wouldn't happen and resolved to handle whatever came my way. I had no friends, so I walked alone. No one wanted to be friends with a kid who stuttered and was constantly being attacked by bullies. I started the trip home which required crossing Highway 9, the only passage into Corpus Christi from San Antonio at the time. It was a two lane highway used by eighteen-wheelers going ninety miles an hour. It was too dangerous for a kid to be crossing, but there I was, taking on the whole world alone. I had no one to help me and went into my first gang fight outnumbered, outgunned, and without hope of surviving. I knew I'd be beaten or killed, but had nowhere to go and no one to turn to. It was a moment of brutal reality, and sadness overwhelmed me. I remember not having any thoughts or feelings other than fear and anger, which turned into an evil poisonous mixture. I don't know where I got the idea, as no one had ever told me, but I took off my socks, filled one with rocks, and put that sock inside the other. The small stones were white chalice taken from the beaches in Corpus. With them I created a weapon which I could place inside my book satchel and hold while I carried it with my other arm. I continued to walk alongside the highway as I noticed the thugs approaching me in the distance. Only it wasn't just the four thugs from earlier, but eight. I didn't know the other four guys, and assumed they must have been their brothers or cousins. I felt a rush of adrenaline charge through me. It might have been the first time in my life I felt alive, and I walked towards them with murderous intent. I noted some had large sticks in their hands and knew that they all carried knives. I remember reaching under my book satchel and feeling the weight of the rocks in my sock. They grew closer and began surrounding me, laughing as they closed their ranks and told me how they planned to beat me down. I was more afraid than I'd ever been. Then suddenly, I saw a white light of pure fury once more. Without hesitation I screamed and charged into them swinging my weapon, cracking one kid on the forehead as hard as I could. He fell as if he'd suddenly realized he was asleep. The blow knocked the kid out and opened a huge hole in his skull. He crumbled to the ground like he'd been shot. As blood poured out of him I continued swinging at my attackers. I hit another on the arm which he'd lifted trying to protect himself. I swung again and the blow landed on his elbow causing it to break. He let out a scream and fell to the ground, whimpering like a dog as my blood boiled and I continued to beat anyone who came near or attempted to help the fallen. I was so enraged I chased some of the bastards as they ran in fear, and then returned to beat those who were lying on the ground in pain. My kamikaze charge lasted less than thirty seconds, but during that time I hit five of the eight thugs and sent the others running in all directions. I remember looking down at the bloody sock in my hand as I stood heaving air in and out, catching my breath and sweating under the hot Texas sun. The traffic zoomed past me going ninety miles an hour into Corpus as I noticed my right hand was also covered in blood. The sock had torn and some of the rocks had fallen out. I tipped it over and poured the remaining rocks onto the ground. All of them were as red as a stop sign. I began to beat the punk who lay closest to my feet, kicking and hitting him a few more times before I let out a ferocious scream into the blue Texas sky. The devils within me must have rejoiced, because I became a monster that day. The demons of vengeance which fed upon my hate must have toasted their victory. I learned I could hurt my enemies and discovered the power to fuck these bastards up. I decided right there and then to hunt every one of these bastards down, and I was reborn into the image of God. I was the one kicking out the money changers from the temple. I was reborn and baptized in blood. I joined the ranks of millions of crazed and angry people who discovered the sweet taste of vengeance. Even though I was only a child I'd been in battle, defeated multiple opponents and counted coup. I was a warrior.

I walked into the fields lost in a haze of adrenaline. Yet, after the fury finally subsided I knew I was in deep trouble. I knew this would not be the last incident and I'd get a beating at home. I was more scared of my father than I was of the thugs who'd tormented me. I knew I could fight back against those bastards, but how could I defeat my father? He was the ultimate bully in my life. Next to Beelzebub, I hated him the most. I ran deeper into the grain fields and sat in one of the furrows. I hid and waited for darkness but cannot remember how long I waited. I had a spiritual experience and all sense of time stopped. I felt at peace and knew that no matter how badly my father beat me, I'd never allow anyone to humiliate me again without fighting back. I abandoned myself to whatever happened and experienced total control and total abandon. It didn't last long. As I sat alone hidden by the grain plants, staring up into the Texas sky, I prayed once again for God to let me die. I couldn't understand why God would let one of his children suffer so much injustice. I'd been told by the nuns that God loved children, yet he ignored my pleas. I only had more suffering to look forward to. The sun was about to set when I made my way home, sneaking through the fields. I feared the gang was gathering reinforcements and would be waiting for me if I walked down Main Drive. I felt like the hunted sheriff in one of those old black and white Westerns. When I arrived home via my escape route I saw cars parked in front of the house. They belonged to the parents of the kids I'd injured. I crept in fearing the worst, expecting to be beaten to death by my father. He shouted at me to come over to him. The parents, along with the kids I'd beaten were standing in our living room. The bastards were now all scared and their heads were covered with bloody bandages. Others were covered with black and blue bruises on their faces. I hated them more than I'd ever hated anyone in my life. The cowards acted as if they'd been innocent of any wrongdoing. In seeing them like this I made a wonderful discovery. I learned all of them were cowards. I could take them out if I could just catch them alone. I vowed to hunt them down and make them pay. I was so angry I must have looked dangerous, because all of them turned away. My father demanded I explain why I'd hurt them. As hard as I tried I was unable to speak due to my stuttering. It wouldn't have mattered as I'd broken someone's arm, given one kid a concussion, and bloodied the others. All the parents were angry and demanded to know why I had done this horrible thing to their innocent children. As much as I hated them, I also envied them. Their parents were standing up for them, something which my parents never did for me.

My father beat me so hard he knocked me out, which is how I believe I got the scars on my face, which I'd never been able to explain. I remember being grabbed by the shirt and hit. He never asked me what happened or why I'd gotten into a fight alone against eight kids. He just beat me until I was unconscious. I don't remember much after the beating started except for my mother yelling at him to stop, which he did only after he had spent all his rage. Aside from knocking the hell out of me, his beating served no purpose and solved nothing. I still had to deal with the consequences and the four bastards who started it all. It didn't help my feelings towards my mother either, as I cannot believe a mother would allow her husband to beat her child without trying to protect him. No one ever asked why I'd fought all those kids. I had no choice. I don't know how I gathered the strength to continue my struggle to exist, as most people would have quit. I don't know how, but despite the terrible beating I resolved to keep fighting or die. I'd seen dead men alongside the road, in ditches and in the river. Some had been beaten to death, and some of them looked peaceful. Their suffering was over. I knew mine was about to get worse.

The word got around school and in one quick moment I'd fought off my attackers, gotten a tiny bit of revenge, and became a "bad kid." In what was to me the most brilliant moment of my life in which I'd struck a blow for all abused children, I awakened a creature that lived inside of me — a monster which personified evil, violence, and ferocious anger. After years of being beaten and humiliated, and before I'd ever heard of Emiliano Zapata, hero of the Mexican Revolution, I concluded that it was better to die on my feet, than to live on my knees. This experience also earned me many new enemies. Now I had the brothers, cousins, and friends of the thugs I had injured to deal with. I knew I would be hunted and it was only a matter of time before they caught me. Once again, I don't know where I got the idea, but I decided to stop being the prey and become the hunter. I knew I could beat those bastards if I could just get them one at a time. I vowed to catch each of them alone and pound the shit out of them. I planned to beat them until someone stopped me or they were dead. Looking back, it still frightens me that a little kid could consider murder as his only method of survival, which proves the brutalized become just as brutal.

I began my hunt by giving up recess and the idea of carelessly playing ever again. I knew I could not live and let live, and instead spent my time standing alongside the playground, not far from the teacher's lounge. I scouted the area and watched the thugs from a distance, keeping track of where they went and what they did. I noticed that Juan Yanez went to gym right after lunch, while the others went to class. One day I decided to ignore the bell and hide in a corner of the building while the rest of the kids and teachers went inside. I waited for the bastard who'd taken so much pleasure in beating me while with his gang. As Juan came walking around the corner alone holding his books, I jumped on him like a panther upon its prey. I caught him completely off guard and scared him so much he never fought back. I pummeled him for at least three minutes, and then I kicked him until my toes hurt inside my shoes. I enjoyed it. I left him beaten and bloody, lying beside the school building on the ground. I went to the bathroom, washed the blood off my knuckles and felt the water sting my hands, and then walked home. It was the first time pain felt good. I'd beaten the first of the guys who'd tormented me for years. I don't know if someone found Juan lying on the ground, or how he managed to get home after school. I didn't care if he died. I hated the bastard, and one ass kicking was not payment enough as far as I was concerned. I attacked him by surprise many more times. I beat him down like a dog every single time and gave him a little taste of what I had endured. I never humiliated him in front of his peers, tripped him, or stole his lunch, like he'd done to me. I just beat the shit out of him for the next five years. I vowed to beat his ass as often as I could catch him alone. I was ready for whatever came at me, but to my surprise nothing happened. The incident had gone unrecorded by anyone. As impossible as it sounds, no one saw what happened. I could have cared less, as I was on a holy mission, a one man jihad of vengeance. If my father beat me, then so be it. I'd make sure my attackers were made to pay. It was the beginning of one of my greatest accomplishments. I became an army of one. My years of hunting taught me patience and how to stalk my prey. I'd learned to attack from a hidden position and gut what I killed. I'd learned to enjoy the sight of blood. A genuine student of this discipline would say I was lucky to have had such a challenge early in my life. However, at the time it was difficult to think of myself as lucky. Looking back, it was an impossible situation without hope of winning, yet I'd *willed* a victory.

I stalked each of my tormentors down one at a time and lived in a constant state of war, often fighting more than one opponent, always alert, never safe, and never off guard. It was exhausting and more than once they tried to corner me. Each time was closer than the last. Yet I outsmarted and outfought them, discovering the power of commitment. By this point I had given up the idea that I'd live to see twenty. I hated those motherfuckers and I wanted to see them all dead. None of them realized I wasn't just trying to defeat them. I wanted to tear out their hearts and eat them.

My personal war against these thugs lasted for years and helped me develop a sixth sense. I moved through the schoolyard like a soldier on patrol, always alert and on guard against possible attacks. I was always watching where I stood so as never to be trapped without an escape route. I expected to be attacked and was prepared to go down fighting. I had no hope of winning and would always be outnumbered, outsized, and outgunned. Later I began carrying a knife and a battery cable, which was my last resort. I knew if they came at me suddenly with knives, I was dead meat. I practiced fighting with everyone I could. We used popsicle sticks, coloring them heavily with red Crayola crayons or chalk, and act as if they were knives. We'd lunge at one another, attempting to cut without being cut. The red markings that showed up on our clothes showed us where the popsicle sticks had struck. Unfortunately, the only help we had in learning knife fighting came from what we saw on TV. We never received any assistance or instruction from anyone. Nonetheless, it helped when I had to use a knife years later. The unbelievable detail about all this was that we were just kids. We should have never had to depend on our own resources to feel safe, nor should we have had to provide our own protection. My father acted as if none of it was any of his business. I don't know if he was just a simple coward, or if he really did not give a damn. Either way, it amounted to the same thing. It was up to me. He taught me that the opposite of love is not hate, but indifference.

I accepted life was not fair and never would be. The best I could hope for was to escape Texas, beyond that there were no plans. If I got into a knife fight I knew I'd be cut. If someone pulled a gun, I'd be shot and killed. I read about Japanese kamikaze pilots who gave away all their possessions, attended their own funeral, and then flew their fighter planes into American battleships. I understood their commitment and fury of fighting against an overwhelming enemy. I lived in a combat zone, fighting for survival and existing on hope that there was life outside of Texas. The world never seemed as dark as it did during those days in which I sought vengeance and fought constantly. I fought some of those guys ten times each. I swore I'd beat their ass every time I saw them, and I did. I don't know if they avoided me, or if they just gave up the idea of having peace in their lives. All I know is they wouldn't go anywhere I might find them and always traveled in groups. The sons of bitches were cowards to the core. Looking back, I'm lucky one of them didn't get a gun and shoot me dead. I did everything I could to make their lives miserable, every chance I could, including embarrassing them in class. I became their tormentor, which proves the tormented become as twisted as their oppressors. The people who say revenge is wrong and a waste of time, have not dealt with humiliation inflicted upon them by a gang of bullies. People who claim revenge is sinful have never experienced continuous torment at the hands of bullies who see it as sport. I believe now, as I did as a child, although I could not articulate it, deliberate malicious attacks are not pardonable. Any deliberate act of malice with intentions of humiliating or harming you cannot be forgiven. Anyone who turns the other cheek is inviting more attacks. What I find amusing is that people who advocate forgiveness are neglecting the fact that in order for a victim to redeem themselves in their own eyes, they must confront their tormentors. An individual who fails to confront his attackers is doomed to live with the memory of the humiliation for the rest of his life. Now as an adult, after having served in a combat zone, I can testify that there are some things which one cannot forgive, and must never forget. I also believe that living with such humiliation is equal to spiritual death. The only person you must learn to forgive is the child you were, who lacked protection and was afraid. Otherwise you will never feel good about yourself, until you seek out those who tormented you and demand payment for their behavior. If you believe revenge against such crimes is wrong, then you would forgive those who would murder, torture, or harm your children. Good for you. A priest would say you are a man of peace, and a man of God. I'd say you're a fool. However, it's your cheek and if you decide to turn it and let someone knock the shit out of you again, good for you. I would not and do not teach my students to submit. I believe peace starts and ends at home. If a bully is tormenting you, then it's up to you to knock the shit out of them, quickly and without mercy. I'd suggest a ninja attack, but that's only a suggestion. As always, you must remember the consequences for inflicting physical pain on a person. The cops don't like other people administering such violence, as they believe only they have that right. I also advocate that sometimes you must fight, and it's always best to fight back at the moment.

There is no such thing as behavior without consequences, and I repeat this constantly to my students. There are many things worse than death. Living with self-loathing because of your own cowardice is one of them. I remind my students that seeking payback for wrongs done to you as a child is not justice. It is revenge, and society will see it that way. This should serve as the ultimate warning, as should driving past the thousands of correctional facilities found across the country. A horrible truth is that no one ever forgets being fucked over. No one will ever forget those who humiliated them or the bitterness of having to swallow their pride. I believe it is better to take a beating than submit to such spiritual punishment. At the same time, I have no illusions of helping others stand on their feet. Not everyone is a Warrior. Revenge comes in many forms. I have no expectations of anyone coming to my assistance if confronted by a bully. I am on my own and may die for taking a stand. All the regrets and apologies afterwards are bogus, as nothing will bring back the dead. Prisons are full of men who acted without thinking or acted against their own interest. A Warrior always chooses their battles, knowing that once the war starts it's never over. It is better to withdraw, knowing that you, as a Warrior, will have the persistence to attack when it suits you to do so. Remember to do it alone.

Anyone who harms you deliberately and with malice should fear your vengeance. Anyone who harms another human being for sport does not deserve kindness, forgiveness, or reprieve. They should be made to pay in the exact manner which they imposed themselves upon you. Beware if you are a part of a gang that once imposed their will upon others for pleasure. You are being hunted. You better find a way to make amends or move far away and change your name. You may have forgotten those who you abused, but they have not forgotten you. Time is not a healer and no one ever forgets. I keep a list of individuals who deliberately wronged me, and I am certain the Universe will present me with an opportunity to balance the scales. You may consider this wrong, which is fine. I am not asking you or anyone else to follow my lead. In fact, I warn all who read this book not to. You would need ten years just to prepare, and you'll have to do it alone. Only a Warrior could accomplish such a worthwhile objective.

Years later while I was standing in front of my house in the dark, as I sometimes did, the Universe presented me with an opportunity to balance the scales. I saw Neto, my old archenemy from elementary school, and former gang leader who disappeared after summer break. He'd just recently showed up on Main Drive again, talking shit and acting a fool. I'd seen him around, but made certain he didn't see me. That night he was walking home from Emilio's, the local bar. Emilio's was a beer joint and grocery store which had been opened by a migrant family. It was a nasty old cantina after dark, where all the Main Drive thugs would hang out. Neto was stumbling home and didn't see me standing alone in the dark, like a vampire waiting for prey. The son of a bitch had been gone for years and forgot about the shit he did to me. He also forgot that no one forgets nothing. I'd been feeding upon hatred for years and yearned for revenge. I knew if I waited patiently, like a hunter, I'd get my chance to pay the bastard back. I followed him about a hundred yards into a spot where the neighborhood lights didn't shine. I crept up behind him and with one swing to the back of his head from my baseball bat, knocked him out cold. I beat him like a dog with that baseball bat, and planned to drag his unconscious body into the ditch to let the bastard drown. During the rainy season the ditches lining Main Drive would flood. Lucky for him it hadn't rained enough to flood the ditch completely. Also, he'd put on a lot of weight, which is what saved him. I was unable to drag him all the way into the ditch before I saw the headlights of a car coming down the street. I ran into the darkness and watched as the car stopped and a group of guys came out, picked him up, and placed him inside. It was the same bastards with whom I'd been at war with for years. The story which made the gossip circuits was that he'd been jumped by a carload of guys from Clarkwood, a rival neighborhood made up of the same kind of thugs. I never saw Neto again. I heard he got married, then was shot and killed in a barroom brawl, but I swear it wasn't me. I wouldn't have let the bastard die so quickly. God works in mysterious ways.

    I finally caught Joe Garza, one of the last of my attackers, off guard while coming out of a bathroom at a baseball park. I was leaving for the Army soon and I had to get him before I left. He was playing baseball and wearing his uniform. I was playing baseball also, for a team called the Apaches. I saw him and followed him to the bathroom and waited outside. As he walked out I attacked him and beat the bastard into the ground. He screamed like a girl as I kicked and stomped him. He whimpered and cried while I laughed and beat him until I was exhausted. I made sure he knew it was me and why I was kicking his ass. I told him I wasn't done with him or the rest of his gang. He cried like a baby, and then got up and ran away. I ran away also, but only because I believed he would return with reinforcements. I quickly armed myself with a baseball bat which I intended to use if attacked. I felt neither remorse nor pity, but only pride in my accomplishment. I would have howled at the moon if I could have. I felt like the biggest baddest monster in the forest. I continued my hunt, all the while watching my back for the attack I was certain would come. I moved like a silent panther, hungry for revenge, always alone with no hope of succeeding.

I've hunted down many of my enemies throughout the years, and some I am sorry to say I have not been able to find. I still have old scars which need satisfaction. Some Warriors believe that to actively seek vengeance is a waste of energy. Others believe that if a Warrior stays *focused* on his quest for knowledge, and lives like a Warrior, the Universe will provide an opportunity for balance without him having to go look for it. While I acknowledge and agree with the concept of the Universe rewarding energy, I do not agree with this in its entirety. Perhaps someday when the time is right I will be in a position to help or hurt those who hurt me. Yet, unless you are a powerful man, you'll never have a chance to hurt someone by something you do, via something you don't do. The Toltec discipline does not say it is necessary to treat 96ers fairly. Everything is situational and depends on your *read* of the person. The one thing that is certain is that you cannot expect to be treated fairly no matter what you do. Deciding to treat others fairly has nothing to do with good or bad, as all that is subject to interpretation, depending on point of view and culture. It's about storing energy, as the Universe only rewards energy. The Universe does not involve itself in judging right from wrong, good or bad. Power is all that matters. Gathering, storing, and not wasting energy is what's important. In the end it all comes down to personal power.

There are many ways to save, store, and maintain your energy.

One of the ways is to avoid interacting with individuals who lack boundaries or have no Code of Conduct. They'll drain your energy. Distance yourself from anyone who brings trouble, lacks discipline, and needs to be carried. Each person must battle their own weaknesses, as no one can do this for anyone else. My experiences have led me to conclusions which you may find troubling, yet they are nevertheless true.

My vengeance upon this group is incomplete, as I never was able to catch Tommy Trejo by himself. The cowardly bastard made certain never to leave his house alone. I'd sometimes ride in front of his house after dark, hoping to catch him in the street. He never went anywhere without his thug older brothers and slipped away like a slug on the ground. I never stopped hunting him, and the hate he helped instill within me fed my urge for revenge, like the sun heats the earth. Tommy was a perfect example of the kind of thugs which thrived on Main Drive. He dropped out of school, knocked up his girlfriend, and ended up working in a junkyard with his brothers. The son of a bitch now has to wonder and worry about another generation of my friends who have his photograph and make regular trips to Texas.

Another bastard who got away from me was an ugly, dark-skinned guy named Pablo Garcia. Contrary to some beliefs, it's not true that you become friends with guys you fought many times and once hated. I hated this bastard just as much after we fought. He was a foul, thick-skinned son of a bitch, who had vampire teeth and a huge head like a wild boar. He had thick greasy hair and could take a punch and keep coming. We fought for nearly an hour once, and I am not exaggerating. We went out behind Main Drive into the empty oilfield and threw punches, kicks, and everything in between for an hour. I beat that hardheaded son of a bitch so long and so hard that the skin on my knuckles was completely gone. Both of my hands were bleeding and swollen from beating him with my fists. I hit this guy so many times. He was bleeding from his eyebrows, his nose, and his mouth, and the bastard wouldn't quit fighting. We finally stopped fighting because it got too dark to see. We made an appointment to fight again, but when my mother saw how I looked, she locked me in the house and refused to let me out. Believe it or not, this fight was over Margie Perez, the same thug chick who liked me and I'd ignored. She was the younger sister of the infamous thug, Curly Perez. Thank God he'd been locked up and was gone during that time. I believe Pablo, who must have been deaf, blind, and dumb, married her. Main Drive had so many lowlife individuals I felt as out of place as an eagle amongst a gang of turkeys. If I could have run away, I'd have done so. Only I had nowhere to go, nowhere to run, and nothing to do but endure. Life was so awful. It seemed like I'd pissed God off by being born. Looking back, I realize I should have joined the military sooner, even if I would have had to lie to do it. Nothing but heartache and disappointment were gained by my staying.

I struggled through many battles and continued to do everything I wanted within my limited resources. I changed and learned the value of changing when necessary. I never hesitated to engage bigger and older bullies who thought they'd pick on me for amusement. I fought so many times with Beelzebub and the thugs on Main Drive that even before I started boxing, I'd gotten pretty good at it. Beelzebub only fought with me, while I fought anyone, anywhere, and at any time. His size gave him an easier path, which is the reason why I don't respect guys who think of themselves as leaders simply because they are bigger. I've learned many times over that size don't mean shit once the fighting starts. A man's courage cannot be measured with a ruler or a scale. I've helped bury many bigger guys who thought themselves better, more capable, and of higher quality. As I've told my students a hundred times, it's not the size of the man in the fight, but the size of the fight in the man. It's true that size matters in a fight, but so do brains, speed, and the willingness to kill the bastard if you have to. Throughout history it has been men of smaller stature who have led armies, built empires, and held the world in their hands. This make-believe fantasy about bigger guys is only true in the minds of those who allow themselves to be brainwashed. Think of Sun Tzu, Alexander the Great, Julius Caesar, Napoleon Bonaparte, and the billions of Chinese, Koreans, and Latinos all over the world. This is not to say that bigger men are not capable of possessing such qualities, only that their size does not guarantee them. I was not as tall as Beelzebub, so I got picked on, but never by the same person twice. Once someone crossed that line the fight was on forever. I never hesitated at using baseball bats and coming out of the darkness swinging it in complete silence, making sure they didn't get up. Not knowing who attacked them or how, caused those bastards nightmares for the rest of their lives. Some guys I fought as many as twenty times over a period of years. I learned to live on hate, as it gave me reason to train, study, and dream of someday getting the hell out of Texas. By the time I joined the military I'd already had experience in hand-to-hand combat situations with pipes, baseball bats, and of course knives. All the military taught me to do was use better weapons. I already had the willingness to seriously hurt someone without a moment's hesitation.

One of the legendary fights I had while growing up on Main Drive was with a loser named Joe Vallejo, whose nickname was "Gordo," or "Fatso" in English. It was all over a girl named Trini. She arrived at Andrew Jackson Junior High School from who knows where. I met her in class and spoke with her as I would anyone else. She wasn't even attractive. She was just different from the girls on Main Drive. I found all these girls about as interesting as algebra. I never made a play for her and never had any romantic intentions towards her, but that loser Gordo did. The problem wasn't Gordo. He was just an overweight loser and wannabe tough guy. The problem was that he hung out with the only real gangster on Main Drive, Curly Perez. The same guy I mentioned before, who was the older brother of Margie Perez, who several years earlier decided that she liked me and I was going to be her boyfriend. This mean son of a bitch was one of those guys you only read about in horror magazines. He was a real psychopath and a real bandido, completely void of any feelings which supposedly make us "civilized." He was the kind of guy who'd take a shit in the middle of the street just because he was pissed at the world, and wanted the world to deal with his shit. To top it off he was several years older than me and much bigger. Looking back, I don't even know what this guy was doing hanging around us junior high kids. I do know that he later married a girl from another loser family, and the endless cycle of giving birth to baby demons continued. At this time Curly wasn't yet the thug who he'd inevitably become in future years. He'd not yet been arrested for murder, armed robbery, or any of his many other alleged exploits. At the time he was the leader of a group of rejects who spent their time drinking, stealing, getting high, and doing God knows what else. He was not someone I wanted to tangle with, as he was in a league above anyone I'd had to fight thus far. His degree of violence and indifference was not something I'd yet learned. Other than the time he told me his sister liked me, we knew each other only by sight, and I had no interest or reason to speak with him.

I hadn't heard the rumors that Joe wanted to fight me over Trini, so I wasn't suspicious when Curly randomly approached me. Although I should have been, as I hadn't spoken six words to him the entire time I lived on Main Drive. I'd asked Trini about her and Joe and she said they were only friends. I took that to mean they weren't involved. Silly me, I should have expected trouble, but my combat antenna was not yet fully developed. Curly approached me during study hall and asked me about Trini. I told him the truth. She and I were just friends, nothing more. Looking back today, I realize I should have just charged him and tried to kill the bastard right there and then, taking him out of the picture. Unfortunately, I didn't know then what I know today. I should have realized that I'd end up having to fight him anyways. If I had attacked him and showed I wasn't afraid, things might have gone completely different, but at the time I was scared and alone. Curly knew I didn't have any backup and he wasn't afraid of my chicken shit brother, the gutless millionaire, Beelzebub. Looking back, I realize I should have done many things differently, but I was just a stupid kid who was not used to dealing with homicidal maniacs trying to humiliate me, other than Beelzebub. I had not yet adopted my kamikaze psychology to the extent of dealing with his psychopathy.

That afternoon as I rode the school bus back to Main Drive I was sitting quietly as I usually did. I didn't have many friends and the few I thought I'd had quickly disappeared when the rumors of trouble spread. There was Ernest Garza, Pablo Garcia, Joe Gonzales, Benito Davila, David something, and Joe Flores, all of whom simply disappeared. I'd grown accustomed to being alone and trouble seemed to follow me like a dark shadow. I'd gotten up to exit the bus, when Joe Vallejo suddenly kicked me in the back. The bus driver, an old redneck, didn't want any trouble and quickly told us to get off the bus. The old redneck bastard, who would have been my only protection, was tired of breaking up fights, so he let kids go fight somewhere else for all he cared. He didn't give a shit about Tejano kids beating each other up, and I don't blame him for not getting involved. I quickly got off the bus and squared off with Joe. We faced each other and were about to fight, when Curly, who'd been standing alongside Joe, said "Come on let's go, we're right in front of his house." Luckily the bus driver had missed the stop, and stopped right in front of my house. My little brother Punk, another gutless wonder, was sacred as usual and did nothing. I couldn't expect any help from him, he never demonstrated any courage. He faded into the crowd and never said a word the entire time. The rumors of an impending fight between Joe and I quickly spread throughout the entire school. Everyone was keyed up and expecting me to get my ass kicked. As far as they were concerned, I was a nobody. I was a former altar boy, not one of the vatos from la Main, or a former correctional facility inmate like Curly Perez. I didn't have a reputation for real street fighting yet. I wasn't a thug or a badass. All the fights I had been in up to this point were for survival, and were more out of desperation, rather than a desire to be a tough guy. I was fending off the thugs who tormented me relentlessly. Curly Perez was in a complete different level than the bullies I'd fought off. Had it not been for my experiences fighting Beelzebub, I would have been even less prepared. This may not sound like much to someone who has never known a mentally disturbed sociopath, but I had lots of experience dealing with one. A genuine student of this discipline would likely suggest I thank Beelzebub for forcing me to learn how to fight. Had it not been for his continuous verbal and physical attacks I might have never become the man I am today.

However, as hard as I try, the best I can feel towards him is disgust. Perhaps I'll thank him after he's dead, or maybe I'll piss on his grave and say I'm watering it.

None of my alleged friends would even come near me the following day at school. One of the few guys who did was a kid named Silverio Garcia. This poor kid was literally half-nuts from a car accident, and had large scars across his face and head. I'd pulled him out of several tight spots and he wanted to back me up. I said thanks, but then asked him to split. He'd be more of a problem than a help. Although now looking back, I should have let him help me. All morning the rumors and gossip were hot and heavy. Much to my disgust, the loser girls whom I'd ignored all my life were speculating about how long I'd last against Joe Vallejo, also known as "El Gordo." There was one loser girl named Suzy Pedarza, who had a reputation for allegedly giving hand jobs and blow jobs on the school bus. I'd often wondered if I could get into her panties, but all that ended with her smirking at me and laughing, while saying "They're gonna fuck you up!" There is nothing worse than a woman's wrath, and up to that point I had no idea she disliked me or even why. I'd never said ten words to her, as I've always found such women disgusting. I never saw sexually overt women as attractive or believable. Who knows why 96ers hate, they just do. I committed a violation by omission, as I'd seen her making out on the bus ride home from school. I'd never approached her or asked her for a blow job or a hand job. Looking back, I realize I committed the ultimate crime against her. I'd ignored her. Worse than that, I behaved with complete indifference towards her. The poor girl was going out of her way to attract attention, and my thoughts of her were that she was a disgusting loser who someone might fuck only in secret. She wanted to be valued, treasured, and validated. The best I could have done was to bang her across the head with a hammer and called it love. She was one of over a hundred people who came to watch me get my ass kicked.

I knew the fight would take place at the little store next to the school, which was where everyone went to eat lunch. Having lunch at the little store consisted of going out behind the store and eating our sandwiches. Some of the older kids would light cigarettes and talk about what they'd done, tell dirty jokes and act like jerks. The younger kids wouldn't do anything. We'd just eat our lunches, have a sip out of someone's coke, and maybe share a few potato chips. There wasn't any real reason for being there, other than it was just what everyone did. My mother made us sandwiches for lunch, which was considered pretty good by those standards. We'd have pressed ham on two slices of white Rainbow Bread with sandwich spread. My sisters were in charge of making the lunches and worked like indentured servants, with no limit to abuse imposed upon them by our parents. I felt sorry for them, but I was helpless to do anything about it. Our parent's reign of terror was all I'd ever known and it appeared impossible to defeat.

After a long morning, lunch break had finally arrived, and with the exception of one guy I showed up at the little store alone. Rudy Hasset, the same guy I mentioned earlier, who I played football with and was the older brother of Angie Hasset, a girl who I once had a crush on, was the only guy aside from Silverio who'd not simply disappeared. I came ready to fight, and although I wasn't afraid of Joe, I was afraid of getting jumped by Curly and his thugs. No one expected me to have the guts to even show up. I knew there was no way to avoid the fight, as doing so would have resulted in my becoming fair game for everyone to pick on. I had to show up and had to fight.

It didn't matter if I took the worst ass kicking of my life. Being known as a coward on Main Drive was only one step away from being called a hoto, or a fagot in English. Being called a hoto also made you the target of abuse and torment. Having been subjected to that at home, there was no way I was going to allow myself to endure any more shit. The entire scene was surreal. There were over a hundred people surrounding us. In my mind it was like a modern-day Western, with me as the good guy, and El Gordo, Curly, and his gang of thugs as the bad guys. I was like the lone sheriff outcast, facing off against the gang of thugs who were tormenting the town. Foolishly, I was more afraid of being afraid than of getting my ass kicked. I'd been beaten up by Beelzebub before and knew I would survive it. I'd also been humiliated and knew that that was more painful than any beating I'd ever taken. I vowed to fight until I was either dead or unconscious. Both were very real possibilities and everyone knew it.

Joe and I were standing facing each other, when he yells something like, "Come on! Come on!" I replied with something like, "This is your shit! You go for it!" He was about to respond when I attacked him. Looking back, I know I attacked more out of desperation than because I believed I could win. I knew there would never be a winner. Once a fight started, it never ended. I threw several punches, all of which missed, and then I took a giant swing which threw me off balance. I fell to my knees and was expecting to get kicked when once again the gods of war interceded on my behalf. The store owner came out of the store and chased all of us away. I got up, hearing dozens of voices saying all sorts of things. I remember I was wearing my Sunday shoes because they had leather soles and were better to kick with. The trouble was they were also slippery on the dried grass, which is why I'd slipped. We all started walking towards the main campus. In the midst of the giant crowd El Gordo and I stopped and squared off against each other again, this time in the teacher's parking lot. We began circling each other like two roosters about to pounce. Again, I am not sure why, but I attacked first. I am not sure that I was braver or badder, but somehow I knew it wasn't only about the fight. I knew I had to demonstrate courage and make an impression on all those watching, because one battle usually led to another. I had to make an impression and plant an image of having guts and being a fighter. Otherwise I ran the risk of someone else trying to use me as a punk to build their reputation upon. I charged with a jumping kick in the air which connected squarely on Joe's chest. As I landed I rained a dozen blows upon him. I must have hit him pretty hard because he was about to go down, and then suddenly the coward screamed out in a whimpering voice, "Curly! Curly!" At the sound of his pitiful screams the baddest and sickest homicidal maniac on Main Drive attacked me. He did so in the exact manner in which I had attacked Joe. The son of a bitch copied my move and leaped into the air with a running start, landing a solid kick to my chest. At that moment Rudy Hasset interceded on my behalf. Curly landed and I squared off with him. Curly smiled at Rudy and told him the fight wasn't with him. Rudy told Curly the exact same thing. The fight of the year had grown into a huge event, and half the student body was now out there watching me face off against this sick bastard. At that moment several teachers came out and stopped the brawl, which caused everyone to start walking away, but I knew it wasn't over. Storm clouds loomed overhead for the rest of the day, and it seemed as if they didn't leave for years.

   The rest of the day proceeded as I'd expected. No one spoke to me, and everyone stared. Some of them stared with anger and others with amazement. Most people were simply surprised I'd had the balls to attack a reputed badass. I was not expected to survive without taking a serious beating, and several of the older kids were taking bets on whether or not I'd get my ass kicked. I had no intentions of taking the bus home that day, as my chances of survival were not good. While walking home after school, again with Rudy Hasset, I didn't expect to be attacked. Even though I knew it was more than three miles from the school to my front door. Rudy and I were almost to the Hererra's store on Main Drive when a car suddenly pulled up next to us. Within seconds Curly, Joe, Angel Flores, Alejandro Longoria, and some other high school guys jumped out and surrounded us. I'd never been in a situation like that in my life, and had no experience fighting multiple opponents of this caliber and severity. I felt I was fucked and couldn't see a way out of there. Alejandro Longoria came up from behind and grabbed me, holding me in an armlock with my arms held behind me. I watched as the baddest, most meanest bastard on Main Drive, opened a green handled knife and stepped towards me. I was more than a little scared, and in an act of sheer terror I cried out, "Rudy!" Once again this guy jumped in and saved my butt. Rudy attacked Curly, kicking at his hand, trying to knock the knife out from it. Curly, who moved like a cat, sidestepped and took a slice at Rudy, who managed to move away before being cut. I am still amazed at the degree of brutality which Curly and his gang was willing to exercise. Curly intended to make an example of me, and damn the consequences. In the meantime I'd managed to get away from Alejandro. I'd jumped across a ditch, thereby keeping it between myself and the gang. Once again the gods of war parted the sky and intervened on my behalf. Mr. Perez, Curly's father, suddenly drove up and yelled for Curly to get inside the car. Then like a cat who'd been caught torturing a mouse, Curly turned and walked away. The other guys quickly followed, jumping back into their car and driving off. Rudy and I continued to walk down Main Drive expecting to be attacked again. I felt like some old-fashioned gunfighter, walking down the main street, on my way to meet another in a life or death match. I never felt so alone in all my life. I knew it was either up to me to fight and win, or quit and die. There was no middle ground on Main Drive. The degree of brutality was beyond description. Life was cheap, blood was common, and death waited patiently for the next battle which would surely come. I knew we didn't stand a chance if we were attacked again. We had no weapons to defend ourselves with, nor did we have the experience of dealing with such coldhearted brutality. Whatever was left of my innocence faded away that day under the hot Texas sun. It was the longest walk I'd ever taken in my life. The hot afternoon sun and the humidity made it even more miserable. The Universe must have been watching, because Curly and his gang of thugs never showed up again. Finally we reached Rudy's house. He said, "See you later," and walked off. He must have been very scared, but no more than I was. I walked the rest of the way home alone, past Curly's house where the gang hung out.

    The days after the battle dragged on with rumors and gossip everywhere. I felt more alone than ever, and I never assumed I'd have help. I expected to be caught or surprised one day and killed, either by Curly and his gang of thugs or their relatives. I expected to be beaten to death or stabbed. I swore I wouldn't go down easily and that I'd take at least one of them with me. I felt like a hunted animal, unable to relax and afraid to drop my guard. This was clearly gallows logic, but in light of my situation, without police protection, or intervention by my family or school administrators, taking somebody with me was the best of all my terrible choices. I tried to remember to always carry a knife, and practiced slicing, stabbing, and killing imaginary attackers. In my mind I imagined myself as the good guy, fighting off gangs of evil thugs and being victorious. In reality I felt like a hunted animal, without protection, solace, or a chance. I had no one to turn to, and asking for help would have been an admission of my fear, which I could not have publicly admitted. Fear crept into my dreams and haunted me. It mixed with the anger I felt and concocted into an ugly and violent potion, which made me capable of murder. I developed the same suicidal tendencies so common amongst poor barrio dwellers. I developed a self-defeating logic which helped me cope with the reality that I might be murdered by a gang of thugs, for no more than talking to a girl. Fear and death became my only companions, which followed me like a dark cloud everywhere I went. In order to manage it, I developed more dysfunctional behaviors. I grew into some kind of half person, half animal, prowling around the edges of society, peering in only to see what I was missing. I grew lonelier than I'd ever believed possible without dying of loneliness.

It didn't take long for Rudy Hasset to grasp the reality of his predicament. He'd placed himself against the toughest group of bandits, thugs, and assholes on Main Drive. I was saddened when he, the only guy who'd been my friend during crisis, simply disappeared and stopped associating with me. After a while we never spoke again. The result of the biggest street fight of my life up to that point was that I'd lost all my supposed friends. I'd also gained a reputation as someone who knew how to fight. Big fucking deal. I never wanted to be a fighter and would have rather been left alone. I wanted to read my books, draw cartoons, read comics, play football, and get the hell out of Texas. I never wanted to become a street fighter. I never wanted to feel hunted and have to look over my shoulder everywhere I went. However, the Universe had different plans for me, and pushed me in a direction I never wanted to go. The reputation I received for standing up to Curly Perez extended beyond Andrew Jackson Junior High School, and I became a street celebrity on Main Drive. I'll bet Suzy would have given me a blow job for sure after that fight. Even the teachers looked at me differently. Foolish me, although I was still desperately frightened of Curly's impending retaliation, I thought it was kind of cool. I was unaware that this new found attention was just the lull before the storm. For instance, my new reputation came with benefits, such as, the make-believe tough guys left me alone. I never had to deal with fake cowardly bastards teasing me or giving me any shit. They saw the fury in my eyes. I must have looked pretty scary, because even the girls were afraid of me. The girls who found my reputation attractive were not the kind of girls I found alluring. I don't know why, but I never found street girls attractive. The more often they made eyes at me, the more I found them revolting. Suzy and her friends had a tremendous impact on me. I found them cruel, veil, and disgusting. I never wanted to associate with girls who'd been passed around by assholes like Curly and his gang of thugs. Girls like Suzy, Margie, Angie, and other street girls thought I was really something, but I thought they were trash. I couldn't understand how they believed guys who acted and looked like Curly were anything more than garbage. I still don't understand, and still don't find street girls attractive, and I've been around them all my life. I have grown kinder towards them, or at least now I don't judge them, but I still won't have anything to do with such individuals. I've learned how miserable and brutalized someone has to be in order to develop such tendencies.

Who would want such a damaged creature with so much baggage?

Much to my disappointment my own brother Punk, whom I had completely misjudged, was one of those who abandoned me. This act of cowardice is what earned him his alias. Looking back, I realize that he was a chameleon. He could change colors and blend in anywhere. Years later I would step into another major battle in his defense, again over a girl. To this day he has never repaid the favor. Oddly, I'd watched him beat the crap out of several guys before, but Curly and his thugs scared him enough to turn his back on his own brother. Recently it has also dawned on me that Punk never developed any bond with me. This magical event which is supposed to take place between siblings never occurred. He never felt anything other than annoyance towards me, and never did anything to help me, no matter how much I needed it. Learning this has solved many puzzles and answered many questions in my life. I discovered a terrible secret, a major contributing factor to my family's dysfunction. The reason why my father and mother never presented a united front during a crisis was that they had chosen sides. Each had chosen their own side, which is typical of 96ers. They were never united as married people. They were always on opposite ends of things. What they lacked in their marriage was also absent amongst their children. There was never any sense of caring or concern. It was everyone for themselves, which put them against everyone else. As a result, there was never a feeling of love towards their children. I found myself comparing the way things were, with the way things were "supposed" to be. I suffered terribly because of the absence of affection amongst us. I just wanted to feel a part of a family. I realize I would have never found the Warrior's path if I'd had a more functional upbringing. Perhaps it was a Hollywood make-believe ideal of what makes the "good guys" different from the "bad guys." I always believed that an older brother was supposed to protect his younger brother, which is what I did for Punk. I'd grown up believing families were supposed to be there for you, not against you. I suffered terribly, and have my parent's dysfunction to blame. Their bad parenting has never stopped tormenting me and I don't believe it ever will. Every time I remember how much I suffered as a child, I am so happy I don't have children. I would never want to harm someone as badly.

By some miracle the school year ended without my being beaten, stabbed, or killed. The entire experience left me assured that I could expect no one to intercede, and that I would not live to see my eighteenth birthday. Each passing year I felt my self-worth lessen, as my parent's indifference and my struggles to survive seemed too much to bear. Looking back, I don't know how I survived, and in truth, I know I didn't. I died inside. The part of a person which is born with hope, love, and goodness died. All that remained was the chewed up spirit of a tormented individual. I still cannot believe I lived through such a horrible upbringing. This is why I made the decision to face these ghosts and rip them away from my soul. I am determined to unload all the negative baggage of my childhood and adolescence via this journey thorough the most painful memories of my life. I feel it gradually loosening its hold on me, even though every step hurts like having a hot branding iron placed on my spirit. After more than forty years on this path I've learned that dislodging painful memories is a never-ending process, and not a simple or singular act.

Texas escapee,

don Jesus M. Ramirez

Chapter Three
No Tejano Football Heroes Wanted

"Some pains are easier forgotten than others. Some wrongs can only be corrected via retribution. Forgiveness is never easily given."

–don Jesus M. Ramirez

I am not sure when I fell in love with football. It might have been in the fifth, or maybe even the sixth grade. Perhaps it was one of the times I walked to the high school football field to watch a game. I really don't remember when, but I remember why. Unless you've lived in the South, you'll never understand the value Southerners place on football. It's a rite of passage and standard of achievement. It's the equivalent of going on a vision quest for Native Americans or a walkabout for Australian Aborigines. In addition to this, next to dancing, women in Texas love football. Or at least Norma Jean Slaughter did, and I wanted so much to impress her. Football hero worshiping has always been a major part of Southern DOEI culture. Like all 96ers I wanted to be popular, be a part of something, and be validated for it. Like all kids I wanted to be accepted, liked, and well-known at Andrew Jackson High School. Looking back, it seems an act of lunacy to risk broken bones just to be a part of a culture that rejected, humiliated, and oppressed you, but I did it.

The first time I saw how the fans loved football players I knew I wanted to play football in front of a cheering crowd. It was tremendous. Imagine living out in the middle of nowhere, and being so poor and average that no one knew you existed, and then being given an opportunity to shine. Imagine being a nobody, never feeling like a part of anything. Imagine being shunned by hundreds of your DOEI classmates, and then having an opportunity to be somebody special. It was like being born again, brought back from the dead. Unless you've experienced this it may sound ridiculous, but at the time it was like throwing a drowning man a lifeline. It was like the parting of the Red Sea, which gave me a path to the Promised Land. Football saved me from oblivion. It gave me self-respect and placed me in the excitement I longed to be a part of. Football in high school made me respected, admired, and acknowledged publicly. I belonged to a team, had a uniform, and was good at it. Even though I knew it was transitory, shallow, and didn't change the fact that I was viewed as a second class citizen by virtue of being a Tejano. It also gave me a chance to hit people and receive recognition for it. Off the field I would have been arrested for similar conduct. On the field I was praised, respected, and held in awe for doing what I'd been doing all my life; fighting back. It was easy. It made the danger and hard work of playing football sheer pleasure. Another detail was that on the field I never had to compete with Beelzebub. I was judged by my willingness to smash into others, and valued for my courage and willingness to take on anyone. On the field I made my own way, based on my desire and ability. I don't know what Beelzebub was doing at the time, and I didn't care. I do know that he went out for football during his seventh grade year, but wasn't willing to put in the work unless he received immediate rewards. He was a bully at home, but outside the house he was a coward. He went out for the team because everyone else did, but quit after several weeks. He tried basketball and failed at that too, and then spent his time making fun of those who played.

He took the position that it was dumb to risk injury for a game. In truth he simply lacked the courage. Like all haters he faded into the background and rationalized his cowardice. It was a pattern which he repeated for the rest of his life.

Another Tejano guy who saw himself as being above the rest was Eduardo Rodriguez, or "Tiny" as his parents called him, because he was so short. He was a few years older than me and became a good football player, and for a time I wanted to play like him. Sadly, as it is with all average people, the attention he received soon revealed his true nature. He thought of himself as a hero and believed I wanted to be like him. I was disappointed with the arrogance I *saw* in his eyes. Instead of being a benevolent role model, the praise distorted him and revealed deep flaws in his character. I was disappointed he became just another delusional wannabe hero. He could have been a great help to people like myself. I had already *seen* him and I wasn't interested in being around him. I didn't want to be a subordinate, which was how he wanted to treat me, instead of like a friend. I remember once asking him for one of his football pictures. He said he wouldn't give one to me, but that he'd sell me one. Looking back, I don't know why I wasn't insulted or angry. At the time it seemed fair, as I knew how much everything cost. It was only afterwards that I realized why he made me pay for it. To him I was a nobody, and in his mind I would never amount to much, at least not at school. Simply stated, he didn't see me worth the cost of a picture. At the time, in my naïve mind, him asking me to pay made sense. I mean, I'd bought several of my school pictures and I had to pay for them as well. Anyway, I paid him. He made a big deal of cutting and signing it as if he were a big football star. Looking back, it's just a bad joke and a reflection of his lack of character. He signed it as if he considered me to be a fan of his. This is what happens to all average people when they receive a little extra attention. This is an example of what happens to all 96ers when people start blowing smoke up their whazoo. It's what happens when you believe the praise you received for something applies to your entire life. Like all ex-high school football heroes, he discovered that an ability to play football has nothing to do with real life, making decisions, or will ever matter after graduation. His disillusioned self-importance, lack of character, and disconnection from reality caused him to believe he would succeed no matter what he did. Like most high school football heroes he faded away into the faceless crowds. He never completed college and failed miserably at life. He joined the millions of former jocks who knocked up their girlfriends, got married, divorced, and then put on another hundred pounds. In truth, he never mattered as much as a fart in the wind, and his arrogance was based on what he saw through his own eyes. All the praise and encouragement his parents gave him amounted to nothing more than an excuse not to leave Main Drive, venture out, or test his mettle against the world.

There weren't many Tejano football heroes at Andrew Jackson. There weren't many Tejano football players anywhere for that matter. As a result there weren't many Tejano fans. The few Tejanos who played football were like a strange creature no one knew what to do with. The majority of Tejano students were never encouraged to participate in any school activities. We were shunned and marginalized, and tragically the few individuals who could have become role models started believing the rest of us were beneath their attention. Guys like Eduardo quickly got caught up in the same self-made fantasy which is so popular in high school. The late Sixties and early Seventies were perfect breeding grounds for self-centered Hollywood versions of reality. It was easy to convince yourself that somehow you were different, special, and destined for greatness. Everyone told Eduardo he'd probably be a high school football coach one day, or some important political figure. The idiot believed all the smoke blown up his ass, and thought he was so wonderful, the racism which denied Tejanos equal opportunity would not apply to him. The little bubble he lived in, created by his parents, burst before graduation, and all those dreams built on ego crumbled. It all seemed like a harmless fantasy, only it wasn't harmless because like so many other popular people in high school, their indifference was harmful. Their self-created celebrity built a wall around them, and average people love to see idols fall.

For example, Eduardo was talked into playing a role in a play someone had dreamed up and presented to the student population during Senior Week. He was booed off the stage and humiliated by the same people he'd looked down upon. He expected to be loved and applauded. Instead he was shamed, cursed, and hated. I spoke to him afterwards. He was so insulted and angry, it was funny to watch. I wonder what he would have said if I'd told him that I was one of the hundreds booing. The wannabe James Dean even bought a new pair of jeans and borrowed my father's old worn-out motorcycle jacket for the play. I hear he's gained a hundred pounds, is divorced, and has a middle management manual labor job for HEB, a grocery chain store in Texas. Whoopee! He expected more than this after believing himself to be such a big man on campus. In the end he was just another unwanted Tejano football hero. Even then I knew he was suffering from the same delusional self-importance which so many high school athletes suffer. Once out of high school they quickly fade away and sink into their own level of incompetence. Eduardo Rodriguez should be the name of an entire lesson on avoiding your own bullshit. I use his name when giving my students an example of how dangerous your own lies can be. The first step to becoming a Warrior is to stop bullshitting yourself. Play the cards you've been dealt and don't try to bluff your way past the goalpost.

I never believed playing football made me superior, it just gave me something in common with a lot of other people. It helped me feel like I was a part of something bigger than myself, but it was all bullshit. I wanted to get the hell out of Texas since I'd been old enough to know better. I wanted to travel, be free, and get away from racism. After football ended I had no reason or opportunity to associate with Eduardo or his friends. We had nothing in common, or at least he thought. I already knew I was going to join the Army after high school, while he was planning to get married. I didn't want to be anything like him. He became just another reason why I couldn't wait to get the hell out of Texas.

It's amazing how much easier life is, simply because your parents treat you like you matter. Mr. and Mrs. Rodriguez were everything my parents were not. They loved their children and demonstrated it via their behavior towards them. Standing on my front porch, across the street from theirs, while living in a nightmare I often wished I had been a part of their family, and not mine. The only real thing I envied about Tiny was his parents. I didn't like his girlfriend, who was just an average looking girl without an education, goals, or professional aspirations. He could have done a lot better, although he had the nerve to say that to me about a girl I once dated. Goes to show how life unfolds in mysterious ways. The poor guy must have banged her and thought he was in love. While he was looking forward to getting married, I was looking forward to getting the hell out of Texas and seeing the world.

I started playing football in the seventh grade, and was prouder than ever when Mr. Rodriguez told my father I was very good. My father however, being who he was, didn't believe it and told me so. He said he couldn't believe I was good at football because according to him, I was so lazy. Nothing I did impressed him and I had no idea why. Looking back, I realize he needed someone to hate, and he chose me. I kept playing football and testing my mettle against bigger kids. It was easy. I'd been fighting for years, so I grew stronger, tougher, meaner, and more determined to succeed. I came to accept my father would never appreciate what I accomplished and stopped telling anyone what I did. It's why I'm good at keeping secrets. Football was the second best thing I liked about going to school. The first was the girls. Third was hitting people, and the fourth was learning. I loved to learn and the more I explored, the more I wanted to know. It was like giving water to a man dying of thirst. I fell in love with knowledge and books as a child, and have been a lover of both ever since.

My first football coach was Mr. Rhodes, who looked like one of those backwoods rednecks right out of a Civil War movie. I don't know how he became a coach or why, as he was not a good person, or a good coach. He was a tall and skinny arrogant man with bushy hair, who wore glasses and had false teeth that moved when he got angry and spoke. He was a typical Southern DOEI who looked down on Tejanos. It always amazed me how people could behave in such a horrible manner and expect no consequences. None of my oppressors realized while they were attempting to squash me that no one forgets being screwed over. How is it possible that it never occurs to such fools that one of the people who they attempted to squash would write about their experiences? I don't get it. Anyways, that year I tried out for the best position on the field, quarterback, and I got it. I loved being in the backfield as a quarterback. I was the leader of the team and loved it. After falling in love with Norma Jean in the fifth grade, I thought I could impress her by playing football. I loved the entire experience. I loved the hard work, summer camp, sweating, hitting, running plays, and just being a part of something. I loved the illusion of having found my place in the sun. On the field I felt special and nobody would mess with me. I stopped being a nobody and in one smooth step changed from being just another Tejano, to being a football player. Plus, I was good. I don't mean I was okay. I mean, I was damn good. I was fast and could pivot, changing directions quickly. I wasn't afraid of anyone, even though I was getting the crap knocked out of me for years. I'd been fighting Beelzebub all my life, so hitting bigger guys was as simple as throwing a rock. I was more afraid of not being allowed to play than I was of getting hurt. I never backed down and stepped up every time there was a fight on the field. I soon got a reputation as a tough kid who liked to fight, and didn't care who with. As I mentioned before, Rudy Hasset, the same guy who pulled me out of a jam, also played football, and earned himself a similar reputation. We could outplay everyone else on the field. It was great. He later joined a gang of losers on Main Drive, and eventually murdered someone, but I was long gone by the time that happened. All of those thugs and rejects on Main Drive became my enemies. It's too bad. We could have been lifelong friends. I once threw a pass to him for a game winning touchdown. For a few magical moments of our adolescence we were football heroes. It lasted as long as the bus ride home. I still have the newspaper clipping from that game.

Anywhere else in the country I'd have made friends for life on the field. The problem was I played football in the South with guys like Robbie Rogers, Sammy Hill, Billy Myers, Bill Shoemaker, Bill Chancy, and other such bigots who would never be more than classmates. These guys had been brainwashed by their parents and South Texas DOEI society to avoid contact with Tejanos. None of them ever invited me to hang out with them, or anywhere else. We were never more than casual acquaintances, even though I'd known them since the first grade. It's the way the Southern caste system works in Texas. Even if one of these guys would have wanted to be friends, the rest of them would have discouraged it. You are not valued as a human being unless you look and think like them. It was a horrible realization to learn that to them I was not thought of as good enough to be friends with. I also knew I'd never see any of these guys again after high school. Therefore there wasn't any point in letting my feelings get hurt. They were as much victims of the racist attitudes of Texas as I, and that's the best I can say. As I've mentioned before, much to my disappointment such behavior was typical of my experiences with DOEIs while growing up in Texas. Which made knocking the hell out of them on the football field fun, and I never tired of it. For a very short period in my life we had football in common, even if it was only a temporary distraction. My willingness to keep trying even after endless disappointments paid off. During the seventh grade, not only was I on the team, I was the quarterback. Just like Tiny Rodriguez, from whom I'd gotten the idea. My first year of football was great and in my mind I'd became a real-life football hero. Trouble was that in a racist society with clear racial boundaries no one seemed to notice. The DOEIs were not interested in Tejano football heroes, and the Tejano kids didn't care. Even I knew it was all a school fantasy, as no

Tejano ever got a scholarship from Andrew Jackson. I never got the recognition I thought I deserved, only superficial approval from teachers and shallow attention from team members. It wasn't much but it was enough to make me want to play harder. I loved football and during the few moments of intense action I was the happiest I'd ever been in my life. Being in the middle of the action became my addiction, and I soon discovered that I only felt alive during moments of intense danger. I also discovered that I was able to function better than the average person while under attack. I loved being in the middle of the fray, and this discovery changed my life forever. I'd become a full-fledged adrenaline junkie, who years later would impress others by being able to control my emotions during moments of intense danger.

As I continued to develop my identity, I noticed my improvements were not met with approval by my father or Beelzebub. Neither of them wanted to treat me in any other manner. As I grew stronger and more confident, fistfights with Beelzebub developed into full-fledged knockdown, drag out battles, with him usually getting the better of me. Stubbornly, I always stood up to him and willingly traded blow for blow, which was stupid, as he was much heavier and bigger. At the time I didn't know any better. No matter how many times he beat me up, I'd always fight him again. It's amazing that I never quit fighting my brother, who would not stop picking on me. His relentless behavior is what taught me that once a fight starts, it never ends until one of you is dead. Only then can you stop worrying about unexpected attacks from your enemy. Our father did not want us fighting, but the fights were becoming so numerous and violent that things got broken, as well as bloody noses, black eyes, and torn clothing. I kept fighting back harder and he beat me only because of his size. I hated him and kept training because I knew someday his size wouldn't matter. I knew there would come a day when I would kick his ass. This is why I started boxing. For the record, I never wanted to be a fighter, soldier, or a tough guy. I would have preferred to play with my toys, read my comic books, and be left alone. Yet, these terrible events became the keys to my freedom.

My father, whom I swear was a barbarian, came up with the most unbelievable and bizarre solution to end the fighting between Beelzebub and I. One Sunday morning, Beelzebub had once again found another reason to pick on me. I have no idea what the hell he was mad at this time. We fought back and forth until the noise got our father's attention. In the most bizarre experience of abusive treatment, he beat us both with a belt, and then made us kneel down as he ordered someone to bring him the salt shaker. He made us strip off our shirts, and then placed salt on Beelzebub's back. He then ordered me to lick the salt off. When I hesitated, he beat me until I did as he told. He then did the same to Beelzebub. I have no idea what this was supposed to teach us. All I learned was to hate him even more. I hated both of them the same way a prisoner hates his jailers. I still don't understand what he was attempting to teach us, as it was his fault Beelzebub was so violent. By beating us, and then humiliating us via making us lick salt from each other's backs, he further ingrained the hate I felt for each of them.

My father and Beelzebub were not the only ones who found my development troubling. The entire population of DOEIs at Andrew Jackson High School found my presence disturbing. They did not want a Tejano football hero who wouldn't take shit or stay quiet. High school was supposed to be the time when young DOEIs demonstrated how much better, tougher, and meaner they were. As it turned out, they weren't tougher, meaner, or better. Their only advantage was that they'd been born DOEIs by accident in a racist society. Other than the accident of birth, most had zero accomplishments, and as far as I could see were no better than myself. In fact, an easy life made many of them soft and of no consequence in a physical confrontation. I was physically fearless, as I had been fighting since I could remember. I outran, outplayed, outhustled, and outdid every DOEI kid on the team, but I never got attention from the coaches because my parents didn't go to the football booster club meetings. Once while playing against our archrivals, Calallen, I played every play of the game and was in every tackle of the night. After we'd won the coach stated that I had saved the game. It was the first public compliment I ever received. None of them ever knew how much I hated being treated as an inferior. Learning that I could play football better, but would never receive the recognition for doing so, was a bittersweet discovery. I would never receive the same accolades as DOEI players in that racist caste system created to oppress people of color. I was so angry, and seeing the unfairness of it made me hate my oppressors even more. The injustice made me want to kick Beelzebub's ass more than anything else in the world, as he was the ultimate oppressor in my life.

In spite of it all I continued to excel and gain more confidence, but it was all part of the same bittersweet pill of *seeing* and knowing what others did not. My ability to perceive and see past people's masks made it nearly impossible to manage. I kept on doing my best, but there was no place on Main Drive or at Andrew Jackson for Tejano football heroes. Those of us who played football were only accepted by DOEIs on the football field. Other than that, we were ignored. I was never invited to anyone's house or any parties, and I never attempted to fit in with the cliques. I went to practice and worked hard. The rule, as per Coach Washington, was that anyone who missed practice twice would not be allowed to dress out on Friday night. If anyone missed practice they would not be allowed to play in the game. However, despite my never breaking this rule, pressure from the parent's booster club, politics, and the principal, found me on the bench, and put the DOEIs who had missed practice on the field every Friday night. It was one of many betrayals I endured by 96ers in positions of authority. The entire experience was a demonstration of how bad parenting affects your life in ways you'd never have imagined.

There is one Friday night I recall in particular. After the game one of the girls came up to me and said, "We're so sorry you lost tonight." I replied honestly, saying that I didn't lose, because I didn't play. The following Monday Coach Washington said he wanted to see me in his office. Upon his request I replied, "No problem, Coach." He knew I had a right to be pissed off, and nothing was ever said about it again. I quit playing football that year. To this very day I remember Coach Washington as one of the people who did me harm for no reason. Coach Washington stole my high school football experience. I haven't forgiven or forgotten his deliberate act of betrayal, which needs balancing. In stereotypical fashion he taught me that life is not fair, and aside from getting pissed off, there's usually little you can do about most of it. He taught me that a man's position has nothing to do with character or the value of his promises.

Soon after denying me the position I'd earned via my hard work during practice, Coach Washington was fired and replaced. I never saw or heard from him again. The new coach was named Milton, but everyone called him "Tear Drop," because he cried after a pep rally once. He only remained coach for one season. I tried playing again, and made the team, but found that after Coach Washington's betrayal the thrill was gone. It made no sense to bust my ass for something that wouldn't mean shit after the season ended. Football and all that it once meant became another symbol of racism and oppression at Andrew Jackson High School. Like I said, life is not fair and there is usually nothing you can do about it.

I had several other football coaches before Coach Washington. One of them literally beat a fourteen-year-old kid named Joe Garcia like an animal during a game. He taught me that violence is the ultimate form of authority, and almost always works. He was never legally charged or fired for beating up a child, and later he began dating one of the students. He eventually knocked her up, and then they got married.

Another coach I had was Coach Rumley, who routinely used his paddle. He taught me that power is justice, or at least what passes for justice in Texas. Surprisingly he also taught me that if you need a helping hand, don't look for it from teachers, or anyone other than yourself. The poor dumbass was so disconnected from reality that he never knew his wife was cheating on him until he got dumped for a dance teacher. These were some of the valuable life lessons I learned while at AJHS, which prepared me well for dealing with bigotry in the United States Army.

My father never saw me play football or box, even though I was considered to be very good by other parents, who told him about my accomplishments on several accounts. He told me he responded to their compliments by saying he couldn't believe how someone who wasn't worth a shit at home, could be such a good football player and boxer. By that time I no longer gave a damn what he thought or said.

I was as mean and as tough as I had to be to survive. What the hell did he expect from me after treating me like shit? He was a horrible parent, and like Beelzebub, he served as my motivation to fight. I hated his guts and vented my rage every time I entered the ring. I did the same every time I fought on the streets, which made me a dangerous individual. I have no idea how many fights I've had or how many individuals I've injured. I have no idea how many of those I hurt were guilty or innocent. I fought anyone at any time and anywhere with equal passion. My objective was to utterly destroy my opponent. While boxing I actually wanted to kill someone in the ring. I believed that if I'd killed someone as an amateur fighter, my professional career would be made. This might scare some people, and it should, because there are kids out there right now who are just like I was. When the bell rang I was out to kill everyone I fought, and I nearly did. Keep in mind, the social structure at Andrew Jackson was set up so that it was completely impossible for any Tejano athlete to be anything more. Racism was so deeply ingrained into every fiber of school culture, that even though I was never considered an accepted hero by the student population, I was still considered a cool guy for being a badass. Not because I won every fight, but because I would fight anyone at any time. The truth is I knew it was impossible to avoid someone who was looking for you. If someone was out to get you, they'd find you sooner or later. My philosophy was that if someone wanted to fight me, it didn't matter why or where. The best thing to do was to find them, call them out, and try to beat them to death. I threw caution to the wind and fought like I was charging the Normandy beaches on D-Day with nowhere to retreat. As you can imagine, I had thugs lining up to fight me after school, at parties, dances, or anywhere they found me. I was fighting all the time. My reputation got so bad that guys would come from other schools and other towns just to fight me. After a while things got so bad that no one, not even the football players, would hang with me. It got so that every time I'd see a strange guy looking at me, I'd drop my books, tighten my shoelaces, and charge. After a while, talking was just a waste of time. I saw no use in asking questions or listening to anymore bullshit. A lot of these guys wanted to give a speech and tell whoever was listening why they were there to fight me. I didn't care. I decided that if they came to fight, they'd come to the right place. Like I said, I have no idea how many guys I've fought, which guy was avenging who, or what we fought over. None of it mattered. All that was necessary was knocking the shit out of all of them one at a time, or as many as jumped me. I'd learned that an ass whipping was better than the fear that ate at you once you knew a fight was coming. I no longer cared if I ever had any friends. No one would associate with me anyways, other than in just a passing manner. Everyone was afraid of me, which suited me fine. I'd grown accustomed to being alone. Even though I hated it, it was better than being afraid. Or worse, being someone's dog.

One of the most famous fights I had in high school was with Eduardo Rodriguez, the self-proclaimed football hero and popular youth leader. I was a sophomore at the time, while he was a senior. During one of the many storms which took place in hurricane season, Coach Washington, the same asshole who'd refused to let me play, had the football team meet in one of the adjoining rooms of the gym. He'd found some old boxing gloves and thought it would be funny to watch the players beat the hell out of each other. He would call out two guys, who would then go out on the mat and put on the gloves. There was no way to back down without being thought a coward. When he called my name, and then Eduardo's, I knew it was all about him resenting my attitude, which I never hid. I thought being pissed off that I wasn't allowed to play was appropriate, considering he was the one breaking his own rules. He wanted to see me get my ass kicked by someone who he believed could do it. Unbeknownst to him, I'd been boxing for two years by then. I'd also been in so many street fights I couldn't count them if I'd tried. I think a lot of people wanted to see how tough I really was. Eduardo and I stepped onto the mat while the entire varsity football team watched. We were the two toughest Tejano kids on campus and were about to get it on for the amusement of the coaches. The tension rose in the room, just like before a real boxing match. As usual I said to myself, "Fuck him! I'm not gonna take an ass kicking from nobody!" The room grew quiet as we put on our gloves. Coach Washington broke the silence by saying something like, "It's only playing around. We're not going for the championship." However, I knew a lot more rested on this than just having fun. Eduardo's reputation, as well as mine was on the line. I knew this fight would be talked about for the rest of my life at that school, and I wasn't going to lose it. I thought to myself, fuck it, there is no tomorrow, and I gotta leave it all in the ring. I took my stance, and Coach Washington yelled, "Fight!" I moved in behind my jab, and then threw my right cross, catching Eduardo square on the chin. I then followed with my left hook, and knocked him back onto his heels. He dug in, came back at me, and we swung at each other like lumberjacks trying to knock down a tree. We kept swinging for about three minutes without stopping, until Coach Washington called time. It was one hell of a fight, and everyone learned just how pissed off I could get. According to my oldest friend, Roger Hernández, I kicked Eduardo's ass. Once word got around people started behaving even more differently towards me. Many left me alone before, but now most avoided me completely. Eduardo also never treated me the same way again, and knew that he'd been beaten. He played it off like it was all just in fun, but I knew that's not the way he felt about it. I expected to have to fight him again and was ready, but it never happened. I'd had my ass kicked so many times by then, I didn't care. I knew once the first punch was thrown it wouldn't matter what we were fighting about, and it would never end until one of us was dead. That's just the way things were on Main Drive. Remember, people were coming back from Vietnam in body bags with flag draped coffins by the dozens. The draft was hauling people away and the rich DOEIs were running off to Canada. The people who had more courage than money were doing all the fighting. It hasn't changed.

Eduardo graduated that year and faded into oblivion. He had dreams of going to college and playing football, but no one gives scholarships to five foot four football players. I don't know why, but he later took a job at Woolworth's downtown as a dishwasher. It sucked because he was working out in the open and everyone could see him. I'd washed dishes too, but I'd been in the back, out of sight from the customers. The real irony was that by then I was working as a shoe salesman at Hardy's Shoe Store, and then as a salesman at National Shirt Shop. I'd see him washing dishes and stop by and say hello. I'd ask him if he had any money he could loan me. He'd usually have some change, which he'd get as tips for bussing the tables. I paid him back many years later. As far as I know, we're even on that count. He was going to college, working, and ended up marrying. That went to hell too. Last I heard he put on a hundred pounds and is now as fat as a tugboat. Like so many early bloomers, he had a great period during high school, but didn't do anything for the rest of his life. Like so many other "leading" people in high school, he let his parents convince him he was something special. Once he was out on his own, and mommy and daddy weren't there to praise him, he folded like a cheap lawn chair. His courage and bravado were put there by the accolades his relatives blew up his ass, but weren't really based on merit. I don't know if any members of the "starting team" amounted to a pound of shit. To my knowledge all of them faded into the faceless masses and disappeared.

Another significant fight I had was with one of the thugs on Main Drive named Adam Flores. Our fight brought me an unwanted degree of prestige. He was tall and skinny with red hair and freckles. He also had a large Adam's apple which made him look like a cartoon character. When I cut to the mettle of it, he was just another bully who'd grown up believing everyone would be afraid of him because he was so bad. The truth is he wasn't bad, or threatening, and I have no idea where he got the idea he was so tough. Once again I am reminded of how different I was, even amongst those wild-eyed, half-mad people surviving on the edge of society. Adam lived across the street from a thug named Rudy Cruz, also known as Goofy. He'd been going to the club dances and we knew some of the same girls. One of these girls was Tina Cantu. She was as beautiful as Salma Hayek, and just as short. She knew me because Beelzebub had gone out with her older sister, Rosie. I wanted to be with Tina, who'd met Adam and was dating him at the time. I first met her when I'd gone to her house with two guys who I was boxing with, Danny Davila and Able Gomez. While we were there she showed me a picture of Adam and asked if I knew him. I said I did, and then she asked me if Adam had a girlfriend. I said he did, because it was true. Tina was shocked because Adam had lied to her and she felt insulted, so she called him to confront him. Adam was just trying to get some, but I wasn't his friend, and had no reason to cover for him. The next thing I knew Adam was gunning for me and wanted to kick my ass. I didn't know if his girlfriend had broken up with him or what happened. At the time I was still trying to fit in, and just got caught up in the mix. On a Friday night shortly after, I saw him at a party where I shouldn't have been, and he started calling me names and so forth. Eduardo was there, and for some reason was trying to play the role of mediator. He was acting all important, like he was some big man or something. I have no idea why. I never asked to be protected. I knew there was no way to avoid a fight on Main Drive. Eventually it was going to happen, so you might as well get it over with. After speaking with Adam, Eduardo came back to tell me that he wanted to kick my ass. I said fuck it, let's go for it. However, due to Eduardo's intervention, the fight was postponed because Adam was drunk and no one wanted a fight at their party. I spent the entire weekend getting ready for the fight. By Monday morning I was mentally prepared and ready to rumble. I got to school late and had to go get a tardy slip from Mrs. Robinson, the school attendance clerk. After I got my slip I started to walk down the hall, when who do I find? Adam Flores. He was getting his books out of his locker. It was an expected event and I had no alternative but to step up, which I did. He turned and smiled at me, like a cat eyeing a bird. I told him I didn't want to fight, but there was no way I was going to back down. He said "I'm gonna kick your ass," or something along those lines. Not wasting any time I threw a high kick at him, and then dropped down to my feet and threw another kick to his chest. I knew I had to charge hard and try to take him out in the first few seconds of the fight. I charged with all the fury of a cornered animal. By this point I was no longer afraid, just pissed off. We crashed into the girl's home economics class, swinging and kicking, trying to kill each other. I landed some good shots to his chin and body, and had no intentions of stopping. The next thing I knew someone was pulling me off of him. I watched him pick himself up off the floor, and noticed it was the assistant principal who had broken us up. The fight might have lasted thirty seconds, but in those few moments I cemented my reputation at Andrew Jackson as a real-life badass. I'd fought every thug, wannabe tough guy, jock, and fool in school. By the time I left for the Army there was no one left to fight. I left without ever looking back or wondering why. The only good thing about coming from such a negative environment is that you never second guess your decision to leave or get homesick. No one realized how serious I was about getting out of that hellhole, and how much I hated the bastards who made my life so difficult.

In a culture that values brute force over intelligence, I grew in status. The amazing result of having fought the meanest thugs on Main Drive was that I became a local celebrity. I was the topic of gossip which spread throughout school and the neighborhood. I had singlehandedly stepped up and refused to submit to any of them. I had refused to take shit from any of them and chose to die on my feet, rather than survive on my knees. Something which was unheard of amongst the average people I grew up with. Rumors spread and the story of our thirty second fight grew into an epic knockdown brawl behind the auto mechanic shop, in which we both beat the hell out of each other. It was the stuff legends are made of, and I never tried to correct the stories. I just went on with my life, while at the same time watching my back and carrying a weapon everywhere I went. While at a party soon thereafter I saw Adam Flores again. I no longer cared or feared him. I knew he couldn't hurt me. I believed I could take him. Also, as usual, the asshole was drunk again. I never got drunk or high. Hell, I never relaxed, no matter where I was. I was always concerned I might get jumped, and knew I couldn't expect assistance from anyone. Eduardo was at that party also, but I knew better than to expect help from him. He was never one for brawling. For some reason no one ever started trouble with him. Sometime during the party I noticed him talking to Adam. I don't know about what, but they stopped as soon as they saw me watching, and quickly called me over. Like I said, Adam was drunk, and for some reason Eduardo was impressed with me. I have no idea what the hell was so great about having to fight off a bully who wanted to humiliate you, but there I was. Assholes... I had somehow become the object of their admiration. Strange thing was I didn't admire shit about either of them. For some reason everyone thought I was such a great guy because I hadn't backed down and threw the first blow. This must fall under the title of stupid male bonding or some other absurd ritual. I expected to be hunted down and attacked, like I would have done to an enemy, not admired. I just wanted to be left alone and certainly didn't want to be friends with Adam, or any of the other assholes he associated with. I had fought back because I hated them, not because I had anything to prove. These guys didn't get it. I was playing for keeps and didn't just want to beat them, I wanted to kill them. I never forgave or forgot anyone who'd ever wronged me. In my mind, once the fight started and blood was drawn, it never ended. I knew I would be seeking revenge for the rest of my life. I knew that if I played my cards right I'd see that bastard again. I knew that if I waited and watched I'd catch him alone, and then I'd fuck him up. I only wished I had at least one friend to back me up, but I never had a soul stand beside me. I would have loved to have felt like one of King Henry's men who fought together on St. Crispin's day, or one of the 300 who fought to the death with King Leonidas. I faced all my battles alone, which is why I hate gangs. Those bastards considered me vulnerable because neither Beelzebub, Bumper, Punk, or my father ever backed me up. I had no illusions of peace or friendship, and knew that although there may be a lull in the fighting, it was always lying there beneath the surface. I knew violence could show its ugly face at any moment and anywhere. I had foolishly adopted a code of ethics which my mother instilled in me about bravery and fairness. Thanks to her brainwashing I never started trouble, but once it started I felt compelled to seek justice. I deliberately avoided being near any of those bastards and watched them from a distance. I longed for the opportunity to jump out at them from the darkness with a baseball bat. Those assholes had no idea how angry and insane I was. They were just trying to impress their friends. I never antagonized anyone, but once someone messed with me, I never let it go. I hated those bastards with the same passion and rage I felt towards Beelzebub and my father. My belief was that fighting was one of the many unpleasant but necessary realities of life. It was best to accept reality in all its terrible ugliness and learn how to do it well. I became a secret avenger and hunted each one of my enemies down. I ambushed them like a rabid wolf and attacked every one of the gang members who once humiliated me. I wore a mask over my face and came out of nowhere, swinging my bat like some maniac out of a horror film. I never said a word, and every time I saw those guys limping, either with broken bones and wearing a cast, or a bandaged head, I pretended I had no idea what happened. I'd watch them watching me suspiciously, and pretend I didn't see them.

Today, I realize the real challenge was refusing to join the ranks of the people I hated. I knew even back then that just because there were more of them, didn't make them right, or protect them from the consequences of their behavior. I'm happy I didn't kill any of them. If I had I would have been doing them a favor. I knew that not knowing who it was, and wondering who attacked them without saying a word, has given them nightmares throughout their lives. The beatings I gave them became the stuff of legends, and the thugs that once considered themselves safe, disappeared. They'd only hang out in groups, and were also armed to the teeth. They'd drive up and down Main Drive expecting to see a stranger walking alone in the dark. They started doing investigations on their own, and things got real crazy for a while when they ended up shooting someone they knew. Not knowing changed them in horrible ways. They made up stories of being attacked by a gang of strangers, others just moved away. I have no idea how they explained it to themselves. Maybe it was fear or their parents who forced them to leave for their own protection. I'll never know, and I don't care. I've always hated bullies and always loved baseball.

  The effects of so much hate also changed me. It distorted my spirit and made me into a monster. I developed a habit of hitting everyone who crossed me or made a passing joke at my expense. I lost as much as I won. Letting go of the demons that possessed me was as difficult as acquiring the suicidal abandon required to confront multiple attackers. It took many years to let go of the anger. During that time it brought about many horrible events, and made my life a nightmare. I should have known the Universe would come to claim its due.

Texas escapee,
don Jesus M. Ramirez

Chapter Four
The Golden Gloves Champion

"Nothing soothes the heart of a Warrior like close quarters combat. It nurtures him, feeds him, and warms his soul. By fighting, a Warrior makes death his friend."

—don Jesus M. Ramirez

Nothing has taught me as much about life as boxing. Boxing has been there for me during the darkest moments and it has never let me down. It has never lied to me, and has always been a source of solace. This may sound strange to many, but I've learned that fighting is clean and pure. I don't mean fighting is good. I mean that violence, depending on the degree, is a purely unholy event. It's a war. Boxing is called a sport, but that's only by the people outside of the ring. Those inside it know it's a ruthless, cold-blooded, and socially approved legal method to kill someone. The demanding requirements have served as a sacred purging experience for me. It was not always that way. As I've stated before, I started boxing because I wanted to kick the shit out of Beelzebub. Had it not been for his constant tormenting I would have never wanted to learn to fight. I would have been perfectly happy playing with my toys and reading my comic books. Had it not been for him I'd be a completely different person. As it is, I've seen more death and destruction than the average person. I never wanted to learn how to hurt or kill anyone, I just hated bullies. I might have been a poet or a farmer. Like most things in my life, I never had much of a choice. It was either fight or surrender, and I'd die before doing that. Bullies like Beelzebub never gave me a choice. He planted the seed of hatred within me, which sparked my desire for revenge and led me to the real calling of my life; boxing. By the time I first heard of the Toltec discipline, I was already well on my way to many of its objectives. A Warrior's spirit must be tempered and able to bend or it will break. It must be both fire and ice. There are no shortcuts to reaching this elusive goal, and most who attempt it only catch a glimpse from a distance. Few are ever able to adopt it into their lives.

Unless you have been tormented by a bully, you might not believe how much I hated Beelzebub. He was the source of ninety percent of all my turmoil while growing up. His senseless random violence and sick sadistic manner forced me to learn how to fight. Looking back, I have to laugh as it must have been maddening for him. I refused to submit, even though he beat the shit out of me dozens of times. I fought back like a cornered animal against a larger and stronger foe, without hope of winning. I learned that size is not as important as fury and abandon. Unless you've been tormented by someone, you will never understand the depth of how it affects you. The constant shootings at schools across the country might give you a slight understanding of how being bullied affects a person. It literally drives you mad. Revenge becomes your sole purpose for living and you spend entire days fantasizing about it. You create plan upon plan as to how you are going to achieve victory over your enemy. Years later I often daydreamed of shooting the sadistic bastard. The trouble is that I'd never be able to kill him enough times to extract adequate revenge for all those years of torment. Christians say one should forgive his transgressors. I've learned that unilateral forgiveness is an exercise in futility. There are six points to forgiveness.

1. The person who offended you must acknowledge their actions and ask to be forgiven.

2. They must admit what they did was wrong.

3. They must promise to never do it again.

4. They must be worthy of forgiveness.

5. They must truly be sorry.

6. You must agree to forgive them.

My sick, sadistic, disturbed brother and father never did any of the above. I believe we are still at war and I must therefore always be leery of them. Beelzebub and my father are both dark spirits, like those spoken of in books by spiritualists. I know that wickedness comes in many shapes.

Boxing was another of my many great adventures. I started boxing the same way I did everything else, just by sheer force of will and determination. I had no resources, no support from my parents or anyone else, and although I had fought with Beelzebub and other bullies countless times, I had no experience fighting in a ring. I knew no one who boxed, and had no idea how I was going to go about it, but I did it. I was thirteen-years-old when the Golden Gloves were announced in the paper. I called the number listed in the advertisement and found out how to sign up. I hitchhiked into town, got the application, filled it out, and showed up at the physicals. It was the first time I had a doctor poke me about my privates and ask me to turn my head and cough. They took my blood pressure and looked me over. I must have been all right, because I passed the examination.

On the night of the fight I showed up early, wearing cutoff football pants and my running shoes. I talked one of the football coaches into going with me to help work my corner. I don't know what possessed him, or why he agreed to help work the corner. He had to get certified and go through a screening. I don't even remember his name. He was the same coach who was banging one of the Andrew Jackson students. He later married her, but that was all after the scandal.

On the first night of the tournament I didn't know who I was going to fight. I was nervous as hell when I stepped into the ring and saw my opponent for the first time. He was a Black kid named Frankie Poke, who was supposed to be a famous football player, although I'd never heard of him. The bell rang and we went for it like old-fashioned gladiators. I stood in front of him and we traded punches for three rounds. Like two robots we stood toe-to-toe and beat the hell out of each other. I must have been crazier, or just didn't give a damn, because I won the decision. The crowd went nuts.

The second night I fought a DOEI kid named Frankie King from Kingsville, Texas. He was about six inches taller than me, and we traded punches like our lives were on the line. My head was still sore from all the shots I'd received the night before. In the third round he tagged me with a right hand that rocked me and put me on the canvas. I was going to get up, but my cornerman, an old guy named Whitey Moore, who would later become my boxing coach, told me to stay down. It didn't take much to convince me. I stayed on the canvas and lost the fight by TKO.

Losing that fight changed my entire life. If I had won, who knows what might have happened. I might have quit boxing, but I doubt it. What I do know is losing that night set up an ongoing love/hate affair with boxing. I swore to never lose again. I hated losing. I kicked myself for months afterwards for not being better prepared and for a million other things. I swore I would not fight again until I was better trained and ready to compete. I did not fight in another competition for over a year. When I did, I won and I loved it. I started training as if my life depended on it, or as if I was training for the world championship. It changed everything about me. I ate, slept, and lived boxing. A lot of guys got drunk and messed around on weekends, but not me. I'd never been a party guy, as I was always too worried about getting jumped. I wasn't a real ladies' man yet, because at the time I still stuttered. I had never been a very good student, or anything else. But I was a real good fighter, and took to fighting like a bird takes to the sky. I flew as I'd been flying all my life. I had natural instincts, fury, and control due to the fact that I'd been fighting all my life with Beelzebub. I loved every bit of boxing, from the smell of the gym to the sound the bag made when you hit it. In the ring I felt totally alive. I loved the sense of danger, and most of all I loved the idea that I was preparing for the day I would beat the shit out of Beelzebub. I also loved the idea that I could beat the hell out of someone and get a pat on the back and a medal for it. If I did that in the streets I might get killed. If not, I'd certainly be arrested. Yet, if I killed someone in the ring, I'd be a hero. I'd receive validation, praise, and recognition, something I'd never received from anyone who mattered. As I mentioned before, I set out to kill someone in the ring as an amateur. It was a decision born out of desperation and a life of brutality via being humiliated and tormented as a child.

Amateur boxing has always been dangerous, but it was much worse back then. We did not have passbooks to keep track of our records and experience, as you must have today. It was a completely different sport with very few records of any kind. Coaches lied about their boxer's experience all the time. There was no real way of knowing if the guy you were fighting had four fights or forty. You might be in the ring with an experienced open class boxer and you'd not know it. Believe it or not, it was left up to the coaches and the honor system. What a joke. Looking back, I'm surprised more guys weren't killed. The average person has as much honor as a politician or a child molester. Back then, when someone wanted to stage a boxing show, they just got a couple of adults to work as judges, referees, and timekeepers, and then rented a wrestling ring. The biggest problem was the coaches would lie like politicians to get an edge for their boxers. There were a lot of backdoor agreements, which today would be completely illegal. Due to several deaths in the ring, today we have more rules, and safety is the ultimate concern. As usual, the biggest problem is corruption by the different associations. Allegedly, USA Boxing, Inc. is currently monopolizing amateur boxing across the entire country. Some smart guy figured out a way to get rich from a nonprofit organization, and it's all about the money. The problem is all the old timers feel ripped off because they were not included in the inner circle of those getting rich. They now spend all their time raising hell, complaining, bitching, and moaning about everything you can imagine.

Whitey Moore was an old timer from the Twenties. He'd been a tough slugger who'd fought way past his prime, and then started coaching. He volunteered to wrap my hands and work my corner during my fights, so I started training with him and his wife Minnie. They were old fight fans who were both too old to be doing what they did, but there they were. Minnie, who weighed about ninety pounds, would teach boxers how to hit the bag. While Whitey, who had to use a cane to get around, tried to teach boxers how to move around the ring. It was kind of funny, but at the time I didn't know any better. No one I knew had any idea about what it meant to be a real boxer. I quickly learned there was a lot more to it than just standing in the middle of the ring, trading punches until one of you dropped due to a broken jaw or exhaustion. Due to the absence of knowledge or volunteers, these two old farts, who were too old to be there, were the coaches. I don't know why I believed they could help, and looking back, it must have been a cultural thing. I'd been told that all adults knew a lot about life and deserved respect. Today I know that age has nothing to do with knowledge or wisdom.

Whitey had been around forever. He knew everyone and everyone knew him, but I learned most of what I learned there from other boxers. Guys like Danny Avalos, Tony Falcon, Blackie Zamora, Able Cannles, Ramon Sarrano, and dozens of other guys whose names escape me. I am sorry to say that Whitey did not teach me very much. Like most coaches, he had his favorites and I was not one of them. His favorite boxer was Danny Avalos. However, what Danny had in talent as a boxer, he lacked in judgment. Like all 96ers he had his head so far up his ass, he could see his lunch. Poor guy ended up in a dead-end manual labor job. With the exception of a guy who I'll refer to as "Mr. Silver," most of the boxers I grew up with turned out the same way. Mr. Silver became a full-blown politician and chief of officials for the country. He once handed me a brand new toolbox filled with tools, for free, when he worked at a department store in Corpus. He gave me a receipt and I walked out of the store. I think he was just trying to impress me because he liked my sister. Who knows. He was a ladies' man. Although he had a girlfriend, he'd keep several others available on the side. I guess all the guys I knew were guilty of the same thing. I never trusted him, but I didn't know why. There was just something sneaky about him, but most 96ers are like that. You have to get to know them before you discover who they are. After I left for the Army he stayed in Corpus and got married, divorced, and then remarried. He is one of the people whom I use as an example of what not to do. I tried to speak with him when I saw him at the National Championships in Las Vegas, but he acted as if I was asking him for money. I apologized for disturbing him and promised never to do so again. I've seen him around several times since then. I believe that a deliberate insult meant to humiliate you can never be forgiven. I've kept my word. I know who he is, whether he knows it or not. I've never kissed the hand that slapped me, or the boot that kicked me. It's kind of funny. You'd think a politician without any real friends would know better. He does not realize that the Universe only rewards energy, not position, job title, or social standing. I predict a terrible misfortune will befall him due to bad judgment.

Boxing saved my life, as I found something to channel my aggression. I found that fighting was my forte, and I loved it. I don't know how, but I had a rock solid chin, and I learned to punch as hard as a mule kicks. Boxing offered Tejanos like me a real opportunity. As a fighter it was up to me to be as good as I wanted. It was up to me to work hard, train, practice and improve, or not. Everything depended on how much I wanted it. I would hitchhike to the gym and hitchhike home after working my ass off. I'd never wanted anything as badly as I wanted to win the Golden Gloves. I trained like a man possessed and took many beatings in the gym, fighting bigger, older, and taller guys. I was as scared as anyone could be, yet I refused to back down. Once a fight was set, I was determined to fight until I won, or died. I refused to let anyone or anything dissuade me from my objective of being a Golden Gloves Champion. I must have jogged a thousand miles around Main Drive. I'd run from Main Drive along Highway 44 to Robstown, which might have been ten or twelve miles. I'd run to the Greyhound Bus Station, buy a soda and an Eskimo pie, and rest in the park for a little while until I was ready to head back. I ran so much I felt like the wind blowing across the open fields. I'd lose track of time and distance. I moved like a well-oiled and perfectly timed machine. By the time the Golden Gloves arrived I was ready to slay a dragon with my fists. I fought three times and destroyed each of my opponents to win my first Golden Gloves Championship. I nearly killed one kid in front of the several hundred people who packed the Memorial Coliseum along the bay front. Alice Zapata, a beautiful girl who I'd been dating prior, witnessed my victory. I didn't think she was going to show up, as I'd broken up with her shortly before the tournament. Spending time with her was interfering with my training, and winning the Golden Gloves mattered more to me than anything. This may have been why she thought I was so cool. I was probably the first guy who'd ever dumped her. I don't know for sure. All I know is that winning my very first Golden Gloves was the most important accomplishment of my life for many years. Being a champion was even more important than having a beautiful woman on my arm. Although, I cannot deny having Alice with me helped make the experience ten times better. We started going out again. Like I said, I only broke it off with her so I'd have more time to train for the tournament. She really was a great person. Unless you've had a beautiful woman on your arm, you've not experienced what it means to be proud. Especially after triumphing over the greatest challenge you've ever faced. Winning the Golden Gloves literally changed my life. Even now, many years later, winning my first Golden Gloves still remains as one of the most important events of my life. I've had hundreds of fights since then, and fought guys from every European country in the world, as I continued to box while in the Army and stationed in Europe. I've also fought guys from Korea, Japan, China, Thailand, and everywhere in between. Interestingly, and as a testament to personal power, while in the Army the Universe provided me with an opportunity to balance the scales. By what would seem to be random chance I was paired against none other than Frankie King, the same kid from Kingsville, Texas, who beat me in my second fight. He was going by Frank at the time. I had spent the years since our first encounter dedicated to the art of boxing, and as a result, suffice to say I extracted my revenge. When looking back, for some reason all my fights become one giant blur. However, the Golden Gloves in Corpus Christi, in front of people who I knew, including Alice Zapata, remains the most significant. My oldest and closest friend for many years, Roger Hernández, was there ringside. My brother-in-law also saw me win while watching the eleven o'clock news on television that evening. Winning the Golden Gloves gave me a title no one could take away. It was a title that no one, including my father or Beelzebub, could belittle or tarnish. I accomplished something they'd never dreamed of doing and broke out of the role they'd placed me in. After that, there was nothing they could do to squash me. I'd climbed the tallest mountain and accomplished something no one in my family had ever done. To this day, I am the only Golden Gloves Champion in my entire family.

Not surprisingly, I soon learned that there was also no place for Tejano boxing champions on Main Drive or at Andrew Jackson High School. Even though I'd made the papers, no mention was ever made of my accomplishment. Principal Liema, who'd pretended to give a damn, never mentioned it at school, and I was ignored and marginalized. Mr. Liema taught me that blindness to racial bigotry is selective. Winning the most important objective of my life meant nothing to anyone but me, and it's always been this way. Not even my brother Punk, whom I defended many times, placing myself in harm's way, ever made an effort to congratulate me. It was a lonely experience, like so many other great moments of my life. Fortunately I had Alice, whom I cared for deeply.

Around the same time I learned another powerful lesson from yet another great educator at Andrew Jackson High School. Mr. Hill, the high school counselor, told me point-blank to drop out of school, as "I was not college material." He taught me that racism and ignorance cannot be cured via an education or job title. Mr. Hill was respected and considered a fine example of a teaching professional. He taught me that a person can be taught to pilot a rocket to the moon, and a person can be taught to speak a foreign language, but a person cannot be taught to not be racist. His upbringing and life in an all-white neighborhood isolated him from the general population, and must have painted a very different picture of what normal was. He must have been blown away when I sent in a request for transcripts before my college graduation.

Boxing taught me more about myself and the world than any book or person ever has. However, as much as I did to earn this victory, I know I could not have done it alone. I had plenty of help. I only wish I could remember the names of all the guys who'd helped me along the way. I thanked them at the time, but had no way of knowing just how much winning that victory would change my life. After having lived the results of this triumph, I wish I could thank them all again personally. Winning the Golden Gloves may have been my greatest victory. I'd never thought of myself as a loser prior, but afterwards, I know I always saw myself as a winner. The victory did not go to my head. I knew I'd soon face tougher fighters. The more I learned about boxing, the more I understood how little I knew. I also discovered that boxing was about conquering yourself. It was a journey into the very essence of my soul. It required a dedication so rarely found, that the only way to actually describe it is to call it a religion. It demands you be a fanatic, a crazy person, and so aware of yourself as to make you dangerous. It empowers you in ways only found in storybooks or in movies. It really is magic.

I continued to box in and around Corpus until I left for the Army. My trophies and medals were all thrown out by my father, or stolen by one of my siblings. I never found all the things I'd stored in the attic after I left. My record collection, clothes, books, and all my things were picked through by my siblings. I lost everything that might have served to remind me of the past. I was furious at first, but after the anger passed I realized they'd done me a favor. I'd have to earn new trophies and achieve new objectives. I had to continue to improve and grow. I have never missed or wished I still had all those trinkets, which might also hold me back. As a Warrior I no longer seek other's approval, neither via trophies or awards. I have my discipline, which demands all my attention.

Winning the Golden Gloves gave me the final strength to leave Corpus Christi, the only place I've ever called home. Visiting Corpus now holds few painful memories. I've exorcised my demons. Now when I return, I only remember the sweetness of my youth, and the excitement and adventures I experienced within its borders. I've rescued the neglected child I once was and nurtured him. I've *detached* myself from my family's negative effects and moved on. Life continues to be an adventure, and I continue to savor life as only a man who knows death is stalking him can.

Texas escapee,

-don Jesus M. Ramirez

Chapter Five
California Dreaming

"Adventure called my name and I went out to win my fame. I lost her somewhere along the way. Lies, betrayal, and disappointments — I found no Angels in the city by that name. No gentle hearts or comfort there."

-don Jesus M. Ramirez

Music was the reason why I fell in love with the idea of California. Perhaps my childish belief of finding freedom also contributed. Who knows. Ever since I was a child my mother spoke of her distant brothers who lived in Los Angeles. She may have exaggerated her stories or just plain lied. I'll never know. My grandmother also lived in California periodically. She divided her time between living in Torreón, México, and Pasadena, California, as well as Corpus Christi. She came to visit us several times from California, although I cannot understand why she'd want to visit my mother, who had such a beast for a husband.

While I was still a young child my brother Bumper left one summer for California. He went with my mother's cousin, Albert, who was her only real connection to her family. She loved him very much and looked forward to his visits. When he called to say he was coming, she'd bake him an apple pie, which he loved. He'd eat as much as half of it while drinking coffee, and we'd get whatever was left over. It was usually only a small slice or less. He was a tall man with a light complexion, and had dark eyes and dark hair. By occupation he was a minister who preached fire, brimstone, and damnation.

He was not a Catholic, like my mother and father claimed to be. However, my father's idea of God and practicing religion was as genuine as his beliefs of fidelity. My father, along with millions of others just like him, are typical average people who convince themselves they can reach heaven simply by going to church on Sundays. I've never met a real Christian, much less a real Catholic. Needless to say, it was my father's hypocrisy that convinced me religion has nothing to do with a man's behavior, nor his relationship with the power average men call God. As a child I thought I heard God speak to me. I never knew I had so much in common with Joan of Arc and Socrates, who confessed to hearing voices. I am happy I never said a word about the experience. We all know what happens to anyone who claims God's love.

    I don't know how my mother convinced my father to permit Bumper to go on this trip. Yet, I know it had to do with making money, as we lived like poor people, even though my father earned a decent wage. He was a cheap bastard who died with several hundred thousand dollars in eleven separate bank accounts. We lived on rice, beans, flour tortillas, chicken, and whatever else my father would spend. Even so, we had it better than a lot of other people on Main Drive. My father believed because he worked like a mule all day long, he deserved to screw around and drink as much as he wanted. All of the major battles between my parents had to do with money and his screwing around. I realize the cause of our present day social problems stem from kids watching their parents behave like selfish adolescents. They want what they want because they want it. They hate rules, but want everyone else to follow them, yet want understanding for sins when it comes to their behavior. As an example we have the entire United States riddled with gangs, poverty, unemployment, and political corruption. All this comes from adults refusing to rein in their behavior and conduct themselves within the boundaries of social decorum. This is why the world as we know it will never have balance. It is run by emotionally unbalanced average people. This is the way they are, and trying to change, fix, or enlighten them is a waste of energy. Warriors accept things as they are, change when necessary, and adjust to their environment. They also avoid average people.

My brother Bumper left for California and didn't return for several months. During his trip my mother would sometimes receive a telephone call from him at our neighbor's house. The same neighbor I've mentioned before, Lily Abundez. She was the mother of Frankie Abundez, the kid who while fighting I sprayed in the face with green spray paint. My mother gossiped about her tirelessly, but never hesitated to accept her assistance. Lily would come over all excited and my mother would rush over right away. She'd return home in tears after speaking with Bumper. I thought my mother loved him most because he was her firstborn. He was also the first to defy my father's tyranny and defend her, an example I followed. My mother shared stories about her brothers and of childhood memories. Sometimes my father would join in on the stories, but then get up and walk away. Evidently his memories weren't as pleasant as hers, and there were many unresolved issues regarding their memories of home. According to my mother, my grandfather's ranch in México, where she'd spent a portion of her childhood, was home sweet home. However, it never seemed as dear to my father. By the time I started examining her stories I'd already figured it out. No one leaves home because they want to. I grew up in a migrant camp and saw dozens of families pick up and leave, only to return months later. They always looked tired and beat down. The only difference is now they were a little bit older.

Years later I learned my Uncle Hector had allegedly punched out my father for hitting my mother. Apparently this was also why my father abandoned her, which led to the birth of my half-sister, who I've referred to as Little Red Riding Hood in this book. It was justification for my father's horrid behavior towards my mother and my sister. My Uncle Hector told me he'd come home from working on the ranch and heard my mother crying. He said their mother (my grandmother) had warned him not to get involved, but that when he'd heard my father hitting her there was no way he could not defend her. I would have done the same thing if I'd heard someone hitting my sister. This also makes it clear that hitting your wife was considered to be common in those "good old days." He said that he went into the next room and actually saw my father hitting my mother. He claims to have said, "If you want to hit someone, hit me!" Then according to him they fought and the fistfight went on for quite some time. During which he claims to have "whipped my father's ass." Average people like to exaggerate, so this may not be true. I've always enjoyed good bullshit, and smiled at the idea of anyone beating my father like I'd dreamed of so many times. Unfortunately, my mother was the one who ultimately suffered, as my father left that night. According to family legend, he was gone for over four years and many thought he'd never return. My sister claims that my grandmother on my father's side of the family had broken my parents up, and then regretted doing so when the Korean War started and everyone was being drafted. She supposedly got them back together, and my father knelt down in front of the Virgin de Guadalupe and promised never to cheat or hit my mother again. Of course this promise, like all the rest he made, wasn't worth a damn. This is the same reason why my mother never called the cops when he beat her. Plus, keep in mind, beating up your wife was not against the law in those "good old days." The laws against beating wives or children didn't arrive until the Seventies. Although, I'm not sure these laws ever arrived in Texas. Keep in mind, just because a law is in the books, doesn't mean it will be enforced. This is especially true in South Texas.

Turmoil seemed to be a common theme in those bad old days, and dark clouds always loomed overhead. Trouble was always on its way, had just occurred, or was in the process. As an eight-year-old kid I needed someone to defend me, but who was going to protect me against my own parents? My father, much like Beelzebub, was only a bully and a tyrant within our home. I never witnessed him behave similarly elsewhere. For instance, he never stepped up to help quell the trouble during church dances. These fights turned into brawls and involved tough hoodlums who'd kill you sure as look at you. There were roving gangs of migrant workers who came in ready for trouble and looking for women. There were brawls involving twenty people which started over someone dancing with someone else's girlfriend. None of the women I knew as a kid were worth that much trouble. In the end, none of it mattered. The guys went to prison or ended up in a grave, and the women found someone to replace them, proving my point that no one is worth the trouble. The trick is to learn when to fight back, because sometimes you've got to fight or 96ers will stomp you into the ground, and then piss on you for letting them. Every interaction with an average person is a struggle. Therefore it is an act of war. As such, someone must win or lose. This only sounds harsh to those who can afford to live amongst civilized people. Those who have to live with the average people of Epitaph in the Valley of Tears, know that 96 percent of them are not worth pissing on if they were on fire.

While my brother Bumper was in California very little was said about him by my parents. It was obvious that for my father he was simply out of sight and out of mind. He didn't like the idea of what Bumper would share with my uncles, who already had reason to hate his guts. Time went by and I'd just gotten used to him being gone, when all of a sudden he returned. He came home with boxes full of clothes and toys given to him for us by my uncles. I was impressed with all the things he brought, along with the changes in him. That's when I got the idea that California was a great place where I could also learn the things Bumper knew. It became a fantasy of mine to someday go to California. The idea of escaping Texas and living in California gave me hope and something to daydream about. I learned as much as I could about California. The cool TV shows said everyone had the right to be free and be who they were. I now had a place to go and began planning my escape from Texas.

As expected, my father wasted no time in making sure Bumper remembered who lord and master of the house was. He started beating Bumper for almost no reason, and he always seemed angry about something. It was like living in a minefield where anything could set him off. It was horrible, and somehow we endured it, but not without lots of tears and deep emotional scars. I have no idea how I managed to keep hope alive, despite the beatings and senseless violence. I steadily grew to hate him even more, and played with the idea of murdering him while he slept. I often wondered if I couldn't just walk up behind him and bash out his brains with a lead pipe, calling it an accident. However, that might have been hard to explain to the cops. Hmm... let's see here. You accidentally hit your father in the head with a lead pipe 25 times? Sure... It was a horrible situation, a double whammy, and a catch-22. All abused children can relate to the concept of hating, yet wanting to love the parent who abuses them.

The trip to California brought about many changes in Bumper, which further enticed my desires to visit as well. He became bolder and quicker to interfere when my father beat my mother, which brought about more violence and beatings. The problem was that life was not only tough at home. It was just as bad outside of our fenced compound. My father never had any friends or spoke to anyone, and as I mentioned before, he built an eight foot fence around our home, supposedly to keep thieves out. Yet like all fences, it also served to keep us in. As a result of this fence we grew up apart from the other kids in the neighborhood. I hardly ever spoke due to my stuttering and never learned how to socialize or develop friendships. Looking back, the isolation did us more harm than good. This is something which parents who attempt to protect their children via isolating them should keep in mind. It does as much harm as it does good. Most importantly, it's impossible to protect kids from themselves. This is especially true if they have no experience dealing with people, which is the problem with today's technological society. Kids spend all their time hiding behind a computer screen and communicating via text messaging. They never learn how to manage their emotions and deal with 96ers, who are utterly and completely corrupt. How is a kid going to learn to deal with corrupt individuals if they never interact with them? The answer is that they don't. My father brainwashed us daily by telling us how rotten and inferior "those" neighborhood people were. I never saw any differences between them and us. Most people on Main Drive were just as wicked and hateful as he was. As far as I could tell everyone was just as miserable, lost, poor, hopeless, and emotionally screwed up. We were no different. We were just as poor and malnourished, and lived just as they did. My mother endorsed my father's position, and never allowed us to play with the neighborhood kids. We had to stay within the fence and were not allowed to venture beyond the wire. I cannot recall how many times my mother said that the neighbors were all good-for-nothing Indians with bare feet. We were told they had head lice, fleas, and diseases, which they probably did. Looking back however, I can honestly say we were just as poor and often went barefoot. We had head lice, ringworm, and every other illness common amongst poor people. I realize now that she was not being honest in her reasoning. She was not protecting us from our neighbors, as she claimed to have been, but acting out her own ignorance and insecurity. She saw control over us as one less problem to have to manage. In her mind, the less interaction we had with our neighbors, the fewer problems we'd bring home. Main Drive was a cesspool of ignorance, which produced angry homicidal maniacs by the dozens.

The oppressive poverty, ignorance, and discrimination we suffered from was the real enemy. Yet in typical 96er fashion, the people of Main Drive victimized each other with unwavering earnest. In reality ignorance and poverty were the cause of, and the combination which sparked violence. Isolated out in the middle of nowhere, Main Drive was a perfect breeding place for contempt, violence, and brutality. Most people didn't have a phone, indoor bathrooms, and couldn't read. The houses were paper thin, poorly constructed, leaked during the rainy season, and offered no protection during the winter or summer. The practice of comparing themselves to one another constantly brought about problems between neighbors. A week never went by in which gossip did not drift into our home about someone's ungodly behavior. Gossip, which generated more gossip, ruined dozens of innocent people's lives. As a kid who never made a sound or spoke, I heard everything as I sneaked in and out, always on the periphery. Through harsh lessons I'd learned not to incur the wrath of my mother's depression or my father's anger. It was a horrible habit to develop — a habit which I've never lost. I developed a sixth sense, the same as our ancestors are said to have had in order to survive the saber-toothed tigers that hunted them. I cannot say I escaped unscathed, as I received emotional wounds from witnessing continuous brutality. I also still carry several unexplained physical scars on my face from my father beating me unconscious. I must have blanked it out. I suspect I received them from the beating he gave me after I injured the group of thugs who tried to jump me in the fourth grade. That night their parents showed up at our house very angry, demanding an explanation for the beating their children had received from me and my sock filled with rocks. After being yelled at, all I remember from that night was being beaten by my father until I passed out. Try as I may, I cannot recall ever receiving the cuts and punctures which the scars above my right eye prove I sustained. I have questioned my eldest siblings, but they either cannot, or will not remember how I got the scars.

The violence outside our home was nothing compared to that which existed within it. I constantly had to watch out for Beelzebub, whose sadistic nature kept him preying upon me. I may never understand completely what he experienced, or why he has such disturbed tendencies. I know my parent's attention didn't help his behavior, and actually made it worse. I recall one Saturday after my parents returned home from a trip into town. My mother walked into the house and announced that she'd bought three shirts. I was young at the time, and Beelzebub, Punk, and I were relatively around the same size. At least as far as clothes were concerned. Therefore, the only differences between the shirts were the colors and pattern of their designs. I'll never forget what happened next. With the three of us standing before her, she turned to Beelzebub and said, "Pick the one you want." She then turned to Punk and asked him to choose from the remaining two. After he had, she threw the leftover shirt to me. I don't recall what it looked like. I don't even remember wondering why I was being pushed to last, or why she would do such a thing until days after. Even then, as an innocent child such behavior felt evil and mean. It was deliberate malice and absolutely unnecessary, as it accomplished nothing and gave Beelzebub license to misbehave. I have no idea why my mother would behave so hatefully towards me. I hadn't done anything and rarely spoke unless spoken to. I wasn't a bad kid. Needless to say, she broke my heart. Worse, and above all, it served to fuel Beelzebub's sadistic dysfunctional behavior. Instead of bringing out a noble spirit, it released the perverted monster which lived inside of him. The preferential treatment fueled his dark side and created the monster Beelzebub became. To this very day, I have not spoken to him for years. I've learned that time doesn't heal anything, because memories don't watch the clock. Such emotional abuse is not healed with time, but only via hard work at soothing and restoring your damaged soul. It is via these experiences, and having to refight all those haunting memories, that I have discovered taking a Warrior's inventory is not a single event.

    It may have never occurred to my mother that the sad expression I wore was the result of her neglect. The ugliest example of a lack of character was her reactive anger when confronted with the sadness shown upon my face. Looking back, I pity my mother, who ran away from her family as a girl of only thirteen. She never had a childhood, never knew love, and never had a life away from my father.

I cannot generate anything other than an indifferent disgust towards my father, who could have created a better life for himself and the rest of us. He could have carved out a paradise, instead of emptiness. He could have created an empire by simply caring for us. I imagine the tremendous things my brothers and I could have accomplished if we had been taught to work together, instead of having to compete for survival and attention.

A common trait amongst the population of Main Drive was pack behavior, or the idea that someone's weaknesses were reason to pounce on them. It still puzzles me beyond comprehension, but it seems to be a common trait amongst 96ers everywhere. Instead of recognizing weakness and accommodating someone's suffering, it becomes the focus of ridicule and laughter. I first experienced and endured abusive laughter due to my stuttering. Experts suggest this is caused by an emotional condition, or on rare occasions it can be caused by a physical condition. Sadly my parents, who inflicted me with this condition, were the first to make fun of me. It's a terrible reality that in most cases someone's faults are a direct reflection of poor parenting. I am sorry to say I also became involved in making fun of people with handicaps and physical disabilities. It shames me to admit it today. Now looking back, I know I was a victim of surviving in this environment. Like hungry wolf packs, the kids of Main Drive learned what they saw from their older peers, and continued the abusive cycle amongst themselves. It's a horrible but honest statement about 96er's lack of quality and absence of conscience. My struggle to survive produced the same predatory characteristics within me that I despised in the bullies who tormented me. It's the same battle against my weaknesses, which I wage every day of my life. Anyone who has survived a similar upbringing will attest to the fact that it's like fighting a war on all fronts. It is impossible to keep from becoming like those who tormented you, as you must adopt certain characteristics, values, and behaviors in order to survive. If you are smaller in size you have to develop a higher state of alertness and can never let your guard down. You have to be faster, smarter, tougher, and twice as mean as your oppressors. It is no wonder people living in crime ridden neighborhoods usually prey on each other. This is why the cycle of misery heaped upon generation after generation of families living in barrios and ghettos around the world is endless. It's a never-ending cycle of random violence and suffering.

The hardships I endured, and the brutal environment I was forced to survive, are what made my desire to find freedom so strong. At the time I believed California held the key that would set me free, and after overcoming tremendous obstacles, constant negativity, and my parent's opposition, I finally earned the money to fly to Los Angeles. I contacted my sister Little Red Riding Hood, who'd offered me a place to stay. She had escaped Texas several years earlier and was now living there. She went to live with my uncle because our mother could not protect her from my father's sexual advances. I had no idea this was going on right beneath my nose. Had I known, I'd of shot the bastard in the head with my 22 cal. rifle, like I'd planned. The idea of him molesting my sister is sickening and repulsive. It's clear my brothers don't feel the same way, as they continued to interact with him until the day he died. I cannot understand how or why they would want to, and not have refused to have anything to do with the dirty bastard. After I learned about this I wrote the district attorney in Corpus, and tried to file charges against him for abuse, neglect, and sexual molestation upon my sister. To my knowledge none of my brothers have ever taken any steps to seek justice for my sisters or my mother. This episode was swept under the rug and stuffed into the closet where all my father's skeletons are hidden. Had it not been for Little Red Riding Hood I would have never known it happened. I had enough reasons to hate him even before this discovery.

All year long I saved every dime I could get my hands on, and at the age of fourteen I made my first trip to Los Angeles. I lived with my sister and her husband for the entire summer in their apartment in Altadena. I planned to work, earn some money, and then fly back home bearing gifts and a new found independence. Unfortunately, my first trip to California was a disappointment. I didn't have a chance to meet many girls, which was too bad, as I'd heard the girls in California were easy. After all, it was the age of free love, drugs, and rock and roll. I did have a chance to go to Malibu and other beaches, and got to see how Mexican and Native Californians of Mexican Ancestry (NCOMAs) in California lived. I was surprised to meet NCOMAs who did not speak Spanish. Everyone in Texas spoke Spanish and it was a shock to discover my own cousins never spoke it, or even cared to learn it. I also met a lot of undocumented Mexican immigrants. I had no idea how different Mexican people really are from those of us who grew up in the United States. I had no idea how different I was from the average person anywhere outside of Corpus. I was slapped twice as hard by the realization that I was different from the average person, even in California. Until then I had held onto the notion that all I needed was to find "my kind of people." People whom I believed I could find in California. Man, was I wrong. I learned I didn't fit in anywhere. I felt as if I had been left here by a space alien, who must have been passing through on his way to somewhere else. I discovered a deep loneliness like I'd never known before. Instead of finding freedom and people to relate to in

California, as I'd hoped I would, I discovered how different I was from everyone around me. I learned I would never fit in anywhere, and slowly came to the realization that for whatever reason, I had not been born under the grace of the same god I'd been taught to believe in. I accepted that my mother and father did not and would not love me, ever know me, or appreciate who I was. I accepted that I had little in common with anyone, anywhere, and I was alone. I admitted that for whatever reason the Universe had played a bad joke on me, and that I might not even be from this planet. I never felt so lonely in my life and actually considered killing myself. Had it not been for music I might have.

I discovered that my mother had done us an unbelievable disservice by lying to us about her childhood. Prior to this trip I'd never spent as much time around Mexicans from México, nor heard México spoken of so raw. I'd never known how bad things actually were over there. Not only was there a complete lack of culture, education, and social justice, there was an abundance of corruption. I mean down deep and dirty, nasty, shit in the streets corruption. A complete corruption of the soul that soiled everything it touched. A corruption so profound as to make me wonder if this was the same México my mother always spoke of so fondly. I'd grown up listening to stories about my grandfather's ranch and the Mexican Revolution. I'd grown up believing Mexican people were good, honest, and hardworking individuals. I'd been taught that Mexican people were honorable, of high moral character, and worthy of respect. Now for the first time these stories were met with reality, and my discoveries were earthshattering. I will not generalize nor speak on behalf of an entire people, but I will relate my experiences. Keep in mind that there are 96ers, as well as Four Percentors, from every country, culture, and race in the world. What I describe is accurate to my personal experiences with those whom I have interacted with. Prior to this trip I'd never known so many lying, deceptive, game playing, loud, and foulmouthed individuals in all my life. Despite the harshness of life on Main Drive and in Corpus Christi, I found that I was sheltered, and compared to them I was a saint. I was disappointed and sick at heart by their behavior and what I heard them say. They turned out to be foul, disgusting, veil creatures that resembled vermin which suck blood and crawl through the mire. I discovered my relatives and all the people my mother placed on pedestals, were just as bad as my father, only thank God, a little further away. I felt as if I had been introduced to my future and it horrified me. I knew that no matter what I ended up doing in life, I would never become as greedy, hypocritical, deceptive, or corrupt as my uncles, cousins, and other relatives had turned out to be. I suffered terribly for years because I kept trying to find a Mexican person with all the qualities my mother described. I searched far and wide for the virtuous Mexican women which my mother had told me about since childhood. To my disappointment, all the Mexican women I have met and come to know of higher economic levels, play so many games in their attempts to seduce and allure a man, it makes plastic seem like a natural fiber. All the fantasies my mother told me must have been learned from watching soap operas, as she ran away with my father when she was just a child herself. This also demonstrates how average people think they desire things they've never known. This is why people think the grass is greener on the other side. The truth is it just looks greener from a distance. Average people are the same everywhere and women in all cultures have learned to manipulate, seduce, allure, and control via their promise of sex. Seekers should be aware of this truth and not be disappointed or surprised.

I've yet to find anyone from México who resembles even a small part of what my mother described. It breaks my heart to think she romanticized her childhood so much as to make it a mere fantasy. Not only had my mother exaggerated everything about México, she deliberately lied about my uncles and cousins. She was a 96er, given to exaggeration. She lied when necessary, and was filled with self-deception. After this experience I no longer sought her approval, and although it never completely stopped hurting, I no longer mourned her lack of affection. I was brokenhearted that I would never have the mother I'd read about in books or saw in movies. I was an orphan with two living and breathing parents, who were as close to pure poison as the hemlock Socrates drank to kill himself.

    I returned to Texas a badly beaten and much enlightened person. I'd accomplished magnificent things all by myself. I'd gone to California and returned a hero, at least in my own mind. I'd been to Los Angeles, Malibu, Chinatown, Newport Beach, and twenty places in between. I learned that I never wanted anything to do with any of my relatives, but I also did not want to live in Texas. I'd fallen in love with the idea of California, not the people. The people were equally as sick and veil as they were in Texas, but I was still hooked on the idea. My vision changed from a dream to reality. Not only had I been where I wanted to go, but I could get there on my own. I returned to Andrew Jackson High School disheartened but with a new confidence born of experience. I'd been to the Promised Land, also known as California, and returned, which meant I could leave again. I learned that if you wanted to change someone, the first person you must change is yourself. My trip to California destroyed my illusion and changed me in profound ways. I learned there was an alternative to suffering and boredom. I learned that you do not have to excuse or forgive someone who deliberately harmed you, even your own father. I vowed to never allow myself to be physically abused again. I also discovered that if I was so different from everyone around me, including my own family, then they could not criticize me, as they did not know or understand me. If I was so different, then anyone who did not understand me could never undermine or make me doubt myself. I'd discovered how far apart I stood from everyone around me. Therefore, they did not matter. Their opinions, thoughts, insults, and etc., should therefore mean nothing. I was not going to let my father or anyone ever make me feel inferior again. I knew it was my father and family who were disturbed, not me. I was still a kid and had little choice in where I lived, but I did have a choice in how I treated myself, and how I allowed myself to be treated. I vowed never to be anything like my father and used him as an example of how I did not want to be. I continue to call him one of my greatest teachers, as he gave me countless examples of how destructive behavior affects those around you. The effects of bad parenting never stop tormenting a person, and only a Warrior can manage it. For instance, no average person who has suffered at the hands of a narcissistic, cruel tyrant would be capable of referring to him as a teacher. This is a mistake. In here lies the crux of a Warrior's discipline. Every genuine Seeker of power knows he can learn from anyone at any time. There is no classroom, enrollment, or qualification for a teacher. A Warrior can and will discern, perceive, obtain, or take energy and information at any time, anywhere it presents itself. Only a Warrior could find useable characteristics, maneuvers, or tactics in their adversary. A 96er will always arrive at negative conclusions and erase any contributions they might have made. This is another mistake, yet standard behavior for 96ers. My father and brother were horrible, corrupt individuals with few redeeming qualities, but via their torment I learned many lessons. This is not to say that their unacceptable behavior has been cosigned or forgiven by any means, but only examined from a *detached* perspective. Seekers who fail to grasp this concept are approaching this material from a position which does not serve them. If you fall into this category, I encourage you to reread this material, as you have missed the objective of this book. This work is not a story written for entertainment purposes, but an instruction manual intended to assist Warriors and genuine Seekers. As one develops an ability to *detach* and view themselves critically, they'll also find that the effects of bad parenting are a demon. These experiences and events will replay themselves throughout your life, showing up at the worst possible moments. They will create doubt, feed your anger, and undermine your best efforts. Defeating these demons is why a Warrior stops asking why. Not of others, but of himself. A Warrior must examine his failure to identify and develop a self-monitoring system that will assist in resolving these issues. The crux is that after you've done so, new situations will arise, and the same monster will show its head again. Then you'll have to continue in your never-ending battle against your weaknesses. This is why I've said, the effects of bad parenting torment a person all their life.

Texas escapee,

don Jesus M. Ramirez

Chapter Six
Blues and the Blue Techniques

"Music saved me from despair. It gave me hope, awoke my spirit, and strengthened my heart. Mozart may have been a better musician, but he couldn't fight worth a damn. Without warriors to protect them, such men would soon become somebody's girlfriend."

-don Jesus M. Ramirez

While a dreamer dreams, their dreams are real, and remain as such until the world imposes its reality. Rebellion and rejection of a bland view of existence is innately within a dreamer's nature. Although eventual surrender to the pressure of the average world is imminent, a dreamer's dreams never disappear — they exist in the twilight between magic and despair. Only those who have learned to silence their *internal dialogue* know magic does exist, safely in this world. The challenge arrives when they realize there are very few who they can share this magic with. This is the aloneness of a Warrior, and why music continues to be my salvation. Music is the conduit between myself and what average men call God. Song and prayer are the essence of existence, like breath is to life. There may never be another story written about a winner who lost so much. This may be the first you've ever read, yet here I am. I have no idea where I got the spunk to do all the things I did, or take the chances I've taken. I don't know how I convinced myself I could be a musician, but I did. Not only did I see myself as having something to say worth listening to, but I wanted to perform, despite my childhood battles with stuttering.

It could have been madness or innocent optimism. I was a snowflake racing through hell, hoping to get out before I melted or the Devil knew I was there.

Music helped me survive life on Main Drive and nurtured my dreams of escaping Texas. I played my brother Bumper's hand-me-down cornet in the high school band for several years. It was fun, but more than that, it showed me a world I hadn't known anything about. In Texas music was one of the ways a nobody could become a somebody. I knew guys in bands that played at the dances and all of them were cool as hell. Everybody knew them. They had the finest girlfriends and seemed cooler than hell. The desire to play my cornet motivated me. However, it was very difficult to get enthusiastic about playing marching tunes, and that was all the high school band played. What really disappointed me was that Mr. Peterson, the band teacher, never gave the Tejano students any attention. As a public school teacher he had to take whoever came along, and I guess that's what he was doing. For the most part he just tolerated me with an air of indifference. In his ignorance and self-fulfilling prophecy, he got exactly what he expected. He expected nothing from me and had nothing to give.

By this time I'd been washing dishes and bussing tables at restaurants along Highway 9, before the freeway was built. I didn't have a car, so I had to hitchhike to and from work. I didn't mind. I hated having to pick cotton during the summer and thought it would be easier to work in a restaurant. I hated it, but it sure beat sweating my ass off and dragging a twenty foot sack filled with over a hundred pounds of cotton for over a mile. After washing dishes for a while I applied to work as a janitor through the high school. Then during the summer of my freshman year I was hired, and began working at Andrew Jackson Junior High School. It was a great job for a Tejano kid. My coworkers were other Tejanos who'd pissed away their youth, never got an education or any other kind of training, and ended up as janitors. It was a dead-end job with nothing to do but wait to die. I mostly helped the janitors strip, wax, and polish the floors. I found out right away how lazy these guys were. They were nothing like I'd expected. They were lying, lazy bastards that hid away in order to not work. I would have fired all of them. It was my first experience working with adults in a job where they didn't have supervision, pressure, or how much they earned depended on their productivity. Up to this point, working had meant earning more money the harder I worked, and I didn't know any other way. It was a learning experience watching how they did as little as possible while earning more than I did. It also became clear why these men were such losers and why they never made anything of themselves. It also said a lot about the racist caste system in Texas, as they knew that no matter how hard they worked, they'd never be promoted. This was the best they could do in a system which never placed Tejano Americans in positions of authority. It was a hopeless, dead-end job, without prospects of improvement. I swore to get the hell out of there and had no interest in hanging out with losers.

  The foreman's name was Jesse. He would tell me what to do, then disappear. Another worker was a guy named Joe, who would go off and do whatever he wanted. Both of them were complete losers. I'd follow and spy on them, watching as they sat around smoking. It was a big game to them. They'd assign me the larger jobs, and then when I didn't complete them, they'd make fun of me. They'd make inappropriate sexual jokes, detailing how they fucked their wives or girlfriends. Who knows what their intentions were, but knowing what I know now, it was probably as vulgar as they were. Most of my impressions of adults were similar to these. I found very little of their behavior worthy of respect. This is common amongst average people. For some reason they love to laugh at people who are exactly like themselves. I knew they were taking advantage of me, and considered me nothing more than a nuisance. They didn't like my unwillingness to tell sexual jokes, share gossip, act tough, or speak about others. I hadn't yet learned to be different around different people. I hadn't yet learned that most behavior was an act, and that all average people attempt to take charge of each other. I hadn't yet learned to play games or manipulate to gain my objectives. I was naïve, innocent, and stupid about the real world. These were all things my brothers Beelzebub, Bumper, and Punk knew instinctively.

After several weeks of enduring this behavior I made up my mind to confront them. Something I'd never do today. I walked up to them while they were hiding behind a wall, just sitting around gossiping. I explained that I couldn't finish the work assigned to me, and would need more time or some help. It worked. They acted as if I'd done something they approved of. They said it was fine, and that they'd help me. I learned a horrible lesson about adults, age, and wisdom. I learned that one has nothing to do with the other, and that adults would lie, manipulate, cheat, and steal just to gain their objectives. It was my first step towards adopting the ways of the world. After that I refused to work as hard or as fast. Looking back, it was not a positive learning experience. Both of these men were operating on a loser psychology, of doing as little as possible. The less they did, the better they felt about themselves, until they only did the minimum to keep their jobs. It's common throughout the country. Average people operate on a less than fifty percent capacity, doing the very minimum to get by. I have no idea what their logic is, but I believe they feel abused, so they never earn what they are paid. The truth is most adults are terrible role models. I lost the little respect I might have had for both of them. I learned age has nothing to do with discipline, knowledge, kindness, or anything else. Like I said before, you can find trash anywhere. I made it a point never to share details of my personal life with them. Neither of them were worthy of anything other than disdain. Through their jobs, both of them watched me grow up. I had been a former student of that school during the time they'd worked there, and they had known who I was. Yet, they saw nothing wrong with taking advantage of a kid. They played it off like it had all been a big joke, but it wasn't funny.

I had my own agenda, and I had no plans of remaining a janitor all my life. My objective from this job was to buy a car so I could have transportation. That way I'd be able to get a better job in town. I also vowed to buy my own car myself, unlike Beelzebub, the lying manipulator, who got a loan from our father to buy a car. I wasn't surprised, as our father always treated him much better. That is not to say I understood his behavior, as I have still been unable to comprehend how my father was able to treat his sons so differently, and do so without remorse or hesitation. I have since observed that he and Beelzebub had formed a mutual bullshit club, wherein they agreed to blow smoke up each other's asses, lie, and make up stories to appease the other. Beelzebub always kissed our father's ass, which was something I never did. I only spoke to him when I had to. He usually just acted like I didn't exist, and only spoke to me to give me an order. I later learned Beelzebub planned everything he would do and say, as well as when and how to say it. I never understood how he could be such a coward and kiss the hand that slapped him, along with the boot that kicked him. I hated them, and flat-out refused to kiss anyone's ass. As a result of my rebellion, I didn't have a car. This meant that aside from hitchhiking I was stranded on Main Drive, out in the middle of nowhere.

After selling his soul in order to buy a car, Beelzebub began attending social club dances in town. However, for reasons which were unknown to me at the time, he never wanted to go to the dances alone. So, rather than being stuck at home, I'd go with him. I had not yet realized he was simply afraid of attending the dances alone. Being afraid had never served me, so I'd pretend I wasn't and move forward. More importantly, I'd grown accustomed to being alone and it never bothered me. I learned to watch out for thugs and was always ready to fight. Attending these club dances was one of the short lulls between storms in which Beelzebub and I actually got along, or at least tolerated one another. I'd earned enough to pay my own way into the dances and give him money for gas. The problem was he wanted me to be subordinate to him, which I refused to do. Therefore we were never close, and it didn't last long.

On one such night after returning home from a dance in Corpus, we were surprised to find our father meet us at the door. It was around 1:00AM, and before I could even say anything he blurted out, "Your grandfather died." My response was a crystal clear reflection of what he instilled in me. It was just as mean, heartless, and cruel, and based upon years of enduring beatings, verbal insults, and humiliation. It demonstrated that not only was I a chip off the old block, but I was also the ax doing the cutting, and I returned cruelty with more of the same. Looking him squarely in his eyes I replied coldly, "We all gotta die sometime." I then walked past him, leaving him standing in the doorway with his mouth open in amazement. He had no idea I had all that hate in me, and my response stunned him mute. He never said anything after that. Unfortunately, this wasn't the only time I demonstrated via example what he taught me during all those years of abuse. I have no idea why he believed any of us cared for his father. His father was never around, and when he was he was a reminder of why my father turned out to be such a horrible person. I felt absolutely nothing for him or his father, who'd also been a drunk, womanizer, wife beater, and the root of my father's dysfunctional behavior. The next moment I was the one left standing in silence, as I watched Beelzebub, who never passed up an opportunity to kiss ass, put on a tremendous performance. It was a horrible explosion of clarity, exposing everything hidden within us. It was also a great act because Beelzebub never cared about anyone other than himself. I never saw him express a real emotion other than pride, rage, or disdain. He hadn't known our grandfather any better than I did, and no one liked him. He'd been an embarrassment and a nuisance to the entire family, who had to put up with him and pretend to give a damn. He had always been a source of irritation for my mother, who hated him, as she had a long memory and never forgot the abuse. I'll never forget watching Beelzebub sitting on the sofa in the living room with my father, pretending to care about someone he never knew. I never said a word to Beelzebub, as I'd always known what a fraud he was. My father never understood what a lying monster he'd created. I have to admit, it was pretty funny watching those two liars sitting next to each other, saying things they didn't mean about someone neither of them cared for. Two actors pretending to care about each other for some unexplained reason makes me sick. The hypocrisy was staggering, but perfectly in line with their character. Neither of them had a sincere emotion or an honest response. I never learned to kiss the hand that beat me or the boot that kicked me. I know that anyone who would surrender their dignity to kiss someone's ass will just as easily stab them in the back.

I continued working toward my objective of buying a car with my own money. Even if my father had offered to help, which he didn't, I wouldn't have accepted. I'd already witnessed and experienced the strings which accompanied his assistance. Every time Beelzebub pissed him off, he'd take away his car keys. He did the same thing with a twenty dollar guitar he'd bought for me while he was drunk. He bought it at the pawn shop next to the bar where he drank. In a moment of drunken frivolity, he paid twenty bucks because he wanted me to play guitar while he sang. It was a cheap wooden box with no acoustics. After that experience I'd learned never to take anything he gave me. After the white pony, I'd already vowed I'd never ask him for anything again. No matter how bad I needed it or what it was. Any interaction with him was an exercise in foolishness, and I wouldn't submit to his tyranny. I hated him and believed he was the lowest form of life possible, and the worst excuse for a father in history. He saw the fury in my eyes, which is why he forbade me to look at him when he spoke to me. He behaved like the alpha dog in a pack, and got angry if I looked at him in the eyes. It was a challenge, and it showed how much anger I felt towards him. He never understood that it was his constant hammering which made me hate him so much. Like an alpha dog, he saw eye contact as a challenge, and he was right. I would have liked to rip out his throat with my teeth.

Unfortunately, my mother was not much better. She had my father's habit of using abusive and derogatory comments. She called me stupid, lazy, good-for-nothing, and everything else in between. Her biggest thrill was calling me "Sam Kane." Interestingly, Sam

Kane was a Jewish businessman who owned a large slaughterhouse and meat packing company in Corpus. This guy had more money than God, or at least that's what was said about him on Main Drive. I never met the man, or even saw him. Somehow my mother got the notion that I was a tightwad, so according to her I must therefore be Jewish as well. It was pure and simple ignorance. My parents, whose lives were completely dictated by racism, were as guilty of it as their oppressors. Don't ask me to explain this. I was her son, but she said that I was Jewish because I was so tight with money. I had no money, and let me add that I knew nothing about Jewish people at the time. I'd not yet learned all I was to learn about the real America and its historical hatred of Jews. Today, as an adult, I've searched for America, that wonderful place which holds liberty and justice for all, and I've yet to find it. I've looked everywhere, and I'd still like to know where that wonderful placed called America is.

    I once carried a large birthday cake for my mother through the darkness for over twelve miles. Like a dog, who despite her cruelty still sought her approval and never got it. At that time I'd gotten a job as a clerk working at a little store called Maverick Market, on Agnes Street in Corpus. I usually hitchhiked home after work. I only had the job during the summer, and my shift was over in the afternoon, so I'd walk home in the dark. I was lucky that I was never attacked or kidnapped. Although, the chances of that happening were small, as there were many unwanted kids wandering the streets. No one cared about another kid walking in the dark. I don't know where I got the courage to do all the things I did, as I've always known the world is not a safe place. After walking for hours holding that birthday cake in both arms, I wish I could say my mother was nice, or even treated me kindly. It was late when I arrived, and I slept in the next morning because I was exhausted. I woke up with the idea of having cake, foolishly believing my mother would have saved me at least a slice. Again, I was wrong. I cannot begin to express how disappointed I was. I felt dejected, sad, and humiliated. All I found was the stained cardboard upon which the cake had been. There were not even crumbs left. It was all gone. I never said a word about it. I do remember my sister, who I have referred to as "Salty" in this work, laughed at me after seeing the expression on my face. My siblings had been so brutalized that they learned to find pleasure and laugh at one another's pain. Don't ask me how or why she found this funny. It was the example we had from our parents, and that's how we treated each other as well. I now know that anger disguised as humor is still anger.

During the summer I was saving to buy my first car, my mother made fun of me for not even buying a taco. I bit my tongue, never said a word, and quietly saved my money. I started bringing her a dozen tacos, which I hand carried all the way home from work. I kept my plan to buy a car secret, fearing sabotage. I wanted freedom and in order to have that I had to sacrifice. I worked the entire summer, never spending more than a few dollars on myself and what I had to give my father as part of my mandatory contribution. I'd already gotten my driver's license via driver's education through the school, which I also paid for myself. This was another incident which caused friction, as I broke my promise to never trust him again, and made the mistake of asking him for help. Apparently, my father had purchased an insurance policy on me when I was a baby. It was not for very much, but as I mentioned before, I had been born sickly and my father suspected I was going to die. He behaved like the man he was, and wanted to make a profit off my death. The trouble was that he was too cheap to take a bigger risk and spend more. Upon my request for help, he got the idea of cashing in the insurance policy. The trouble was the insurance policy check was in my name, so he forced me to sign it. Apparently I had signed it incorrectly, because he later returned extremely angry. I was just a kid and I had no idea what happened. He angrily forced me to become a part of a fraud. The insurance check was to be cashed under the pretense that the money would be used for my education, not go into his pocket. He had agreed to pay for my driver's education class, but true to his nature, once he got the money he changed his mind. He told me he wasn't going to pay for a damn thing, and that I should consider myself lucky to still have a place to live. Once more Beelzebub was there to witness my disappointment and rub it in by laughing. I never understood why Beelzebub got such a thrill out of making my life miserable. I never gave him reason to hate me, at least none that I know. I stayed out of his way and avoided contact with him. My father refused to help me pay for my driver's education class, which only cost $35.00 at the time. He received several hundred dollars for the insurance policy, which he'd bought for $15.00 the day after I was born. It had been growing ever since. I never saw a dime of that money. Only God knows what he did with it.

  I earned the money to pay for my driver's education class by working odd jobs doing whatever I could find. I worked for Mr. Rumley, the football coach, on several weekends. I busted my ass working hard for him. I must have done a good job because he paid me more than we agreed and was happy with me. I bought a 1955 Chevrolet. It was old even back then, but they were great cars. I purchased it from the Chevy dealership in Corpus Christi. True to the greed so common amongst car salesmen, he overcharged me. I've never trusted salesmen since then. I don't know how that guy could look at himself in the mirror. The car had a three speed transmission and a six cylinder engine. It was in need of a paint job, and had rust in several spots. Otherwise, it was white and turquoise. It needed tires and an overhaul, but I was happy and proud of my car. You'd have to understand how much I struggled and saved to get that car. I have no idea what anyone thought about my buying my own car. All I know is the old bastard never said a word. True to his evil nature, Beelzebub made fun of it, Bumper criticized it, and my mother pretended I hadn't done anything worth noticing. It didn't matter. Buying my own car was a triumph worthy of Caesar. I had outmaneuvered and won against impossible odds.

My '55 Chevy was beat up, old, and in need of repairs, but it was in my name and no one could take it away from me. This was my first covert successful maneuver against overwhelming odds and set the tone for the rest of my life. I never retreated because I feared taking on a challenge. It was an invaluable lesson at such a young age. It taught me to set my sights on a goal and work covertly to accomplish it, without asking for permission or approval from anyone. These acts of rebellion and independence were the keys to my freedom. It proved that amongst the many talents necessary to succeed, *will* and *intent* are essential. Most importantly, it severed ties to my father. It also presented a challenge to the rest of my family, as I demonstrated I could achieve success without their approval. Via a dedicated struggle, the war with Beelzebub, my father, and the thugs on Main Drive went into overdrive. There was no turning back. As it was with Caesar when he crossed the Rubicon River in Northern Italy, the dye was cast. I moved towards the coming battle and hardened my heart, never expecting anything from anyone, and prepared to die if necessary.

What appeared to be a seemingly insignificant accomplishment at home was met with a completely different response by my peers at school. Everyone noticed I had a car and assumed my parents had bought it for me, as theirs would have. When they learned I'd purchased it myself with the money I earned during the summer, it seemed to go unnoticed. No matter, I alone understood the significance of it and walked with pride, even as I walked alone. I loved my '55 Chevy, and in order to give it a better appearance, I bought two cans of rubbing compound and dug up every rag I could find. I started rubbing and polishing the car in the morning and polished it all day long. When I completed, it looked great, or at least I thought so. I even got a compliment from David Delgado, a loser who lived down the street and hung out with the thugs on Main Drive. He'd never spoken to me before, but getting a car meant something, especially in that barrio. The fact that I had a car meant I was ahead of the average teenager on Main Drive. However, it was much more significant. Not only did I own a car, I'd bought it myself. My car was the wings that gave me freedom and opened up the world of beaches, drive-ins, dating, and the club dances in Corpus. This was quite an accomplishment by anyone's standards, but my parents never paid my achievement any attention. As far as they were concerned nothing I did amounted to anything. Yet it didn't matter. Somehow I knew I'd climbed a very tall mountain. I realized that with this same determination I could accomplish anything. I proved I was somebody they'd underestimated, betrayed, and lost. I hid a secret desire for revenge and hatred for their refusal to acknowledge my accomplishments. I had been playing football, doing well in school, joined the school band, ran track, had my own job for years, knocked the shit out of dozens of local jerks in the streets and in the ring, learned how to play guitar, and been to California. Yet, the more I did, the more adamant they were about ignoring my accomplishments. I hated their refusal to validate or acknowledge anything I did. They taught me several extremely valuable lessons that still hold true today. The first is that once an average person dislikes you, nothing you do will ever matter. Second, no one will play a game they cannot win. After so many years of seeking their affection, I discovered it came with too many strings and was not worth having. I accepted reality and vowed to get the hell out of Texas as soon as possible. There was never any question about where I'd go. The Army was my only option and Vietnam was the most likely place I'd end up. The dead were piling up and news coverage was filled with imagines of bodies arriving in towns across the country in flag draped caskets.

Having a car my father could not take away from me opened up the world. Keep in mind that this was before mandatory insurance, when regular gas was 34 cents a gallon. Corpus Christi was a teenager's paradise and there were a hundred things to do. The youth scene was exploding. People were dropping out, dropping acid, smoking weed, and everyone was openly rejecting the concept of a pre-made mold we had to fit into. The Vietnam War was going full tilt and draft dodgers were headed to Canada and México. Music was flowing across the ocean from Europe and it was destroying the established order of things. There was magic in the air and life was exciting, precious, and real. There were rap sessions, coffee houses, halfway houses, dances, clubs, parties, the beach, Padre Island, and five girls for every guy. It was great. I started going everywhere, every chance I could. My search for the white pony had already taught me the world was huge and exciting, and not as depressing as Main Drive, where I'd learned the harshest lessons of indifference to suffering. It was a little scary at first, but I'd learned enough to avoid the big problems. Although many people remained focused on the war, the returning bodies and wounded, I shamefully admit I was too busy having fun to worry about it. I had broken free of the shackles that chained me to an inferior position under the tyranny of my father. Freedom was more wonderful than I'd expected, and I loved it. With all the problems it contained, freedom was worth every bit the trouble and hard work. My spirit, which had been continuously crushed and humiliated, began to soar, and I flew as close to the sun as Icarus.

At home I was a nobody, but as soon as I left I was someone special. I was a handsome guy with a car, a job, and the courage to go after what I wanted. I was more afraid of not trying than of failing, and soon discovered that having friends was a lot easier once I had a car. I never lacked for company and there was always somewhere to go. We were all poor kids from Main Drive, but we'd pitch in a dollar for gas, buy some cokes and junk food, and drive all over town. Up to that point it was as close as I'd come to happiness in my life. We'd go to the club dances every Friday night and cruise along Ocean Drive Boulevard to Staples Street, to Ayers bowling alley, and the Ayers swimming pool. Soon I had friends at Miller, Ray, Carol, and Moody High School. I sought out parties, parks, and places to go. I lived two separate lives, like a superhero who had to take shit from a tyrant during the week, but became someone else on weekends. I was the target of ridicule at home, while a pretty cool guy outside. At home I was the black sheep, but on the streets of Corpus Christi I was a somebody. I'd been boxing for over two years, and I'd done well enough to have earned a reputation amongst the toughest kids in town. I wasn't a thug, and this was demonstrated by how I dressed and the fact that I have always hated bullies, and anyone else who would gang up on someone. I'd been in enough scrapes to develop a reputation as someone who could and would fight. At the time the greatest compliment I ever received was from Curly Perez. The same crazy sadistic bastard who several years earlier jumped me with a gang of thugs, then tried to stab me. Over the years he had evolved into a badass old street veteran, who was much more crazy and dangerous than his younger self. He told me, "I hear you know how to throw your hands." Keep in mind, it sounds a lot better in Tejano Spanish. This should also give you an insight into how distorted my values were at the time. Today, I'd laugh at anyone who'd say such foolishness. Yet at the time, to have someone like Curly, the foulest lowlife I knew, say that meant something, at least to me. Looking back, I realize it was Curly, who I hated as much as I feared, that taught me you can never back down from bullies, and that revenge is sweeter when it comes as a surprise. You've got to match their behavior with *focused* violent fury and strike with serious intentions. The downside is that there could be fatalities. He also taught me that once the fight starts, it doesn't matter who threw the first punch or what you're fighting about. It's never over, and no one forgets nothing, no matter how long it's been. You'll never be able to forget about the enemy you harmed unless you kill him. Even this only eliminates him as a physical threat. Looking back upon my experiences, I know you can never forget the soldier you confronted and whose life you took, even under the disguise of national pride and war. These are all valuable lessons, because the toughest challenge a Warrior will have on this plane is dealing with average people. Some of them will be violent thugs like Curly, while others will be people in positions of power, but equally as dangerous. The secret is to strike covertly from a distance, by going outside their circle of influence, then continue to attack until they are utterly defeated, gone, or dead and no longer a threat. Curly also taught me that real freedom comes from knowing you have no alternative, you cannot run, and if you won't accept being publicly humiliated, then you have to stand and fight. This is an important detail and contradicts all those pie in the sky stories of living happily ever after and finding peace. There is no such place, and you'll never find peace on this earthly plane. Average people will always be around to screw up even the nicest day. The only solution is *detachment, forbearance, timing*, and no pity. It seems no matter what you want to do someone will accuse you of being a showoff, and tell you flat-out that it will never work.

For example, throughout all this time I'd been playing guitar and trying to learn as much as possible. I'd learn what I could from whomever I could. I was also singing in a band. I might not have been very good back then, but I could carry a tune. One night at a club dance I met a guy who claimed to be in a band. After talking for a while he invited me to his house to play, and I happily went. He knew a bunch of guys from Moody High School, and some who I had known from Cunningham and Wynn Seale Junior High. His house became a hangout for me. I'd be over there as often as I could afford to pay for the gas. My '55 Chevy became the focus of my life. Every dime I made went into it. I'd even taken auto shop classes in school to learn how to keep it running. Through this guy I met more and more people who were into music. Keep in mind that in Corpus, the best thing a Tejano could do was be a musician. It seemed to me those guys had all the fun. They always had the finest women and were the most popular guys in town. Everyone knew them and everyone wanted to be their friend. At the time Sunny and The Sunliners were a big deal. Then there was Little Joe and la Familia, The Ray

Camacho Band, and a bunch of other smaller ones. One of these bands was Tony and The V-Jays. I don't remember how I met Tony, but I tried out for his band as a singer and got in. I became part of a band while still in high school. It was another great accomplishment which proved I could become whoever I *willed* myself to be. I proved I could break out of the mold my parents had put me into. I was on cloud nine. In a very short time I had gone from a stuttering, scared kid, to someone people wanted to know. We'd play at the Carousel Club at six points in Corpus Christi. As clubs go, at the time it was a big thing in Corpus. I was popular, sought after, and invited to parties. People came up to me and introduced themselves. I had become the kind of guy I'd grown up wanting to be. It was a short period of my life, and it seemed all the planets lined up in my support. It was great, and the closest I'd been to happiness.

One door opens another, and being in a band was great. I sometimes played backup on my trumpet and also did lead vocals. My favorite songs were "I Wish it Would Rain," "Knock on Wood," and "Rainy Night in Georgia." I did backup for other songs, but these were mine. I did them solo with the band backing me up. I was flying close to the sun, and just like Icarus, I didn't notice the wax that held my wings together was melting. I'd go to the dances and lots of people knew me. The best part was that after so much trouble, I'd learned to dance. Let me say plainly, if you cannot dance in Texas, you might as well donate your penis to science, because you aren't ever going to use it. Women in Texas love to dance, and if you don't dance, well, you're going to be lonely. As they'd say back then, I had it going on. I had a car, I was a singer in a band, I was a Golden Gloves Champion, and now that I was driving I had a cool job in town. I was working as a salesman for Hardy's Shoe Store in downtown Corpus on Chaparral Street, the heartbeat of the city. This was before the malls came in and screwed everything up. Everyone, and I mean everyone, would go downtown. It was the place to be. As they'd say, I was so cool I needed shades just to stand the spotlight.

    Life outside of my home was great. All I had to do to feel like a real person was leave the house. I'd go home only to sleep, wash, and eat. Other than that I was in my car going somewhere, usually with a girl. It was great. My solo independence was a trend I'd follow the rest of my life. I was never afraid of being alone. As a matter of fact, I noticed a lot of the guys who I thought were tough, were just like me, or I was like them. I never needed to be a part of a group to feel safe. To this very day I don't care for groups of people who hang out together, just because they don't want to be alone. In my eyes they are just gang members, and all gang members are cowards. Anyone who needs a crowd to feel brave and powerful, or belongs to a clique that deliberately excludes others, is a loser. The fear of being alone is simply a manifestation of the fear of death. Those who fear being alone and seek solace in company are delusional. For some reason they believe if they are not alone, then death will not touch them. Only in their minds can such a ridiculous concept exist. Such nonsense is both comical and pitiful. Above it all, and thanks to Beelzebub, my father, Curly Perez, and many others like them, I hate bullies. I had no problems pushing my boundaries, taking chances, or worrying about failing. It was at this time I came to learn another lesson which still holds true today. I am more afraid of not trying, than of failing something I attempted. To this very day I have relatives laughing at me for trying to grasp as much of life as possible. They don't understand death is stalking them, and they'll never have time to do all the things they wanted. This is why a Warrior grabs onto as much of life as possible. Not to own or conquer it, but only to experience it. There are hundreds of experiences I'll never have. Not for a lack of courage or imagination, but simply because time, age, and death will not allow for it. I've learned that it's usually those closest to you who undermine your innermost dreams and make your life miserable.

For example, I made the mistake of sharing details of my life with my cousin, who I will refer to as "Rosie." This is a mistake I have chosen not to repeat. I've cut all such people from my life and apply *controlled folly* whenever I associate with them. It's not the way I'd prefer it, but I've finally accepted that average people are limited by their weaknesses. I'm always polite, courteous, friendly, and very calculated about what I say to each of them. None of them will ever know freedom. It's too bad Rosie never understood I wasn't pretending or playing games. I was engaged in *stalking* my own weaknesses and unburdening myself of my old baggage. Due to her averageness all she saw was someone like herself, going about their mundane existence, trying to fill the void in their life with no hope of actually succeeding.

Of all the qualities necessary to demonstrate good character, appearance is the least, and yet our society emphasizes looks more than essence. This was probably why I got hired at Hardy's Shoe Store by the boss, who knew me as a customer. You used to be able to get a great pair of shoes for less than twenty bucks back then. I started buying my own shoes at twelve-years-old, when my father told me on my eleventh birthday, "This is the last pair of shoes I'm gonna buy for you." My father, who failed miserably as a parent, has been one of my greatest teachers. He is the reason why I decided not to have children. I never believed there was a need to clone myself. My mother was no diamond either. I still cannot understand why they believed they should make babies, knowing what they knew about themselves and their parents. My father never missed an opportunity to remind all of us what a burden we were to him. The strange thing was he wouldn't wear a condom, have a vasectomy, or allow my mother to use birth control. He burdened her with a child nearly every year until it killed her. This was the same man who bought Beelzebub his first car, but never helped me with mine. This is the same man who took an opportunity to make a profit from my death, yet was unwilling to use the money for my education, as was stated in the insurance policy. After forcing me to sign over the check, he took the insurance money and never gave me a dime to help pay for my driver's education class. Looking back after all these years, I realize he actually did me a favor by being such a complete asshole. He never gave me double messages about what he thought of me, and I grew up expecting no help from anyone. I grew up knowing I was alone, something the Toltec discipline requires we acknowledge. At the time I was angry at his unfairness, as I had to work all summer to buy my car without any help from anyone. I also had to overcome continuous obstacles put up along the way. Both of my parents openly disliked my refusal to beg and kiss their ass, something they considered essential. I believed such behavior draconian and unacceptable. They actually expected me to kiss the boot that kicked me, which is why I often wondered if my real father wasn't from outer space. As of today, I don't know why or where I'd gotten such an outrageous idea, but I refused to kiss the hand that beat me. I wasn't going to beg for affection from the people who belittled, tormented, and ridiculed me, even if they were my parents. They validated a lesson I found via the Warrior's discipline, which is, everyone is alone. My response to their treatment was to hate them, refusing to ask for their assistance or share any part of my life with them. I became silent, sullen, angry, and filled with rage. This was met with their rejection, which pushed me further. In true average person fashion I responded by pretending it didn't matter, staying further away. The ugly cycle of average behavior, fed by the seven deadly sins, widened the gap between us until there was no hope of returning. The more independent I became the more they disliked me, and the less I needed them, until I eventually learned to do without them completely. It was a Greek tragedy in the making, only no gods came down from Olympus to rescue or assist me. If the Christian god who loved children never noticed my suffering, it might have been because Main Drive was on the dark side of the moon, or perhaps beyond his concern. Either way, by this time I'd already given up hope of his intervention.

Even before I got my car I'd been hitchhiking into Corpus, spending days hanging out downtown. I first discovered downtown as a young kid, when my parents brought me out there during the summer. My father forced me to buy all my own clothes, including underwear, shoes, t-shirts, and etc. Although according to Texas Child Labor Laws I wasn't old enough to get a job, I was forced to pick cotton all summer to pay for everything on my own. It was a hopeless existence. Thank the Universe I found music, which changed my life forever. After sweating for weeks working in the cotton fields, I bought my first transistor radio on layaway from Kress Five and Dime, a store which no longer exists. Music fed my spirit and nurtured me at such a deep level, it's difficult to describe how much it helped. Music became my companion and my only friend, as no matter how alone, miserable, scared, or discarded I felt, I always got a little help from my transistor radio. Buying it was equivalent to believing I could fly and escape Texas right there and then. I paid a lot more than it was worth, and in terms of cash value I got ripped off. Yet, it was the best buy I've ever made. Keep in mind that I bought it against my parents' wishes, who thought it was a complete waste and absolutely unnecessary. I sweated like a dog to buy it with money earned from picking cotton, dragging a giant sack weighing over a hundred pounds for over a mile. Then carrying it to be weighed and emptied into a trailer. I hated everybody a little less while I sang along with the top forty hits and learned the words to the songs. Music, a desire for vengeance, and my *will* created the bridge I stepped across to gain freedom. I owe music more than I'll ever be able to repay.

      I hated picking cotton under the hot sun all summer. I also hated being around all those Main Drive losers, who were satisfied with their horrible lives. As soon as I was old enough to legally work, at least according to the Texas Labor Laws, I quit picking cotton. I hated breaking my back for a dollar per hundred pounds of cotton. Even working like a mule, I never earned more than six dollars a day. It never bothered anyone in authority that the Texan land owners were exploiting us. The entire state of Texas was founded on cheap labor via the exploitation of Tejanos and other people of color. No one in Austin, the state capital, considered it unlawful that these alleged "God fearing Christians" were acting against God's laws, along with everything they claimed to believe on Sundays. Texas' history is a trail of tears, made up of the exploitation of enslaved and nearly enslaved people of color. It is no wonder DOEI Texan immigrants massacred and exterminated entire Native American populations. The same was done to Africans, who were brought over in chains way beyond the end of the Civil War. Growing up in Texas, a normal day consisted of watching the poor work all day, while barely earning enough to eat. If it were not for the intervention of the federal government, people of Mexican ancestry would still be treated like animals. Unfortunately, racism continues to be popular, ugly, and violent, which is why the war in Vietnam and the civil rights movement sparked so many battles on the streets of Corpus between NTOMAs/people of color and DOEIs. Tejano, Black, and other veterans of color refused to be stepped on by the same government that was sending us to die for democracy in a foreign land, while it squashed our civil rights in our own backyard. This brutalized environment and hypocritical system had a tremendous impact on me, and as a result I spent all of my teenage years angry, hating the injustice and all those who perpetuated and benefited from it. I hated living in Texas as much as Jews in Nazi Germany hated living under Hitler. All Texas lacked was the concentration camps and the ovens. The racist legal system still supplies the executioners, the prisons, and the gallows. Knowing what I know today about Texas, I'm ashamed to say I once considered it something to be proud of. What's wrong with Texas? Let me count the ways.

I sought employment out of the cotton fields and out of the sun, which is how I got my first inside job, washing dishes at the Holiday Inn on Highway 9, across from Highway 9 Bowl. Both these places are gone now. At the time the problem with restaurant work in Texas was your coworkers. For the most part they were all adult losers who never amounted to much due to poor life choices. They were the perfect examples of average people who were being punished by their sins. They'd spent their entire lives partying, getting into trouble, and were now working as cooks and dishwashers on the edge of society. Ninety percent of all of them were lowlife individuals who'd blown their chance, and were now barely surviving by working in manual labor jobs. The Holiday Inn was straight down Highway 9 from Main Drive and I could easily hitchhike there. I still worked my butt off, but it was not as hard as working in the cotton fields. Anyone who lacks motivation or a reason to study should wash dishes for a while. They'd quickly learn what they have to look forward to without an education. Neither of my parents did anything to lessen my burden or acknowledge my accomplishment of getting a job. Although I knew finding a job was a big deal for a kid my age, no one ever gave me any recognition. I never got a pat on the back or an attaboy. Even though washing dishes was a horrible job, I took orders from my boss and shit from coworkers, and continued learning what it takes to earn a dollar. Silly me, I was proud to say, "I have to go to work," even if it was only washing dishes. I gained real self-esteem via being responsible. I learned to be on time, every time, and do the job according to their standards. Neither of my neglectful parents ever took notice of anything I did. I worked for minimum wage at a horrible job and held my head high with pride in my heart. Looking back it seems funny, but just getting a job was the equivalent of my Emancipation Proclamation, as it meant my state of enslavement was over. I cut the chains to my father and took one step closer to escaping Main Drive, Andrew Jackson, racism, and Texas. Even though it was still a long ways away, I could finally see light at the end of the tunnel.

Life continued with thugs and racist Texans giving me shit outside the house, while my father gave me hell at home. His violence, drinking, and outbursts of abuse continued unabated, and we all lived in a continuous state of war. I maintained strict vigilance because I'd discovered the moment you dropped your guard, you'd get caught in a whirlwind of violence. My father was like someone out of a horror story. He was a total and complete tyrant, absolutely lacking any redeeming qualities. He and my mother always battled after he came home drunk. She'd start arguing with him over his drinking and driving, something he didn't want to be bothered with. It was horrible. Even after all the beatings and child abuse she never reported him to the police. To this very day I am shocked my sisters continued to interact with him throughout their adult lives. As a former child protective social worker, I still don't understand how they could stand to be around him. I believe child molesters should be taken out and shot. Fuck treatment, and let God forgive them if he wishes. As far as I am concerned, there is no place for such monsters in this world. I watched him beat my mother and siblings too many times to be able to erase it. This is a perfect example of why taking a Warrior's inventory is not a single event, but a continuous process requiring many years of tremendous effort. Defeating self-importance is an endless process, as is obtaining and implementing the knowledge that death is stalking all of us. Therefore all of our acts and behavior must be worthy of our lives, as they may be our last on this plane.

My biggest dispute with my mother was that she knew my father was sexually molesting my sisters and did not kill the bastard. She knew what a monster he was and should have done something. As you can imagine, such experiences make people crazy. I understand why my sisters are so emotionally unbalanced, highly volatile, and won't take shit from men. The experience of having him as a father stole their chance for happiness and a normal life with their husbands. I am still disappointed my mother didn't kill him. I am disappointed she did not even call the police, or have her bothers (my uncles) come down and kick the shit out of him. I certainly would have. It demonstrates just how beaten down and dehumanized she was. My poor sister, Little Red Riding Hood, was already a little crazy to begin with. She'd sometimes go off into fits of rage, beating up my younger sisters or anyone who got in her way. She was very strong and used violence to solve any dispute. The story makes me even sadder for my mother, who endured all this for years without being able to tell anyone. I think shame prevented her from telling her family, and fear of poverty stopped her from reporting him. Her actions taught me that there are many things worse than death.

My father certainly deserved to die after what he had done. Luckily for him I did not learn of his transgressions until 33 years later. Had I known before, I honestly believe I would have shot the bastard with his own gun, and then claimed he committed suicide. Though it might have been difficult to prove how he shot himself nine times with a 45. I would have most likely ended up in a correctional facility, which is probably why my mother never told me. She knew I hated him. However, I doubt even a racist Texas court would have convicted a fourteen-year-old kid of murdering his father, after learning he was beating him and his mother, and sexually assaulting his sister. I could have claimed insanity and self-defense, which would have also been correct. I certainly had enough scars to prove a history of violence at his hands. I probably should have shown my teachers the bruises which his beatings left on my back. Silly me, at the time I never knew other parents didn't go into fits of rage, picking up whatever was available, and using it to beat their children. That bastard beat me with garden hoses, extension cords, broom handles, and etc., as if his hands weren't enough. I never understood why he felt he needed to use something more to beat me with. He worked as a mason and his hands were as rough as crocodile hide, and just as calloused. My cowardly brother Beelzebub always managed to be gone when our father beat our mother. I never saw him once try to stop him. I made that mistake several times and he beat me down as if beating a stranger. I was suicidal and had more balls than brains, or at least that's what I'd been told. The problem was that afterwards my mother forgave my father, but he'd still be angry at me for intervening. Then she'd behave as if I'd never done anything to protect her. She was the first person to teach me that nobody likes heroes. Oh yea, they say they do, but not really. You see, heroes are only necessary during emergencies. Once the danger passes, most people want to forget what happened. Heroes don't forget anything, and neither do the people they fought in someone else's defense. My father never forgave me for having the guts to stand up to him. He'd beat me down, but I'd square off with him the next time. Then he'd beat me down again, and I'd do it again. This went on for years. When I describe my life as a state of war, you probably thought I was only using a metaphor. This was another reason why I got the hell out of Texas as soon as I could. My father stopped talking to me after the first time I intervened when he was beating my mother. It was the last time he beat me like an animal with a rubber hose, and I vowed if he ever hit me again I was going to kill him. I am the only person I've ever known who actually planned to murder his father. Of course it now seems ridiculous, but I planned to kill him and then escape to México to live with my cousins. I had four hundred dollars saved up and hidden away. I even bought a 22. cal rifle and sawed off the barrel, with intentions of shooting him in the head while he slept. I also planned to stick the knife I carried into the bastard's eye the next time he came at me with a hose or an extension cord. Thank the Universe I never shot or stabbed him. If I had, I'd be in prison for sure.

    I owe my sanity and escape from Texas to the music of the

period. The songs of Bob Dylan, The Beatles, Simon & Garfunkel, The Beach Boys, The Rolling Stones, and hundreds of others, too many to mention. I turned thirteen when The Beatles had five songs on the Top Music Billboard. Their songs gave me hope and lifted my spirit, something I never had before. To call music my salvation is an understatement, as it continues to play an important role in my life. Back then, local musicians were local celebrities, and I wanted to be one of them. As I mentioned before, through my connections with several guys in different bands, I managed to win a position as a singer with Tony and The V-Jays. It was a local band, not well-known or very good, but it was "inside" the mix. I was a singer in a working band and there was nothing cooler in Corpus Christi. This was during the civil rights movement and the height of the youth rebellion, when getting high was cool and considered harmless fun. After cutting my teeth on stage with Tony and the V-Jays, I decided to start my own band. I formed "Blues and The Blue Techniques." It was made up of guys from Main Drive. There was Pablo Mendez, Benito Davila, Noe Portales, Johnny Ruiz, Louie Garcia, Henry Guerrero, and myself. I had adopted the nickname of "Blues," after watching a cool flick with Peter Fonda called *The Wild Angles*, about a motorcycle gang. It was a horrible film by today's standards, but it was the coolest thing in the world at the time. It was about freedom, doing your own thing, getting away from oppressive adult rules, having fun, music, and everything vogue at the time. I didn't give a damn about people's opinions and can honestly say, even looking back with these eyes, and no bullshit, I was cool.

  I adopted a nickname because I didn't want people on Main Drive to know anything about me. I wanted to keep myself a secret. Nicknames have always been common in Tejano culture. The problem is that they are usually given to you by a bunch of assholes, and few of them are complimentary. I'd also read about Geronimo, the Apache War Chief who had a name which he used for war, and another for peace. Since I was always fighting, I selected mine from the film *The Wild Angles*, in which Peter Fonda played a character named Blues. I thought he was the coolest guy in the world and that's how I introduced myself. No one cared. I got a few weird reactions at first, but I never cared about what anyone thought. I knew I was leaving as soon as I graduated. Plus, it made sense to have a codename. Geronimo, the Apache War Chief, believed if people knew your real name, they'd have power over you. The French call it "nom de guer."

I soon discovered having a nickname like Blues also had other benefits, like protecting me from my own behavior. Other than the guys in my band, no one on Main Drive knew me by that name. I had two identities and discovered via experience the power and flexibility of anonymity. Plus, it made people curious, and my unwillingness to be clear with strangers made the mystery stronger. I created a false history which protected me and prevented anyone from discovering who I was. Their curiosity proved helpful, as I must have seemed the ultimate bad boy, because I had more girls than I had time for. It was great. The down side was that there were a lot of pissed off guys looking for me. Today, looking back, I find it amazing beyond words that I unknowingly practiced the discipline of a Warrior, before I knew it existed. I erased my past, built a cloud of mystery around myself, and hid while standing in the open. I never compared myself to anyone or gave out personal details, years before I ever heard about the Toltec discipline.

As the leader of a group I soon discovered the opposite side of the coin. I learned average people love to put others on pedestals, and love tearing them down and watching them fall even more. Blues and The Blue Techniques performed at the most popular club in Corpus, The Carousel Club, at six points. This was where all the cool guys hung out. It was stressful as hell, as a lot depended on our performance and was not as much fun as I'd hoped it'd be. I'd put this band together by sheer strength of will. I don't remember if we sounded smooth or clean, but all of us were willing to go on stage and put it on the line. We played several songs by Sunny and the Sunliners, as well as a few by other bands. It went by in a flash, and I was the most scared I'd ever been while still having fun. Doing something outside of my comfort zone became a trend for me, and set the tone for the rest of my life. Today, I make my students do things so far outside their comfort zones they can only do so while pretending to be someone else. One of the many disciplines of a Warrior is to act as if you are in control, knowing you're not. I was doing this before I'd ever heard of *controlled folly* or total abandon. I don't know why, but I invited a silly girl from Main Drive to come with me to our show. I guess I was playing the games which one plays at such an age. It was the one and only time I ever dated someone from Main Drive. I think her name was Vicki, but I'm not sure. After the show she had gotten angry because Joe and Pablo were drinking beer, which she found inappropriate. I was feeling powerful because I had just broken another of the many chains which bound me to an inferior role. I was once again flying up around the sun, and just like Icarus, couldn't see the wax holding my wings together was coming loose. She ended up getting a ride home and the rest of us went to Cole Park to drink our beer in peace. I was so amped I ended up being disappointed. I discovered that being the leader of a bunch of average people was more work than it was worth. Looking back, I realize I was implementing another aspect of the Warrior's discipline. I was pretending I knew what I was doing, while actually being as confused as everyone else. The episode went into Main Drive legend and caused mountains of gossip, but no one ever mentioned or asked me about it.

That night was the last time Blues and The Blue Techniques performed as a group. It was also the last time I was with all those guys together. I lost interest after realizing those guys were so far behind me, I was actually alone. I had real dreams of making it in California, while those guys were just pretending. One of the problems with being so determined is that it's nearly impossible to find others as dedicated. Besides, I knew it wasn't safe for me to be hanging around those guys. None of them had real street experience, and when it came down to it they were scared of everything. I didn't want to babysit them or get arrested because of their stupid behavior. That night after we finished drinking our beer we headed back to Main Drive in my '55 Chevy. I drove home along Ocean View Blvd, admiring the lights of Corpus Christi. I knew my time was running out. While the war in Vietnam was raging, I was already enlisted, and now I was saying goodbye, just marking time until after graduation. I continued towards the Corpus Christi Bridge and got on the freeway towards San Antonio. I used the freeway because there would be fewer cops and it was safer than staying on city streets. I glanced at the old courthouse and jail where I'd spent several nights. I didn't want to get locked up again, for any reason. We sped home through the hot and humid, stinky summer night to Main Drive, where despite its inhabitants I felt safe again. I felt I had reached another goal and raised the bar, but I was wrong. The next morning everyone at home acted as if nothing happened, and once again my accomplishment fell into a dark hole of forgotten events.

I saw Vicki at school, but I never spoke to her again. There was no way I was going to end up with some stick in the mud silly girl from Main Drive. I could meet someone with an actual personality just by driving into town. I wanted someone I could relate to, someone with an imagination, goals, dreams, and an urge to get the hell out of Texas as well. No one on Main Drive wanted to get the hell out of there and none of them were much fun to hang out with. I had very little in common with any of them. I couldn't understand how they could be satisfied with life on Main Drive or in Texas. Looking back so many years later, I realize those people had no reference point to compare it to. The average girl on Main Drive wanted to find love and get married. While I wanted to get away from everything that reminded me of Main Drive, Andrew Jackson, and Corpus Christi.

Blues and The Blue Techniques faded into memory and the band members went their separate ways. Benito "Gordo" Davila gave up playing guitar and became a dope dealer. Keep in mind, this was way back when weed was a felony in Texas. I have no idea how he expected to get away with it. He was a great big huge guy, and his girth alone attracted attention. I believe he just wanted to stop feeling like a fat slob and impress people. After a short time he got arrested and became the gossip of Main Drive when he went to prison. It turns out he wasn't a very nice guy after all, and for all I know he may still be there. The world won't miss his guitar playing, as he became just another loser of the highest caliber. He joined the ranks of losers that make up the history of Main Drive, and added another layer of shit already on the streets of that barrio. Noe Portales married an average girl from Main Drive, knocked her up, bought a house, and moved away. Pablo Mendez died from a heart attack and Henry "Do-Rock" Guerrero got lost in the whirlwind of time. Little Johnny

Ruiz got married and actually became a professional Tejano musician in San Antonio.

My learning not to care was the only way to survive so many disappointments, and the result of having been brutalized. Brutality is highly contagious and impossible to cure. I'd stopped displaying emotions and tried to hide behind a Kirk Douglas grin and reckless laughter. In the absence of a male role model, I adopted behavior I thought was cool and reflected how I wanted to appear. It took me years to learn how to express emotion, and I literally had to force myself to show different expressions. While at home I had to act as if I had no feelings and could never show weakness. All the while I was dying inside, hopelessly searching for solace and someone who cared. Acknowledging I didn't have such a person in my life made me angry. It's no wonder I got into so many fights. I wanted someone to love, someone who would love me. My being so well-known had its positive sides and I'd been dating lots of girls, but no one I cared for. While on a date I'd often ask myself, "What am I doing here?" I learned that pretty faces and great legs have nothing to do with what's inside a person. This was a great period in the history of Corpus Christi, when the boys and girls social clubs literally controlled social events for Tejano youth. These social clubs created the social environment and it was a magical time. I'd never seen so many beautiful and eligible women, and felt as if I'd found King Solomon's Temple. I have never found anything close to that environment anywhere else I've lived since then. In that aspect, growing up in Corpus Christi during the Sixties and Seventies was the best thing that could have happened to me. Looking back, I realize I foolishly imagined it would always be like that. Today, the young Latino scene is dead and there is nothing going on which compares. Everyone who was a part of that wonderful movement got old, married, died, or moved away. Today Corpus Christi is only a shadow of what it once was. Today's Latino kids in Corpus don't have a common enemy or ugly monster which they can point at and say, "Let's unite and defeat it." Racism and discrimination still exists, but it is nowhere near as blatant as it once was. Worse, the Latino kids have given in to apathy, which is a disease that's eating away at the spirit of the Tejano people.

    Life outside of Main Drive was wonderful and it was a great time to be young, wild, and free. One of the highlights of the period was when I was asked to be the bow for one of the girls clubs. I was asked to be their male sweetheart. The bow was like the official "guy" of the club, and his role was to accompany members to events so they never had to go anywhere alone. The bow would escort the ladies to award dinners, school functions, and etc. The real benefit, at least in my mind, was that everyone who mattered at the time knew me. I knew so many girls it was difficult to keep their names separate. I never had any trouble meeting women, getting dates, or being invited to parties or anywhere else. Sometimes I'm sure I was invited just so I'd show up and people would see me there. It was such an ego boost. I had an entire page of Norma's, Alice's, and Sylvia's in my little black book. I'd say hello and always got it right. A lot of guys wanted to hang out with me and be my friend. They knew I knew lots of girls, and knew hanging out with me they'd meet some. As it is today, it's all about appearance. If they like the way you look, you're in. If not, it won't matter how great a person you are. It was equally as shallow back then, and being popular was a game. It was bizarre to be so well-known, validated, and popular, while a nothing at home. It's probably the same reason why I never let all this go to my head. I always knew it was as shallow as a coat of paint. I was popular based on my appearance and nothing more. None of them ever really knew me, or wanted to know me beyond being seen with me and having fun. It was the same crap I'd grown up with. It was as sick and screwed up as all the fuss being made about people on TV today. I wish I could remember the names of all the girls I dated, just so I could recall their faces. I would also like to thank them, even the ones who dumped me. They probably taught me the most. I wasn't ready for a relationship, as I was devastated by my abusive parents. I broke hearts, told lies, and love came back to claim its due.

Texas escapee,
-don Jesus M. Ramirez

Chapter Seven
The Knife Fighter

"I was neither brave nor bold, just unlucky to have been born amongst miserable human beings. I joined the ranks of reluctant warriors, swept up in a wave of senseless violence."

-don Jesus M. Ramirez

I have no idea what other kids did during the summer, and admit I never cared. I had to work. I was told to earn my own way and that was that. I had to buy my own clothes, underwear, shoes, and etc. Unfortunately, the only job available to me at that time was picking cotton. This would have been child abuse anywhere else, but not in Texas. As an adult I've read about sweatshops and illegal child labor in Third World countries. If someone had reported our subjugation to the authorities, I doubt a DOEI Texan judge would have given a damn. This is why I laugh when I hear people talk about the "good old days." They must have lived a different reality. The DOEI population in Texas didn't give a damn about Tejanos as long as we stayed in our place, didn't vote, or make any trouble. They couldn't have cared less if we were murdered or died of hunger, as long as we did it quietly and out of sight. Many reading this may scoff and minimize my statements, which only proves my point. This is why I despise bullies. DOEIs of my generation from Texas are guilty of the same indifference demonstrated by prewar Germans, who stood by and never spoke against injustice, permitting Hitler to harm so many innocent people. It's ironic that Texas will become the first state in the country where DOEIs will no longer be the majority.

By the time I was in high school I had plenty of reasons to be afraid of my surroundings. Texas was in a state of war against its native Tejanos during the late Sixties and early Seventies. The DOEI conservatives were preaching a return to the good old days, before civil rights, when Southerners held lynchings in the city's courtyard. Life was scary as hell, and like many Tejanos, I carried a knife for protection. This is a sign of how desperate things were in Texas, as stabbing a DOEI meant a life sentence or death by a police shooting "accident." Life out in the backcountry had proven that it's better to be too well armed, than not at all. I did not carry a knife because I wanted to fight. I carried a knife because I knew I'd have to fight more than one opponent at a time, and those opponents usually carried one too. I wanted to live long enough to get the hell out of Texas. I'd accepted the idea that I'd have to use my knife someday. In line with this thinking I also started carrying a large handkerchief, because everyone gets cut in a real knife fight.

Everyone on Main Drive carried a knife, and it was common to see people playing with them. Throwing them, sharpening them, or practicing opening and closing them. I cut myself many times by accident doing the same, and so had everyone else I knew. My brother Punk actually drove a knife through the palm of his hand while cutting wood. As I mentioned before, as kids we developed deadly games with popsicle sticks to get better at using our knives. We'd steal red Crayola crayons or red chalk from school and use it to color the popsicle sticks. We'd then practice slicing each other with them. If you had red markings on you, you'd know you'd been cut. This is the same concept which 15th century French swordsmen used to score points in a contest, before it was outlawed by the king. It was our way of managing fear and acting out our own destruction. The older guys had the same fascination with knives. It was like an epidemic. One guy named Lupe carried a dagger which he could throw with great efficiency. He became famous for throwing it at a dog and killing it after he'd supposedly been attacked. I suspect he just wanted to see if he could stick the knife into the poor creature. Cruelty and laughing at another's suffering was common on Main Drive, as it is everywhere in America. The story became a barrio legend and circulated faster than a bad smell.

One summer I was hired by a labor contractor to work for a rancher whose ranch was just outside of Robstown, Texas, about seventeen miles away from my house. Several people from Main Drive had already been hired to work there. The first day I was assigned to unload a huge truckload of firewood into a large barn. It was hard backbreaking work. I was working alongside a freckled-faced DOEI kid, who I'd gotten into a dispute with because he wanted to boss me around. He ordered me to go get him some water, and I told him to go fuck himself after he kissed my ass. I'd thought I knew all the DOEI kids through school, but I'd never seen this guy before. At the time I thought he was the strangest looking creature I'd ever seen. He had large orange freckles that completely plastered his face. Orange hair, pink skin, pasty white hands, and eyes like a rabbit, which he hid behind sunglasses. John Steinbeck, famous for the lies he told in *The Grapes of Wrath*, would have called him a real American, or an Okie. In his book he portrays Okies as hardworking, down on their luck, good people. What he doesn't say is that they were also racist, ignorant, violent rednecks, and for every Okie the farmers hired, one farmworker of color lost his job. He also neglected to mention that their hatred of everyone, including other DOEIs is legendary, as is their violent history. These new migrant workers, who had actually owned land in Oklahoma, followed the same migrant trail which the Native Tejanos had for years. They were taking the only jobs that many Tejanos and other people of color had had for years. Steinbeck, who'd grown up in the Salinas Valley in California, supported those whom he identified with. He did what all 96ers do when they cannot find something truthful to say, and just made shit up. Steinbeck had no problem lying and describing these half-mad people as heroes, who crossed America along Route 66 coming to California seeking a new future. The trouble with his fairytale is that it disregarded and omitted what their presence meant to the people who had lived in California all their lives. He romanticized their hardships, and deliberately overlooked and omitted everyone else's. One must wonder if John Steinbeck was in fact a bigot, or just a delusional perpetuator of lies. Regardless of his personal agenda, racism is deeply ingrained within the American experience due to centuries of brainwashing. Everything from the size of a person's skull to the Bible has been used to support delusional racist lies. The DOEI farmers, descendants of other DOEIs who had stolen the land from the native landowners, were racist bigots as well. They preferred to hire someone who looked like themselves, and quickly removed the Mexican American, Filipino, and Japanese workers.

The freckled-faced little bigot who I was working with was just doing what he'd seen being done all his life. After I told him to go fuck himself he replied with the same kind of remark, and we started fighting. I guess he actually believed what his daddy had told him about being innately superior, because he couldn't fight worth a shit. I was knocking the hell out of him with every punch, and he couldn't hit hard enough to save his life. I got tired of outboxing him, so I tripped him to the ground and stomped on him about a dozen times. He got up with a bloody nose, then suddenly pulled out a knife and took a slice at me. I stepped back just in time to avoid being slashed across the chest, but wasn't fast enough to avoid being cut across my forearm. It hurt and bled like hell, and it pissed me off. It was a duck-billed blade, commonly used for castrating animals. It had a brown handle and a blade about six inches long. I had my knife on me, and of course in my mind I was the "good guy." I'd gotten this crazy idea that "good guys" never drew their weapons first, but only after the "bad guy" drew his. In my confused mind this freckled-faced bastard was the bad guy and I was the hero. Looking back, I know that Hollywood bullshit would have quickly been lost on the rednecks who owned the ranch. However, at the time I wasn't scared, but excited that I'd finally have a chance to fight someone with a knife. Only, it was still a game to me. I drew my knife and smiled at the son of a bitch, and quickly noticed he wasn't smiling back. He was enraged that someone whom he considered inferior had not only defied him, but had steadily kicked his ass. He came at me with murder in his eyes and again took a slice at me with his knife. It finally caused me to realize that he was trying to kill me. I also realized that this was not a game, and that I might have gotten myself into something I didn't want to be a part of, but it was too late. We sparred back and forth, with each of us swinging our knife at each other in a deadly contest. I think I had actually dreamed this would happen, but the reality of it killed that dream. It was an empty feeling, and I quickly decided I had to get the hell out of there. At first the large barn we were fighting in had plenty of room, but it was getting smaller and smaller. The freckled-faced bastard kept attacking and swinging his knife from left to right, then turning it in his hand trying to stab me.

I remember his expression and pinkish red freckled covered skin as he sweated, bled, and cursed at me. I don't know where I got the idea to do what I did, or where I might have learned it, but the next time he swung at me, I let the knife blade move past my face, then kicked at his elbow with my front foot. I'd hit him perfectly. I don't know if I broke his arm or if I just hit him correctly, but he dropped his knife and grabbed his arm in pain. He then spun back around and I took a slice at him, cutting him from his forehead, down his face, and to his chest. One long slice that created a river of blood, which poured as he let out a terrifying scream. I knew it wouldn't kill him, but man it looked awful. He screamed like a woman while still holding his arm, then stumbled backwards out of the barn before he turned and ran to God knows where. I had no idea anyone had witnessed the fight, but quickly realized several of the workers had, and recognized some of the men were from Main Drive. Keep in mind, none of them intervened or tried to stop the fight. One of the men stepped forward and wrapped his handkerchief around my bleeding forearm. In Native Tejano barrio Spanish he told me to get the hell out of there, because the kid I'd just fought was the foreman's son, and he had lots of uncles and a large family. In English it would roughly translate into, "You better get the hell out of here. He's the boss's son, and he has lots of relatives. They're going to skin you alive, before they cut off your balls and roast them as they watch you bleed to death." I had no idea he was the foreman's son until that moment. They'd be there as soon as he ran and told them. I don't remember the man's name who told me to run, but I'd seen him drinking at the Stella's cantina before.

    I hauled ass out of there as fast as I could, and as I ran the fear hit me like a bullet. I felt a wave of terror sweep over and completely envelop me as I realized what I'd done. I might have killed him. I knew they'd call the cops, and there was no way DOEI cops were going to take my word over his. I knew there was no way I'd be considered the "good guy." I was the Tejano underdog, without anyone to speak up for me. Chances were I'd be killed trying to escape. I'd probably be found dead with two bullets in the back of my head, or face down in the river. Perhaps I'd disappear into some unknown cow pasture on a lonely ranch, alongside other dead Tejanos who stood up against similar injustice. If I survived I'd be found guilty and sent to prison, but only after I got the beating of a lifetime. As it got dark I started walking through the huge cotton fields towards Corpus Christi and Main Drive. Keep in mind, the ranch I was working at was outside of a town that was about seventeen miles away from my house. I don't know how I found my way back home, but I remember spending most of the trip hiding in the fields. I was afraid of hitchhiking because I was certain the cops would be looking for a Tejano kid walking along Highway 44. I was also afraid his relatives would see me walking and shoot me on sight. I walked across huge empty fields under the bright Texas moon for most of the night, arriving at my backdoor just as the sun was coming up. I was exhausted, and I don't know how I made it home. I had a fever and my arm hurt like hell, but the bleeding had stopped. My wound throbbed as I grabbed an old tarp, wrapped myself up in it, and laid down on the back porch. I stared up at the fading moon as I drifted off to sleep, still expecting to be ambushed by his angry relatives or the police.

Once again, by some miracle, the entire episode vanished into some dark hole. I later learned one of the men who saw the fight told the rancher he didn't know me, and that I was from another work crew, as they had several working at the same time. The DOEI foreman never took a look at me, and was therefore unable to identify me.

I guess he thought we all looked alike. The guy saved my ass, and that's for sure. The incident faded, but it didn't completely disappear. The same man also spread the story of the fight around Main Drive, and in no time I had a reputation as a knife fighter. I was a Chingón, and a real, honest to goodness badass. At the time it seemed like a good thing. There were few higher titles amongst the lowlifes of Main Drive than that of a knife fighter or former convict. I was respected by the guys who'd returned home from prison, as well as the hardcore badasses, who for some reason or another now found excuses to show me their scars. Each scar and story held details which might have put several people back in prison. Several of these stores were so awful I cannot repeat them even now, so many years later. Even then I was aware that there are many levels of being a badass, but I didn't know just how vast the differences were. The truth was I was no badass. I was only trying to stay alive. A small part of me might have been trying to actualize a Hollywood fantasy and be a barrio hero, but that quickly ended when that kid sliced my arm. I never set foot on that ranch again, and I'm still keeping an eye out for that red-haired, freckled-faced bastard who carried a parrot-nosed blade. I'd stared death in the eye, and it scared the shit out of me. I'd never seen such a crazy DOEI in my life. That kid was the first real badass DOEI I ever met who scared me. Not because he was bad, but because he was so full of hate. At that moment my entire life changed, as I knew I'd have to watch my back for the rest of my life. I knew he had a scar across his face which would never let him forget me. I already knew that no one forgets nothing. Strangely enough, no one in my family ever said a word to me about all the gossip. No one ever asked what, when, or where. It was as if it never happened. Once again, my accomplishments or giant disasters fell into a dark vacuum of indifference. The only difference was that this time I was glad it did, as I would have had no explanation.

I stayed away from everywhere I thought I might run into that guy. This was pretty hard to figure out. How do you avoid going to places where a scary knife wielding bastard might be lurking in the shadows ready to kill you? I don't know how I did it, but I did a pretty good job. A few months later I went to the Thunder Bird Drive-In Theater, a hotspot where mostly teenagers went to bang their girlfriends in the backseat of their cars. I must have been half-drunk and not paying attention that night, because without warning I was suddenly attacked. That red-haired bastard I'd cut months earlier jumped out from behind a car and charged at me. He must have seen me in the snack bar and followed me. I have no excuse for not seeing him or sensing he was there, except that I was thinking about getting laid. This is the problem with drinking, smoking weed, and having a pretty young thing rubbing on you. It tends to make your combat antenna shut down. I remember seeing his face in the flash of the movie projector, then noticed the gleaming blade in his hand. I instinctively reacted to his attack, but wasn't fast enough. The red-haired bastard stabbed his knife into my left hand, and then hauled ass into the darkness, passing dozens of parked cars. I never had a chance to defend myself. If he'd had more balls he would have killed me. I reacted without thinking, which probably prevented him from slicing my face, as he had intended. I'll bet he was trying to get even for the scar I'd given him to wear for the rest of his life, as a reminder of our little sticking contest. I tied my handkerchief around my hand and ran back to the car. I don't remember who I was with, but I remember it hurt like hell. I got out of there as quickly and as quietly as I could. I never got laid that night and never went to the doctor. My thumb wouldn't work properly for the next several months. I had trouble holding onto things and couldn't make a tight fist, which becomes a real problem when you're supposed to be some kind of street fighting badass. I did get a little memento from our second meeting, as the son of a bitch left his damn knife stuck in my hand. I still have the damn thing. The experience validated a valuable lesson. Once a fight starts, it's never over. Once you fight someone, it's on forever. It may take years, but no one forgets nothing. I am still hunting that cowardly bastard. I'm sure he still has that scar across his face, and thinks about me whenever he looks into a mirror.

    The reality of this event massacred my fantasies, removing any remaining illusions about having God's righteousness on my side. Once a fight starts, it's just ugly and murderous rage. In here lies the crux of fighting and training, as discipline and physical courage plays an undeniable role. The average person foolishly believes that anger not only provides them with an upper hand, but gives them a right to lash out. Usually this emotional reaction is simply injured pride disguised as righteous indignation. The end result, regardless of how it's justified, is catastrophic. A real fighter, someone with actual experience, knows that once the fight is engaged all that matters is surviving. A real badass, someone who seeks confrontation, enjoys the adrenaline rush. Facing an opponent with training and the ability to manage their emotions is equivalent to facing a natural disaster. Such a person, and there are many thanks to America's endless wars, are extremely dangerous. These individuals exist in society, and truth be told, we need them. Without such people, Americans would not enjoy the freedom they waste. The difference is that these combat warriors have no fantasies about justice or allegiance to a code of ethics. They can and will hurt you. They don't have to be angry, or even have a reason. Yet the typical American thinks they know how to fight because they watched others fight on television. Those I speak of are not armchair warriors, who tell great stories but have zero experience in the field. At the time of this knife fight I was not a real badass, or even close to one. I had however been tested and bloodied repeatedly. I'd had to fight bigger and tougher guys since I could remember. My opponent on the other hand, had not. He actually believed what his ignorant daddy told him about being innately superior. He'd witnessed his daddy cow others into submission and believed he could do the same, simply because he thought he could. The crux of this dilemma is that the world does respond to fiction. The law of attraction applies, and for every action there is a reaction. The Universe placed us on a collision course, and his attempt to be the alpha dog, exert dominance, and be in charge ended the moment we met. His self-importance led him towards death. He failed to evaluate whether our fight was a fight he wanted, could win, or should engage in. There was no advantage for him, as we were both hired help, working to unload the same truck. We could have just done our job, possibly even become friends, or at least acquaintances. Instead he chose confrontation, which led to conflict and battle. The urge and thrill of dominance is an innate weakness of the average man. I've had many confrontations with alleged top dog wannabes who made the mistake of underestimating me. After many similar problems, I make it a policy to tell individuals trying to subordinate me to not confuse my reasonableness for weakness. Unfortunately, they never listen. As a mentor and guide, I've learned that all I have to do to hurt someone is stop talking. Beginning Seekers often confuse following direction with capability, overlooking the fact that while a Warrior is able to set his ego aside, he rejects all efforts to be subjugated. This mistake has been made countless times by many prospective students. Their epiphany only arrives after they realize that their view of themselves, the world, and of me were wrong. What's comical is that I cover protocol, roles, and procedures at the beginning of any association. The problem is that average people do not have a reference point for interacting with a Warrior. Everyone they've ever known has been a reflection of themselves. Therefore, they mistakenly assume that my word is as meaningless as theirs. As a Warrior, I have no need, use, or tolerance for fools who cannot apply simple discipline. I do not give second chances. If a prospective student is not able to alter their behavior upon demand, set aside their ego, and acknowledge their role as student and mine as teacher, then they are not worthy of my association.

I continued to have slicing contests along the way, and it's hard to remember them all. The problem with being a kid and doing insane shit like knife fighting is that you tend to talk about it. Having a scar to prove your story helps. The guys I hung out with spread the story. Only according to them, I'd fought back and had actually sliced up the guy who'd attacked me. I cannot remember doing that, but it didn't hurt my reputation. I also cannot explain why I felt proud of being thought of in such negative terms, but at the time it seemed like the right thing. I was a man of reputation while I was still a kid. This kind of stuff never works well when you're poor, young, and stupid. I had been bloodied in several dozen fights. I'd seen the "elephant," as combat troops returning from Vietnam would say. I'd seen death, been bloodied, and hadn't even joined the Army yet. It was a storm waiting to catch up with me. Sure as day follows night, several weeks went by and it did. I was picking cotton with a labor contractor from Main Drive, a man whose name was Tonio Garcia. He was a coldhearted crook who robbed me and dozens of others out of our social security deductions. I hope the bastard burns in hell. I cannot imagine ripping off all those poor people, but that's how things were in South Texas. Cruelty and brutality gets passed down and not even the children are spared. At the time my only consolation was that a guy who I'd beaten up knocked up Tonio's daughter, then left her without a dime. Soon thereafter my ex-buddy had gone ballistic and beat the hell out of her after a night of drinking. He got locked up and did a long stretch in prison. So, I know he paid some dues. I don't know why that gave me satisfaction, but at the time it did. I guess it shows how brutalized all of us who'd grown up around cruelty were. Later it seems Karma returned to claim more dues from Tonio. His oldest son got ran over, his wife left him, and his youngest son went to prison. His daughter, who was beautiful, later married a jerk who beat her, then knocked her up again and abandoned her. Call it poetic justice if you like.

    I was picking cotton the day the storm caught up with me. It was hot as hell, without the slightest breeze or cloud in the sky to give us shade. I was weighing my sack, which often held as much as 125 pounds of cotton. The greedy farmer was only paying us a dollar per hundred pounds we picked. Tonio would automatically deduct ten pounds for the sack itself, and another pound for the leaves. He was a real son of a bitch. He also sold snow cones, which were simply shaved ice with colored sugar flavors. I'd just bought one on credit and was busy eating it when a guy named Hector Garcia decided he was going to take it from me. He was a short little ugly kid, with buckteeth and kinky hair. He had a light complexion and spoke with a funny voice because of his buckteeth. He just came up and tried to grab it out of my hand. I moved away from him and said something like, "What the hell do you think you're doing?!" He replied with something like, "You're eating my snow cone." I told him to go fuck himself, to which he responded by charging at me. I dropped my snow cone and prepared for his attack. He looked like an easy fight, as I'd fought dozens of wannabe tough guys just like him. I was good at throwing my hands and kicking, and was a lot faster than most of the guys I'd fought. I quickly established myself and he soon realized he was getting his ass beat. He took a step back, wiped his bleeding nose, and then drew his knife. It was what we called a banana knife, because it had a long blade about the length of a banana, and was about the width of a pencil. Unfortunately, this was one of the few times I didn't have my knife on me. This ugly bastard attacked me by swinging his knife like some kind of wild fool. I wasn't afraid of him and believed I could take the knife away and continue beating his ass. However, the cotton sack which I'd rolled up and wrapped around me came loose, and I tripped by stepping on it, causing me to fall backwards. The son of a bitch continued to attack, and as I fell he came at me, slicing down towards my face. I moved my right hand up to protect myself and he caught me, nearly cutting off my right thumb. The blood shot right up towards him, and the expression on his face quickly changed as he realized he'd cut me. He saw the blood gush out of my hand and took off running. I have no idea where he thought he was going, as we were out in the middle of a field, ten miles from anywhere. Tonio's wife quickly wrapped a handkerchief around my wrist and let out a continuous stream of foul curses at Hector, who now stood as still as a statue in the distance. She packed me up and drove me home. When we got there she quickly told my mother, who screamed and had the neighbor let her use the phone to call my father. Things got worse because my mother had to call my father at work. He came home in a hurry and took me to the doctor. His dark eyes blazed as if the Devil had possessed him. I am sure he would have preferred to beat me, but feared killing me. I must have looked pretty bad from the loss of blood. We arrived at the doctor's office at Spohn Hospital in Corpus Christi. The DOEI doctor suspected I'd been fighting and was not pleased with having to treat me. He took my arm and placed it on the steel bed, then, placing his knee on my forearm, poured a bottle of alcohol onto my wound. I screamed like bloody hell. The sadistic son of a bitch was inflicting his version of due punishment on me. His eyes widened and his mouth opened to a half-smile, as I jumped up off the bed and blood started flowing again. I guess my screams alerted the nurse, who'd come in, as did someone else. The fucking doctor quickly changed his manner, as if he were an actor on stage, and then quietly stitched up my hand. I lost the feeling in my right thumb for years, and still carry the scar, a clear reminder of how much it hurt.

A cruel example of my father's indifference occurred on the way home, when he stopped at a drive-in for a hamburger. You'd think the son of a bitch might have offered me one as well. Sorry, but no. I sat in the seat next to him in pain, watching while he ate his hamburger and drank a soda. He never asked me for an explanation or offered one word of comfort. I never said a word to him about what happened or why, and I never asked for anything. He stared at me with his ugly blazing eyes and quietly ate his meal, as if he were watching television. I don't know which traumatized me more; getting cut, the sadistic doctor, or witnessing my father's indifference.

Hector Garcia, the guy who'd cut me, was killed later that year. He was hit by a car while crossing Highway 9. I'd thought about killing the fucker myself, but I swear it wasn't me. I also swear I wish it had been. Again, my reputation grew, only this time I'd been badly cut. This event had also been witnessed by people from Main Drive. Those who didn't see the fight saw the bandage, my swollen hand, and the stitches it took to keep my thumb attached. I knew I had to get the hell out of there. If not, I was going to end up dead or in prison.

I still believed I could find the California of my fantasies and started making plans to do so. I needed to save up enough money for my ticket, plus I couldn't arrive empty handed. I continued to work and save my money, while struggling with the endless and senseless violence, so common on Main Drive. Fights were also normal in the hallways of both junior high and high school. Violence could erupt with serious and often bloody consequences at any moment. I knew my days were numbered after almost having my thumb cut off and a knife stuck into me. I knew I had to get out of Corpus Christi and Texas all together. I never wanted to be a badass. I just didn't want people giving me shit because they thought I wouldn't fight back. I'd learned that if you start running away, they wouldn't let you stop. The trouble was that if I fought back, someone might get hurt, and it could be me. I was desperate to get the hell out of Texas, so I worked my ass off and saved every dime. I earned enough money for my second trip to California while still in high school. I cannot say it was a great trip, or that I had any earthshattering experiences. It was just about working and saving my money. I mostly proved to myself that I could make it in a strange place, around stranger people. Yet, as I look back today, it's always been the same. I never fit in and I never belonged to a clique or a group. I was lonely, often sad, and always angry. My relatives in California proved to be a different, yet same version of the people in Texas. I returned to Corpus older, wiser, and less willing to risk life and limp over an insult. Although I made many important self-discoveries along the way, I never expected to live long enough to utilize them.

One day while feeling like some kind of hero because I'd been to California twice, I shoplifted a pair of cheap shoes, even though I had money in my pocket. It was one of the dumbest things I'd ever done in my life, up to that point anyways. I even tried to escape from the cops who'd arrested me. Talk about stupid. The cop, whose name I still remember, but choose not to say, would have shot me over a fucking pair of cheap shoes. I saw the look in his eyes as he reached for his gun. He was a coldhearted bastard. I hope this son of a bitch gets cursed by God, and like Pontius Pilate's gatekeeper who struck Christ on the day of his crucifixion, is doomed to walk the earth until the end of days. I'd seen this type of hardcore redneck bastard a hundred times, as they exist everywhere. They thrive on hate and anger, like vampires feed upon blood. I have no idea what kind of evil befell this man, but it must have been awful. I never knew so much hate existed. I'm still in awe at all the cruel stonehearted bastards I've had the misfortune of knowing. After being arrested I ended up at the county jail in the old courthouse, which has since been abandoned. As of today it still stands facing the Corpus Christi Bay, but plans are in the works to have it demolished. I had a great view of the port and the Gulf of México from my jailhouse window. It was scary as hell. I was just a kid and the heartless bastards stuck me in a cell filled with grown adult thugs. They never gave a damn that I might have been raped, beaten, or who knows what else. These acts of calloused indifference were referred to as justice, which served to show young lions like myself to stay out of trouble. It didn't matter that over 600,000 rapes occur in the correctional system every year. As they like to say in Texas, "Tough shit." Or, "You want to fuck with the bull, you get the horns," another saying which makes about as much sense as the first. I didn't want to be in the cellblock with all those thugs, so I volunteered to be a dishwasher. However, I had a problem which wouldn't allow me to do so. I didn't have any shoes. Luckily for me a guy I'd never known before named Robert gave me a pair of his old shoes. He probably saved my life. I wish I could have done something for this poor bastard, besides thank him. I started noticing peculiar behavior which told me something was going on, and things were about to get worse. The DOEI cops knew there was going to be a fight inside the main cellblock, and started giving the DOEI prisoners food, toothbrushes, toothpaste, and soap. The Black and Tejano prisoners were then given whatever provisions were left over. When the guys in my cell learned I was going to work in the kitchen, one guy asked me to steal silverware for them, so they'd be able to make weapons. Some of the guys were heating up their toothbrushes, and then embedding a razorblade into the handle, with the intention of using it as a slashing blade. The Universe must have been watching out for me, because I was moved out of the main cellblock that day. I was put into the trustee cell, where everyone just did their time and prayed to get out. Just as I knew it would, a huge fight went down and the cops used hoses and long batons on the prisoners. They waded into the cellblock swinging the batons like baseball bats. The dispensary was filled with injured men, while others had to be transported to the hospital with broken skulls, arms, and legs.

I learned all I wanted to learn about Texas justice, racism, and what I could expect if I stayed. It was a lesson in cruelty which I never forget, especially when I look at the arrogant, shit talking deputy sheriffs walking around Epitaph. The overwhelming deaths of Black prisoners comes as no surprise, as I know what's hiding behind correctional officer's eyes, and it isn't to "serve and protect." If there is a hell, there must be a special section reserved for correctional officers in Texas. Even now, years later, I realize that being in jail was the absolute worst experience of my life. I had no idea so many things could be so bad at the same time. The Texas justice system is something right out of the dark ages, from some Third World country. Man, I hated Texas and racism before, but it was nothing compared to how I felt after that experience. For years I had nightmares of being arrested in Texas and taken back to that same courthouse. I was once told by an old French psychic woman that in a past life I'd been executed in a French prison. I don't know if that's true, but I do know that going to prison scared the hell out of me. I swore I'd never do anything to get locked up ever again. The following day another major battle broke out inside the cellblock and several guys were seriously injured. The cops came in again with batons and beat the hell out of everyone. I saw all these guys later, as I brought food to their cells. It was ugly and very scary. The cellblock looked like an ancient dungeon right out of a movie, complete with moaning and gnashing of teeth. The sounds of all those beaten men in agony changed my life forever. It's impossible to convey the depth of these experiences, as they seemed surreal. Today it seems impossible that I survived.

My brother Bumper came to bail me out, as my father would have left me in there to rot. I told him what happened and wondered if my father felt any responsibility for teaching me to steal as a child. I was very embarrassed. The worst and most impactful part was when I got home and had to face my mother. It broke my heart to watch her cry and see her filled with sadness and despair. "What's going to become of you?" was all she said, as she continued to cry. I never felt more remorse for anything I'd done in all my life. I had the equivalent of an epiphany, only there was no god in the room. Instead there was Satan and his legions of demons smiling at me, as if to encourage me towards more insanity. I had a rare moment of clarity and *saw* myself, which disgusted me, and I knew I had to change. I swore to make something of myself, if not for me, for my mother. I believed she deserved to have a son who she could be proud of, not someone like me. I learned later that the district attorney dropped the charges because the shoes I stole were worth less than twenty dollars. This made the realization of my brutal experience even more powerful. These bastards would have allowed a young Tejano kid to be raped, beaten, and murdered for less than twenty dollars. The record of the arrest remained on file, which has always been a subject of embarrassment. At that moment I vowed I was going to be somebody someday, and I was going to take my mother away from my father and all the shit she'd had to endure. Unfortunately, I never got the chance, as she died several years later. I know the Universe still has that promise written down on some magical list somewhere in its vaults, as it does all promises, no matter how foolish. Her death may have cleansed the record clean. Who knows.

My father never said a word to me about getting locked up, not that it would have mattered. His indifference had already been recorded and he'd stopped talking to me when I'd returned from California. He didn't want me around and he didn't want me doing things he couldn't control. No one ever asked me what happened or why I did it. No one ever asked me anything about my experience in jail. Once again, the entire episode just fell into the same bottomless pit of indifference. It seemed no one in my family cared or wanted to know what I'd learned and experienced while in jail. I don't know what bothered me more; getting locked up for something as ridiculous as stealing a cheap pair of shoes, or knowing that no one gave a damn. I learned firsthand about the depth of despair that existed in the world. It was devastating and that knowledge weighed on my soul. I already knew misery, injustice, and cruelty existed in the world, but seeing it to this degree firsthand was so frightening, it literally stole my breath away. I witnessed the inhumanity of Texas justice and its indifference, and it scared the hell out of me. I was not a criminal, just a kid who made a stupid mistake and stole something not worth enough to trouble the courts with. Yet, I'd been arrested, nearly shot, and jailed with known hardened criminals. I might have been raped, murdered, or beaten to death by any one of those thugs. Between living with my father and Texas Justice, I realized my chances of surviving here were nonexistent. The war in Vietnam actually began to look like a better chance of survival than staying in Texas.

Several months later I ran into Robert, the same guy I met in jail who gave me a pair of his old shoes. He was a heroin junkie who claimed he'd gotten hooked while in Vietnam. The poor loser was all fucked up when I saw him while hanging out downtown in Corpus. I said hello and reminded him of where we'd met and thanked him again for the shoes. He was trying to score some dope and had no time to chat. I remember he had a tattoo which read, "No hope without dope." Later that year I read in the paper that he'd overdosed and died.

Another guy who I'd shared a cell with was shot and killed in a barroom brawl in Clarkwood, not far from where my sister lives today. I remembered him because we'd talked a lot about life. He said he'd been on his own for years, moving from town to town working at dozens of shitty jobs. He shared a story with me which took place not long before he got locked up. Apparently he returned to his apartment one night, which he'd shared with another guy, only to find all of his stuff was gone. The apartment was completely empty and his roommate was nowhere to be found. He later found the guy in a whorehouse in Juárez, México, and had one of the pimps kill him. He claimed the pimp dumped his body in an alley after stripping him. The guy became another John Doe who was never identified. I don't know if he was lying, but I don't think so. Sometime after we were both released we had a beer in the very same barroom where he would be killed later that year. The shooting became famous because the owner of the bar never cleaned up the blood. It was the only building available and big enough for the neighborhood kids to celebrate their first Holy Communion. A place where the blood-soaked walls and floors served as testimony to what happens to tough guys in Texas. Dressed in their white outfits the kids would see the dried blood on the wooden floors. It seeped through the cracks, fell on the ground, and attracted rats. Mufasa from *The Lion King* would have felt validated, as it was a perfect example of the circle of life, at least a Texas version of it. I helped cut the cake and serve the hot chocolate to the kids at one of the celebrations. It seemed strange at the time that none of the parents made any attempt to cover the blood or keep their kids from stepping on it. Looking back today it makes sense. It was normal, and death as punishment for your sins was considered as having been sent by God himself. I can still see the dark bloodstained walls and floor. Like I said, life was cheap in Texas and anyone could be the next victim. Danger, violence, and fear were my most faithful childhood companions. My father never did anything to make us feel safe or secure. His only concern was that we not cause him any trouble, money, or problems.

I don't think I was a bad kid, although I've met many real bad people who say the same thing about themselves. I lived during very troubled times in a very bad place. The country was ripping itself apart due to the war in Vietnam and the civil rights movement. Many DOEIs were angry that people of color were no longer willing to submit to their tyranny. Kids were challenging the government and antiwar demonstrations were going on across the country. The Kent State massacre added fuel to the fire of anti-establishment. The Black Panthers were carrying guns in Oakland, Bobby Seals was murdered in prison, Angela Davis was arrested for murder, and Kennedy was assassinated. I learned many years later that Ramiro Martinez was a distant cousin of mine. He was one of two officers responsible for killing Charles Whitman, the sniper who climbed the tower at the University of Texas at Austin. He became a hero, and later a Texas Ranger, then a judge. Whoop-de-do. Fear, love, and smoking pot were in at the time. People were dropping out and dropping acid. The Brown Berets were talking about open warfare against the cops and we were afraid of being drafted. Life was dangerous, yet wonderful and full of adventure all at the same time. It was about this time that Little Joe Hernandez joined the Marines on an early enlistment program. Sometimes he and I would drive to the Corpus Christi Airport to meet the flag draped coffins of the dead American soldiers — soldiers killed fighting for democracy in Vietnam, while we did not have it ourselves in Texas. It was the only time Tejanos were called "Americans" by those who sent them to die. We'd stand alongside crying parents and the color guard, knowing our number would soon be up. It was surreal, like playing a part in a movie I didn't want to play. The world was crushing in upon me. I was running out of places to hide and I had nowhere to run. I'd soon be out of high school and the draft was sure to get me. There were no jobs for dumb kids without training or an education, and I couldn't afford to go to college. My father never gave me a single word of advice about what to do, where to go, or how to get a well-paying job. I had no idea that so many years later I'd still be suffering from the effects of his bad parenting. Back then I never expected to live long enough to consider looking back and writing about it. Things were desperate and I had no option but to volunteer to join the Army. I was running out of time and had nowhere else to go. I had to move out, as I'd already been thrown out by my father. I vowed to get out of Texas. I'd join the Army, go to war if I had to, and somehow manage to survive to fulfill my dreams. My time in the military was an adventure, complete with castles, battles, flags, and beautiful women. A Warrior's life is always a challenge and an adventure.

Texas escapee,

don Jesus M. Ramirez

CHAPTER EIGHT
ACCIDENTAL GUNFIGHTER

"The Devil may have invented guns, but it was already man's evil nature to kill."

–don Jesus M. Ramirez

As a former cop, today I might say my adolescent self was developing a pattern of lawlessness and violence. Others might add that the best indicator of future behavior is past behavior. I swear I was not interested in being a badass. None of the fights I was involved in had anything to do with gaining recognition or power. I was not fighting for turf or money, nor was I motivated by anything other than a desperate desire to survive. It was as if the gates of hell were opened, and Satan himself reached out and stuck his claws into me. It seemed everywhere I went troubled followed, or got there right before me. As I mentioned before, after purchasing my '55 Chevy I started going into Corpus every chance I had. I refused to stay on Main Drive or be at home. It was an ugly bottomless pit of hopelessness and despair. Home was endless monotony, followed by sheer terror due to my father's drunken behavior. Life in that environment was intolerable, and there was no reason to want to be around him or his foul temper. Main Drive was a nonstop tragic comedy, complete with weekend barrio heroes.

At this time in Corpus' history the social scene for Tejanos was controlled by the social clubs, which had spun out of the local high schools. I don't know who came up with this idea, but man, they hit the nail on the head. The clubs proved to be a great source of entertainment and gave all of us something to do and look forward to. They competed amongst themselves for who'd put on the best dances, hire the best bands, and throw the biggest bash on New Year's Eve. There was always somewhere to go and something to do. I'd become well-known amongst the coolest surfers, bikers, and boxers in Corpus. As a result I was asked to join the Royals Boys Club, which had formed out of Ray High School, but also had members from Moody and Carol High School. Now, I don't know how this crazy situation developed, but as usual it started out innocently enough. It was another hot and clear summer Sunday afternoon. I was hanging out at a cake sale fundraiser which one of the local girls clubs had held at West Gulf Park. I'd gone with a guy named Richard Rodriquez, who I'd recently met at one of the club dances. His girlfriend, who was named Ester, was a member of the hosting girls club, and because I was the bow for another girls club, attending was a part of my duty. The girls were looking great and I was having a blast. I loved being around so many beautiful women who thought I was cool. It was pure fantasy come true. Sometime that evening one of the girl's boyfriends had gotten into an argument with a pachuco, who'd shown up at the park unexpectedly and tried to pick her up. These groups of pachucos were migrant workers who'd come to Corpus during the summer cotton picking season. They'd show up in large trucks containing extended families, including wives and children. At times five or six families traveled together, like bands of roaming Gypsies. Although this may sound ridiculous to most people today, back then it made sense to travel in packs. It gave people protection, strength in numbers, and helped the group survive. You gotta keep in mind that life along the Nueces River was a lot rougher than it is today. These were modern-day tribes of Mexican American Gypsies. The trouble was that they had no idea how to get along with anyone outside of their group. They operated like nomadic tribes, moving across the country raiding, killing, and taking whatever they wanted. It was like something out of a movie, only much worse, as real life has no soundtrack or censorship. Their idea of getting along was to get drunk and take a woman. If anyone complained, they beat the hell out of them, stole whatever they found on their bodies, and disappeared into the Texas night. I'll bet there are hundreds of unmarked graves out in those huge lonely Texas cow pastures. After taking one look at these guys, I knew them well. I'd been fighting the same kinds of jerks on Main Drive my whole life. I knew who I was dealing with. These guys would go to any extreme and were capable of anything. These wild mother fuckers were cruel, brutal, hardcore, soulless gangsters. I have no idea how to explain their survival in light of their horrid behavior. They were dangerous men, who were mean and completely without an ounce of commonsense. A fight with any of them would be to the death or until someone was unconscious. After fighting these same types of assholes all my life, I was not looking forward to doing so again.

I was playing the role of escort as per club protocol, so I had to backup Richard when he stepped in to support the guy who'd refused to allow the pachuco to take his girlfriend. When I say take, I mean the asshole was literally dragging the poor girl against her will into his car, where I assume he was going to rape her. The guy didn't give a damn that she didn't want to go, or that it was broad daylight and in front of a dozen witnesses. He knew that by the time the cops showed up, he'd be long gone. He must have been high on something, because he didn't give a shit. Richard punched the pachuco and six other thugs got out of the car and jumped on him like a pack of wild animals. I jumped into the mix without thinking twice and started banging heads with several of these drunken bastards. Before you knew it the entire building emptied, and eight more male club members jumped in to help beat the hell out of those rejects. The problem was, these guys were nice city boys, not badasses from my part of the woods who knew how to fight. They were quickly outmatched and taking a beating from these thugs. Suddenly, as if by some silent message, and for some unexplained reason after what seemed like a hurricane of violence, it ended as quickly as it started. I knew it wasn't over and that those rejects would be back with knives and possibly even guns. I knew this because I lived with the same kinds of bastards on Main Drive all my life. These people operated on a tribal mentality, and if you hurt one of theirs, they'd come back with fifty more seeking revenge. I knew I should have left, but I couldn't without losing face, along with all the friends I'd made. This is one of those moments when death whispers in your ear and advises you to go, but like all average people, I didn't listen. So against my better judgment, I stayed. I'll admit to being scared, as well as a reluctant participant. Yet I was a victim of brainwashing, trapped by the bullshit my mother had put into my head about being a brave man, like her father who'd fought in the Mexican Revaluation. I'm sorry to say that her stories were probably all made up, yet as a kid you actually believe what your parents say. I'd been in several of these knockdown, drag-out, free-for-all fights before, and all of them were ugly and bloody. There were always several seriously injured people and I didn't want to be one of them. The cake sale was terminated quickly after the fight ended, and only a small cleanup crew remained to close up the building and put the tables and chairs away. Amongst these few were Richard and myself. I'd warned him about what I knew would happen. So he went to his car and returned with a chrome plated 38 caliber revolver. It had wooden handles and belonged to his father, who worked in law enforcement. He said his father carried it in his trunk for emergencies. I looked at him with surprise, as I'd never have guessed Richard, who seemed like a cream fed powder puff, would carry a gun. Yet there it was, a big, ugly, fully loaded gun, ready for action.

We were busy loading someone's pickup truck with folding tables and chairs when out of nowhere, the same car filled with drunk pachucos came flying into the parking lot. The sounds of obscenities and screeching tires filled the air, as one pachuco hung out of the window firing a gun. I remember seeing the guy's face. The car suddenly stopped and several of the thugs piled out, including the gunman. I'd been shot at before, but never from this close. I heard the hammer click back as the enraged drunken bastard shot at us. Luckily the fool lifted his gun over his head and only brought it down to fire, like they do in old Mexican movies. Although I knew he'd never hit anyone the way he was moving his hand, I still hauled ass out of there. Everyone was running away screaming as shots were going off. A second later a bullet hit less than six inches from my head. I dove behind a car, and then got up and ran into the park, just trying to get some distance between us. I looked over and saw Richard running next to me, holding the 38 in his right hand. He looked at me and then suddenly stopped, turned around, and fired at the car. The boom of the gun sounded like a cannon. I heard the bullet strike one of the car's headlights, shattering the glass. I knew it was a lucky shot. Richard turned to look at me again, and the very next instant I heard another shot, and saw a bullet strike Richard square in the chest. The impact of the bullet lifted him off his feet and slammed him onto the ground three or four feet away. When he landed, blood gushed out of him as if he'd been squeezed. With his eyes and mouth wide open he kept saying, "I'm alright, I'm alright," and then he went limp. The gun fell out of his hand, and like an enraged animal I picked it up. I shouted obscenities as I shot back at the pachucos, who were now piling back into the car. I took my time to sight in on them and squeeze the trigger, firing three shots in three seconds, but didn't hit anything. The car burned rubber out of the parking lot and roared away as if the Devil had appeared. I screamed for help and three guys ran towards me and Richard. One of the guys ran back and grabbed an old army blanket which we wrapped Richard in. We picked him up and carried him to a pickup truck and placed him in the bed. He looked dead and was bleeding badly. His girlfriend Ester was screaming and tried to stop the bleeding from his chest with her hands, but the blood kept coming. I don't know how or why, but I had sense enough to wipe the gun clean using my t-shirt. I then threw it into Richard's car, not knowing if anyone had seen me shoot it. I was just trying to get rid of it. Since the gun belonged to Richard's father, who worked in law enforcement, I knew there had to be a record of the serial number somewhere. I watched as the pickup truck, followed by several cars, raced towards Spohn Hospital, which is less than a mile away. I ran back to my '55 Chevy that I'd recently bought with the money I'd earned from my summer job working as a janitor. I climbed in and raced out of there with all the power of its six cylinder engine. I was scared to death and had no fucking idea how I was going to get out of this one. I didn't know if anyone saw me shoot the gun, or if Richard was dead. I knew they'd run a test on Richards hands to prove he'd fired the gun, but I had no idea if they could tell how many times he'd fired it. I didn't know what I would say when the cops questioned me, but I felt certain I was going to prison.

I knew I'd come a hair's breath away from being killed and my luck couldn't last much longer. If those guys had come back with more than one gun, I'd have been dead for sure. I didn't return to Corpus for several months and avoided places that might give those bastards a chance to catch me off guard. The news of the shooting was all over the television and newspaper. Several suspects were being sought for questioning by the police and a citywide manhunt was underway. I was scared as hell, and felt certain the cops would show up at school or at my house and drag me off to jail. I didn't get much sleep for weeks. The thought of living in a jail cell was more frightening than getting killed. Several weeks had gone by before I learned that no one at the cake sale remembered seeing anything. Due to my use of a nickname, no one there could identify me by my real name, so I was never questioned by the cops. I thanked Geronimo, whose story had given me the idea of using a nom de guer. My real name and presence at the scene was never mentioned. By some miracle no one saw me pick up the gun, fire it, wipe it off, or throw it back into Richard's car. Even Richard, who lost a lot of weight, but lived, couldn't remember how many times he'd shot the gun, or if he'd hit anyone. He was charged with firing the gun in public, but it was ruled self-defense. I'm sure the fact that his father worked in law enforcement didn't hurt the outcome. Unbelievably, everyone's attention was on the thugs doing the shooting. Once again, the shots I'd fired faded away, as if swallowed up by a black hole. By the end of the summer I'd gone from a club member with a beautiful girlfriend, to an accidental gunfighter. I knew that despite my use of a nickname and supposedly not being seen shooting the gun, with all the gossip, I still wasn't safe from repercussions of vengeance, or the long arm of the law. Texas has zero tolerance for bad Tejano kids, and it was common for kids to disappear for years after being sent to correctional facilities. Suddenly they would reappear as changed creatures, old before their time, squeezed and drained of life. I feared I'd either end up dead or in prison if I didn't get the hell out of there. I was still in shock at seeing Richard bleeding, lying half-dead on a small hill in West Gulf Park. I vowed not to die like that.

Soon thereafter Richard married Ester. He was a good guy. Unlike me he wasn't into brawling or raising hell. As far as I know they still live in Corpus Christi, and he still believes he unloaded the gun. The episode might have saved his life, because the wound gave him a deferment from the draft. The war in Vietnam raged on and body bags arrived weekly. As America bombed the hell out of North Vietnam, life for me slowly went back to normal. I knew I had to get out of there soon or I'd get caught by those thugs or others, and end up in a hole in Seaside Memorial Park, where Selena is now buried. Richard was just another innocent bystander who got caught up in the insanity of violent and homicidal maniacs prevalent in Texas.

I slowly crept back into town, trying not to attract attention. I knew I was pushing my luck when I went to Alice, Texas, about forty miles outside of Corpus towards the Mexican border. I was with two boxers I'd known from the ABC Boxing Club. One of them was called Oso, "The Bear," because he was a huge guy with dark greasy hair that stuck out. The other guy was called, Cucieo, "The Blade," because he'd supposedly killed a guy in a knife fight and got away with it. The reason I don't remember their real names was because everyone had nicknames, and both Oso and Cucieo disappeared soon after this episode. It was another hot summer Saturday, without a breeze and plenty of sun. On the way back from Alice to Corpus we stopped for gas at a solitary gas station. The bathroom was out of order so we stepped around back to take a leak, where we found a small group of people. These out of the way gas stations often sold beer to underage kids because their friends worked there and would sell it illegally. The kids would hang out behind the gas station drinking beer, smoking weed, and making out with their girlfriends. This was exactly what was going on that day. Oso recognized one of the guys drinking beer and started talking to him. One of the other guys in the group was passing a joint around and had a 38 automatic in his waistband. Very few guys were crazy enough, or had the balls to openly carry a gun while smoking a joint. Guns and marijuana were usually hidden from sight. It was a rare and reckless thing to do, as marijuana was a felony back then. For someone to openly smoke a joint while carrying a gun openly said a lot about what he thought of himself. I think the guy's name was Ramon. He kept staring at me as if he knew me. Who knows, I might have kicked his ass before, or perhaps one of his relatives. It's difficult to remember so many faces. When I caught him staring at me, I stared back. It was the only thing to do amongst alpha dogs, as to look away in fear was to invite an attack. To stare back might buy enough time to get the hell out of there. I knew this guy was looking for trouble, and my response would either result in him looking away or exploding. It was too late to do anything about it. I turned to Oso and asked him if he knew the guy who kept staring at me. Oso said he'd never seen him before. There was nothing else I could have done. I was with them and had no ride home. There was nowhere to go. I was between a rock and a hard place. Ramon then walked up to me in an aggressive manner and tried to pass me the joint.

"No thanks, man," I said calmly.

"You're a fucking narco, aren't you?!" He replied, staring me in the eyes.

I wasn't expecting that response, so I smiled and laughed. "No man, I'm no fucking cop. Ask these guys," I said, looking at Oso and Cucieo.

"I say you're a fucking cop!" the bastard shouted, and then he slapped me hard across the face.

The slap sounded like the crack of a gunshot and everyone stopped moving. I was more surprised than hurt. In a nanosecond every demon that possessed me screamed out in rage, and I felt as if someone opened the gates of hell and released every monster that lived within. I felt myself grow white with anger. I stepped backwards and instinctively reached for the small six shot 22 caliber pistol, which I started carrying since the shooting at the park. I feared the pachucos were looking for me and didn't want to get caught off guard. I pointed my gun at the son of a bitch. I'm surprised no one else had a gun, because if they had, there might have been real trouble. I must have looked more surprised than pissed off, because Ramon didn't seem impressed.

"What! So you're pissed off?! Well, fuck you! Shoot me if you got the balls!"

He then stepped back as if giving me more room, but for some reason, still unknown to me, he never reached for his own gun. I pointed my gun at his balls, looked into his eyes, and then squeezed the trigger. I felt the kick of the gun and saw realization, then fear in his face, as the shot rang out. The pistol had a one inch barrel and sounded like a cannon. I intended to shoot his balls off, but the bullet struck him below the belt and a little to the right. The 22 caliber bullet knocked him off his feet and onto the ground, and suddenly he lost all his bravado. He stared up at me as I cocked the pistol again. The son of a bitch pissed his pants as I walked up to him and pointed the gun at his face.

"Why, mother fucker?! Why were you fucking with me?! Why?!" I shouted at him.

I then pulled his gun out from his waistband and put it into my belt.

"Please don't kill me! Please don't kill me!" he kept begging as he lay on the ground crying.

I might have shot him again, if one of the guys I was with hadn't yelled for us to get out of there. I pointed the pistol over the crying thug's head and fired a round. I then cocked the pistol one more time, pointed it at the ground and fired another shot. The bullet hit close to the hand he was using to support himself. He let out a cry and fell backwards, screaming out like a scared little girl. I was filled with rage and kicked him in the face. I looked up at all his buddies who were frozen in place. If any of them had any ideas of helping him, they didn't act. I slowly backed away from the group. Though they appeared to be afraid, I didn't know for sure if any of them were thinking about getting into the mix. I walked away, got into the car, and we roared out of there into the twilight and setting sun. The road to Corpus was empty and we didn't come across a cop car for at least twenty miles, so all of us felt safe, which was a silly thing to do. The Devil seemed to follow me everywhere I went, and the bastard wouldn't stop.

I realized I'd come too close to shooting the coward in the head. I also knew I'd end up in prison or dead if I stayed in Texas. I had to get the hell out of there, and soon. I never learned what happened to the guy I'd shot. I never heard about the incident again. I assume someone took him to a doctor. Ever since then, I still look behind me every time I visit Alice, Texas. The last time I was there I stopped at the same gas station, isolated out in the middle of nowhere. I even went around back to take a leak, and sure as hell, there were a bunch of kids smoking weed and drinking beer. The more things change, the more they stay the same.

Texas escapee,
don Jesus M. Ramirez

Chapter Nine
Fall of a Tyrant

"Demons walk amongst us disguised as people, lacking the quality commonly known as humanity. They are not ugly, deformed creatures, like those seen in horror films. Rather they are comfortably average, as if they and evil conspired and sought not to attract attention. We must be able to identify and avoid them, but more importantly we must be able to identify and defeat the monsters within ourselves. This is the real challenge of a Warrior."

-don Jesus M. Ramirez

My great search for the white pony taught me to always have a plan, always practice, and always *focus*. I hated Beelzebub so badly, and I'd been planning my revenge against him for years. Like I said, I specifically started boxing just so I could knock the shit out of him. He was the reason why I entered into my first Golden Gloves tournament, and why after my loss I started searching for a boxing club. Knowing I'd never outgrow the bastard, I wanted to learn how to fight. That was when I found the ABC Boxing Club ran by Whitey and Minnie Moore. In school I'd play football, which helped me develop confidence, but I knew it wasn't going to teach me how to outfight the bastard. He was bigger, heavier, and two years older.

As time went by I'd proven myself dozens of times and no longer feared or avoided him. I'd been fighting every thug within the city limits, as I seemed to attract trouble. I'd be standing alone, minding my own business, when some guy would randomly come up saying this or that, and take a swing at me. I never backed down and always fought back. I'd fought every thug on Main Drive, including Curly Perez, Rudy Hasset, Tommy Trejo, Joe Vallejo, Juilo and Nacho Chapa, and dozens more who showed up to challenge me. Guys from different schools would even show up at the bus stop just to test my reputation. I had no idea who they were or why they came. I'd just set down my books and go for it, never saying a word. I fought some of these guys six or eight times each. I'd gotten so good at fighting that kicking the shit out of thugs was as easy as throwing a rock. I could hook, uppercut, and throw a right cross that could knock out a mule. I got a bad reputation and most people avoided me. During all these battles with multiple opponents Beelzebub was conveniently absent. He never backed me up, even though I was getting jumped by three and four guys at a time. He is the reason why I've never attributed qualities to bigger or taller guys simply because of their stature. Most of them have never been tested, unlike guys my size and smaller. Positive traits are usually assigned to them because of their appearance, not their accomplishments. It should be noted that just like most things, there are no absolutes. As I've mentioned before, Warriors come in all shapes and sizes.

There was no joyous homecoming like in the movies when Beelzebub returned home from Basic Training. No welcome home party or cake and coffee with all of our friends from the neighborhood. Not even the priest showed up to say hello. I certainly wasn't happy to see him. Like everyone else in the Army at the time, he had orders to go to Vietnam. True to form, like the drama queen he was, he asked me to place a package of Marlboro Lights, a lighter, and a bottle of booze in his coffin if he was killed. I guess he thought this was romantic. Who knows. I said "Sure," but was really thinking,

"Yea right, you fucking asshole. I'm gonna piss into a jar for a week, and then spill it out on your grave." He romanticized his life and neglected to mention he was a clerk typist in the Army, not a combat infantryman. He was not even in a combat unit. I wouldn't have done shit for him and found his dramatization humorous. The self-deluded jerk lived in a fantasy where he was the center of the world. Lots of guys were going to Vietnam and many were killed. I expected to go myself, as life and death had always been a reality on Main Drive. Life was cheap, as it has always been. One more dead Tejano would not have made a damn bit of difference.

It didn't take long for Beelzebub's old self to emerge. All of his delusional crap died after a few short days, and everything came to a head after he tried calling every girl he'd known before he left. I was watching TV when he came at me pissed off, red in the face and ready to fight. He'd just called Alice Zapata, who he'd taken out once, long before her and I had even met. She told him that she and I were going together, and he was furious. He began saying obscene things, claiming to have had sex with her. I knew he was full of shit and was just trying to get back at me. I also knew Alice well enough to know she'd never risk engaging in such behavior. He then attacked me just as he had so many times in the past, expecting to beat me down. However, this time, and true to my training, I did all the right things. He kicked at me with his left foot and I stepped aside, just the way I'd planned to do for months. I caught his foot, then pulled and lifted it, causing him to lose his balance and fall onto his back. I started kicking and stomping the shit out of him, the very same way he'd done to me so many times. All the years of hating him erupted within me. I wanted to kill the bastard. You might not understand the fury I had inside of me after all those years of taking abuse. In those few moments I released all of it, and it poured out in gushers. I literally wanted to beat him into the floor, and I might have, if our father had not intervened. He'd been in his bedroom, doing whatever the hell he did back there, when he came out and saw me kicking the shit out of Beelzebub. This was not what he was used to seeing, and I don't know how he'd figured out that it had been Beelzebub who started the fight, but he did. He started screaming at Beelzebub, telling him to get the hell out of his house. Beelzebub dramatically stormed out, playing the part of a mistreated hero in some Hollywood movie. I don't know where he went, and I didn't care. I also don't remember what my father said to me, and didn't care about that either. I had set my goal and after years of training, I'd accomplished it.

Boxing helped me defeat the most hated bully of my life. As far as I was concerned, Beelzebub had never been my brother. He had never behaved as a brother before, during, or since. He went off to Vietnam without saying goodbye, looking back, or giving a damn. I couldn't have cared less. I knew he wouldn't be killed. Evil people do not die young. Beelzebub, the chicken shit combat clerk, was in a rear area company, not humping through the jungle looking for Charlie.

It was six years before I saw or spoke to him again. When I did, I wasn't impressed. He'd not changed one bit. He was still the same delusional, egotistical deceiver he'd always been. I have no emotions about him, except for disgust. When I let myself think of him, the best I can generate is pity, disgust, and loathing. This is on a good day. Like I've said from page one, no one forgets nothing.

Texas escapee,

don Jesus M. Ramirez

Chapter Ten
Love Is Hard to Find

"Of all the treasures in the world, love is absolutely the only one you cannot live without."

–don Jesus M. Ramirez

It's difficult to remember if I loved any of the girls I dated in Corpus Christi. At the time I might have thought I had, as I certainly knew lots of them. I say this with all due respect, because much to my disappointment, I did not have sexual relations with any of them. This may be difficult to believe for many of the people who thought they knew me. The truth is no one really knew me and I made sure of that. There is no advantage in having too many people know you. This was years before I'd ever heard of the Toltec discipline. Today, years after my initial Warrior's inventory, I feel stronger about it than before. The reason why I was not pressuring my girlfriends into having sex was because I'd been having sexual relations with a married DOEI woman, whose name I shall not disclose. I refuse to throw dirt on her. She probably helped me more than anyone else, and I owe her more than I can repay. I lost track of her years ago, but discovered she married a congressman from the mighty state of Texas. Wherever she is, I hope she is happy. I know it was wrong to be with her, even if she was separated from her husband. Looking back, she probably saved my life. I knew she was having problems in her relationship and knew it could never be me. I was planning to leave Texas. She was older, but it didn't matter. She was like cool water to a man dying of thirst. I kept our secret not just to protect her, but so as not to ruin the great thing we had. Imagine being a kid with raging hormones and along comes a beautiful mature woman willing to share her endowments. I know she could have gotten in serious trouble if I'd told anyone. I don't believe she molested me, as it would be called today. Knowing her was the first of many wonderful experiences the Universe had in store for me. It was a validation of my personal power and proof that the Universe only rewards energy. Even as a child in school, I always set my sights upon what others might have considered impossible. I thought of it as a game. I knew that in all games, no matter how good you are, sometimes you don't win, but it doesn't mean you lose. Some might call my luck a blessing, although I doubt the Church would consider such things God sent. I most certainly did, and still do today. We never went anywhere in public or to the drive-in movies. Once we went to a walk-in theater, but a lot of adult DOEIs stared at us with hostility. She was attractive and neither of us wanted to create a scene. We'd meet at prearranged locations and spend the day making love. I never told anyone about her. She was a wonderful person whom I hope the Universe rewards. She was the first to see I was an old soul even as a boy in high school.

Other guys my age were busting at the seams to have sex with their girlfriends. I had my sexual needs satisfied and was therefore never insistent. I must have appeared like a gentleman. It was no wonder I was able to make advances towards so many women who were out of my league. I knew that what appeared as confidence on my part was simply knowing those teenage girls were children, while I had grown accustomed to a woman. Confidence is often misunderstood and superficial, yet very attractive. The question no one ever asked me was how I got to be so confident. I would have never said a word, but it was because of her. She had one of those Mona Lisa smiles and brought so much pleasure into my life. She spoke with a sexy Southern accent, had dancers legs, a magnificent smile, and a devilish sense of humor. She loved classical music, the ocean, staring up into the sky at the clouds, life, and me. She taught me things every young man needs to know about women, but rarely learns. She taught me how to touch a woman. She taught me a woman's skin is a sensitive sexual organ, and so many other things it would be impossible to list them all. I am a very lucky person, yet some might say my guardian angel must be part devil. Whatever the truth be, she filled the emptiness in my life. She gave me hope and understanding. An understanding that even though I did not know what qualities I possessed, I had something women wanted. I'm sure her heart must have gotten slightly banged up. I made certain I never spoke her name and never bragged about our relationship. I wasn't surprised when I learned she married a congressman. It's easy to see how such a powerful man would want to have her, as she was alluring. I've seen them together in pictures, but I've never shared our secret.

  I had several liaisons with older women in Corpus, but she gave me the confidence to make the advances. She taught me that what might seem impossible is not. She taught me that I should be more afraid of not trying than of failing. She was also the reason why I wasn't ready to fall head over heels for a naïve girl. My experiences with her saved me from being wrapped up in all their foolish games and insecurities. She taught me to appreciate mature women, which I still find much more interesting and attractive. Young girls are cute, but not in the way a man needs a woman to be. If it weren't for her, I might have knocked up some poor young thing and ruined her life. I'd planned to leave Texas no matter what.

I was always surprised when a high school couple got married, as it seemed stupid beyond description and suicidal. There was no way it was going to work, as every card in the deck was stacked against them. I'd seen dozens of guys get married, and a year or so later they'd be out hitting the streets, chasing women and partying. Except now they were burdened with child support payments and squashed by the knowledge and shame of their inadequacies. They weren't supposed to get married so young, without first having experienced the world and tasted its fruits. The poor bastards who knocked up a girl were doomed to a loveless marriage, trapped in a cycle of poverty and despair. They were chained to a worthless job and hated what they saw in their futures. I saw this scenario played out over and over and swore it wouldn't be me. I promised myself that my senior year at Andrew Jackson would be my last in Texas, and I would never live in such a backward place again, where race meant more than your worth as a person.

I knew I was leaving Texas when I dated Amy Lopez, who was the only girl I dated that came to my mother's funeral. I met her at the Memorial Coliseum when I was fifteen. I still remember what she wore and how beautiful she looked. She was fourteen at the time and had eyes that would have stopped traffic, and a smile that made it seem like everything would be all right. Her voice was sweet as strawberries and cream and gentle as a summer breeze. She wore her hair like Cher, which was very cool at the time. She was wearing a white blouse and a pleated green and black plaid skirt, like the ones Catholic school girls wore. We remained friends for many years, long after I moved away. She eventually married a loser named Richard, who everyone called "Tiger," after getting pregnant. I have no idea what she saw in him. The poor guy was a pimpled-faced, greasy-haired loser, who hung out with a bunch of druggies. He smoked dope, drank a lot, and never said a word. I still cannot understand why she married him. She might have married me if I had asked, but I never wanted to get married. I wanted to get out of Texas, not be tied to it, and she was certainly beautiful and wonderful enough to tie me down. Unfortunately, her father was an alcoholic who drank himself to death. Her mother, whom I only knew as Mrs. Lopez, was a kind and gentle soul who took pity on me, often feeding me. I must have looked like a stray dog without anyone to care for me, or even a place to call home. After the death of her husband Mrs. Lopez later remarried. I hope she found happiness. All of her daughters were beautiful creatures whom I was very lucky to have known. Unfortunately, her children brought her a lot of grief, as they also had the urge to drink and misbehave. I hope Amy and her family, who were kind to me, found happiness.

I dated a girl named Pat Sanchez. She was a sexy young thing who reminded me of Greta Garbo. She was a beautiful girl with snowy white skin and wore makeup on her magnificent legs. She had a beautiful, smooth and delicious voice, big brown eyes that hypnotized, and always wore just the right amount of makeup. Her sister was also very attractive, but not compared to her. Pat loved to dance, which is how I met her. The day we met she was wearing a red ribbon in her hair. I don't know how I managed to entice her, as there were many pursuing her. By this time, via my experiences with older women, I believed young girls were no match for me. I knew I would eventually win her heart and know her kisses. We went out for over two years before she met a guy named Able Garcia. Able was just another drunk, a drug user and bottom of the barrel loser. I have no idea what he offered Pat, or how he managed to get her to sleep with him. She also got pregnant before being married. When I returned from my first tour of duty she was married, content, and had no interest in speaking with me. We spoke briefly at a dance, but she was with Able. He knew we'd dated and although we had been stablemates at the ABC Boxing Club, we were never friends. I didn't want to risk insulting him or being the cause of a problem. I sometimes catch myself wondering how she's doing and if she's still as much fun and as beautiful.

I dated a girl named Tina Cantu, who I can easily describe. Just imagine a young Salma Hayek, and you got the picture. She was short, simply gorgeous, and had physical features that might have been cast in a Hollywood movie. Plus, she had the voice of an angel, something I've always found irresistible. It seemed honey dripped from her lips as she spoke, and her kisses were just as sweet. She was gorgeous and I was so proud to be seen with her. Unfortunately, she was also clingy as hell. She'd been betrayed by a former boyfriend and was jealous and desperately insecure. It didn't last, and she broke up with me right before Christmas. Her dumping me was a double shot of disappointment, as Christmas had always been filled with sad memories. She later married a guy who was killed in a work-related accident and is now financially well off due to the lawsuit that followed. I was very sorry to hear about her sorrows. She had a tender heart. I have always wished her the best and pray she finally found love.

Being in a band as a teenager in Corpus had many positive side effects, and meeting plenty of beautiful girls was one of them. One of the girls I met was named Margie Davila. She was short, cute, and belonged to one of the girls clubs. She had beautiful bosoms and great legs. She also had a funny looking tooth that stuck out when she smiled. We kissed, but never made love, nor got close to it. I never asked her to be my girlfriend. We dated and she met my parents, although I never met hers. This should have told me something, but I didn't care. She was too Mexican and conservative for me. I wanted to have fun, not prepare for marriage, which was all she was looking for. She had many of the hang-ups I was running away from. I hated the idea of marriage, and up to that time I had never seen anyone in a happy relationship. I couldn't understand why anyone would want to get married at all. I also couldn't figure out why anybody would want to have children. I don't know what happened to Margie. I saw her when I came home from the Army to get the rest of my stuff from the house, but I wasn't interested. She was working as a secretary in a basement office of a building uptown. This was many years later when I'd come back for something having to do with my military benefits. I hadn't even noticed her until she said hello and walked me to the office. I said thank you, and goodbye. I never saw her again. She smiled like a raccoon, but I wasn't interested in some girl from Texas.

    I dated dozens of other girls. I wish I could remember all of their names. I wish I could say something about them all, if only as an effort to thank them for helping ease the rage which dwelled within me. Their faces fly past me like photographs in an old album, but not their names. This might give you an idea of how emotionally disconnected I was during the time. It was the effect of witnessing so much brutality as a child.

    I knew a lot of people but had very few friends. One of these few was a young woman whom I mentioned earlier, Samantha Rojas. She was the sister of Jamie Rojas, who later married my brother Punk, and then dumped him for cheating. I made fun of her and was often unkind. Although I have apologized personally, I know that at the time my words caused her tremendous grief and added to her despair. I know it's impossible to undo the damage I caused. Samantha lived eight miles from my house before I had a car, otherwise I'd have been with her much more often. She was attractive, smart, and articulate, but lived in a made-up fantasy world based on television, magazines, and movie stars. I can certainly understand why she created such a make-believe place. Our fathers might have been brothers, as one was as mean as the other. Both of them seemed to spend all their lives worrying about their daughter's sexual organs, and how to avoid possible penetration by unworthy mutts. Her entire family was handsome, well-mannered, and out of place in that rough and tumble area. This may explain why while in high school she fell in love with an older married man, who got her pregnant and then abandoned her. The man's wife went into a rage and instead of venting her anger on him, targeted Samantha, who was sent off to Houston to have her baby, and then put it up for adoption. I can only imagine the pain and heartache she suffered. I have no idea how she survived the ordeal. Typical to men of that period, instead of protecting and shielding her from the world, her father disowned her. She went through many stormy years of acting out in a self-destructive manner, but no more than I did. She later married an attorney, who was elected judge, but divorced him because he was cheating on her. She had two daughters with him, and I understand she is now happily married and living the good life with a rich real estate tycoon. I hope so, and I wish her all the happiness in the world. I often think of her witty sense of humor and regret I did not appreciate it more.

    The only girl whom I truly cared for was Alice Zapata, and she was the finest human being I knew in Corpus Christi. She was wise beyond her years and beautiful as a morning sunrise. She was as enchanting as a wind chime and her voice would have soothed the wildest beast. Her mere presence calmed the monsters inside of me. She became very popular in Corpus after winning the best legs contest at Moody High School, which is where she attended school. She'd also been voted "sweetheart" of the Paracodeen Boy's Club, and crowned "queen" of several beauty contests, and if you'd seen her you'd instantly know why. She had long reddish hair, coffee colored skin, big brown eyes, a great smile, and the neatest expressions. She had the kind of personality I wished I could have had. Everyone liked her. She was popular, intelligent, and attractive. Most importantly, she was nice and interesting.

I still don't know why she took an interest in me or responded to my advances. I guess she fell for my "bad boy" reputation, only she never knew it wasn't an act. I really was a badass and angry at all the unfairness I'd endured. A single look or slight insult would ignite an explosion of biblical proportions. Looking back, I know I was one of those foolish guys worth a dime a dozen, as there are millions of angry young men who feel mistreated and misunderstood. I was a cliché, lucky beyond words she found me attractive.

After we started seeing each other I actually broke it off with her twice, because seeing her was interfering with my boxing training. I had to choose between getting ready for the Golden Gloves and spending time with her. I chose boxing. This was one of the best decisions I ever made and it must have blown her away. I don't believe anyone had ever broken up with her. Who knows. I once told her she was beautiful beyond my ability to describe, which may be as close as I came to saying I love you. Everything about us was right except for the timing. The Vietnam War was raging and many from our group had been drafted or volunteered. Every month someone else was gone and there were dozens of guys in their uniforms at the dances. I knew I'd be leaving soon, but it never occurred to me to ask her to marry me, which would have been the only way to keep her. I knew I wasn't ready for that. I wanted to get the hell out of Texas, and dreamed of living in California and going to college someday, which is why I joined the Army. The G.I. Bill promised to pay for college if I survived the war and completed my tour of duty with an honorable discharge. Somehow I knew it would be years before I healed enough emotionally to marry. She was too nice of a person and I knew my abusive childhood experiences had left me emotionally dysfunctional. I had no idea how to have a relationship, what I wanted, or how to find it. All I really knew was that I wanted to stop hurting. It would have been wrong to inflict my desperate need for affection upon such a nice girl. She needed a husband, not a dysfunctional immature basket case. This was what my brothers chose to do to end their suffering. They got married, knocked up their wives, cheated on them, and just ended up hurting them, spreading our father's illness to someone who they claimed to love. I guess most guys in my place would have pretended to be in love just to get laid before leaving for the Army. It was during a shooting war and lots of guys were coming back in body bags, or worse. Amongst her many qualities, Alice was a lady, and I didn't want to use her like that. I think I might have actually been in love with her, although I didn't know it at the time. I knew she liked me, but she never told me so, nor I her.

   Alice and I continued to go out until my very last day in Corpus. When I left for boot camp she came to see me off at the Trailways Bus Station in downtown Corpus Christi, across the street from the pawn shop where I bought my first guitar. It was also across from the bar where my father liked to get drunk and meet his barroom women. She wore a gray dress with a black belt that day, and her long, wavy, reddish hair was pulled back. She stood on the sidewalk in front of the bus station and waved goodbye to me. It would be the last time I ever saw her. When she said goodbye I thought it meant we had something going, but I guess I was wrong. She only wrote to me once while I was in Basic Training at Fort Lewis, Washington. Having her dump me while I was experiencing one of the toughest challenges in my entire life felt like a betrayal. It felt like she forgot all about me and went on with her life as if I'd never existed. It hurt like hell and made me feel like a damn fool. She taught me a lot about love. Her rejection showed me in detail how fickle and unpredictable love can be. Even though I never told her I loved her, I mistakenly assumed we had an understanding. I was under the impression we were exclusive. I realize now that such an attractive young girl required a declaration of love and a ring. I gave her neither, which shows how naïve I was. It also demonstrates what a hopeless romantic I was as well. Even though she never wrote me, I must have written her a dozen letters during Basic Training. I shared everything in my heart with her. I gave her a blow-by-blow description of what I was going through, but she never answered. Basic Training was a lot of work, a lot of stress, and very little of anything else. Plus, the drill sergeants kept the idea of going to Vietnam in our face. War was a reality and men were dying. Her abandonment just added to the mountains of emotional crap which I was already under and I accepted it. I had nothing to offer her. I was just another of the hundreds of thousands of guys in the Army during the war. Although I was very philosophical about her rejection, in truth it felt like I'd been kicked by a horse. Looking back, I probably should have asked her to wait, or at least asked her to be my girl. The least I should have done would have been to say I loved her, but I didn't. I never told her how I felt. I left without telling her how much she helped me, how much I needed her, and how proud I was to be seen with her. I don't blame her for moving on. She was thinking about her own survival, fighting to get out of the life of poverty she'd been born into. She lived in La Armada housing projects, which are still there today. I thought she was a great human being, but as 96ers always say, "I shoulda, coulda, woulda," but it's too late now. If I had another several lives, I'd make certain to dedicate one to loving her. She was one of many women I misread, misunderstood, and mistreated.

  When I came home after Basic Training I never tried to see her. I never asked about her, but of course I heard she was seeing someone. She was much too attractive to be alone and I let it go. I rejected my affection for her, as there was nothing else I could have done. I had nothing going for me and I was escaping Texas. It would have been wrong to make promises I never planned to keep. My objective was to escape Texas and live in California after the Army. I knew Alice cared for her mother and her younger brothers, who kept her tied to Texas, so I stayed away. Even though I had Advanced Individual Training at Fort Sam Houston in San Antonio, I never made an attempt to contact her again. I hardened my heart and was tough as I had to be. I'd been kicked in the teeth enough times to know it was best to suck it up and save a little of my dignity. She wrote me once while I was stationed in Germany, but by then it was too late. I wrote her back an angry letter and reproached her abandonment during the war. I planned to get a European Out and remain living in Germany as a civilian. Years later I heard she married a guy in the Air Force and moved to Virginia.

For many years I was haunted by what might have been. Generally I moved throughout my days planning, calculating, and maneuvering past life's obstacles, and I was fine. However, there were times while alone when questions crept into my mind. There, alone in the darkness, I found myself asking why I didn't ask Alice to marry me. It would have made life a lot easier for me. It would have ended the loneliness, even if only for a moment. It was a question without an answer, and there was no way to find out. I am certain this is why so many people go to their high school reunions.

I am no longer burdened by regrets of my past, as I've offloaded these memories and regard them like old films of someone I once knew. I smile each time I think of her, especially when old songs play on the radio and I can see her smile. Losing her helped me learn that it's possible for a person to disappear from your life. If it were not for her I might not have had the courage to ask my wife to marry me. I think of her with fondness, and now realize her rejection made leaving Corpus Christi easier. I treasure the memory of her company, her smile, her laughter, and her sparkling happiness. Though I've often wondered what happened to her, and hope life has been kind and that she's found love, I also know that to continue on this theme any further would be self-indulgent. I am certain I did the right thing by not asking her to marry me and entangle her life with mine. I am afraid I would have caused her tremendous disappointment and besmirched her memory of me. I am certain it would have been a disaster. I've made a million mistakes and suffered their consequences, but not marrying her was perhaps the smartest decision I've made.

A student of mine once asked, "What happens if you meet the right girl, at the wrong time?" The question tore through me like a bullet and made me realize how it's not true that time heals all things.

Time don't heal nothing. Memories don't watch the clock. They go on living nonstop, and in the end, we're all just doing time. It's up to us to dedicate ourselves to living a purposeful life. Nothing is handed to you. You must struggle to give your life purpose and meaning, and it's up to you to live it for all it's worth. Even if you do, living a disciplined life holds many questions. After all these years on the Warrior's path, I've learned that disciplined individuals also wonder what might have been. I've released her memory to drift amongst the stars, where such a fine human being belongs, and send her happy energy every time she crosses my mind.

Willie Nelson's song, "To All the Girls I've Loved Before" tells of how grateful he is for all the girls he's known. I've also written many such songs, although mine are not as well-known. I once believed Willie Nelson and I could have been great friends, as I can relate to his music and the lyrics of his songs. Although, I've come to realize that those who make music are just average people who make music. Unfortunately, my experiences amongst musicians and song writers have proven to be a tremendous disappointment.

Texas escapee,

-don Jesus M. Ramirez

Chapter Eleven
Death of a Tyrant

"Imagine what kind of world it would be if Quasimodo, the hunchback of Notre-Dame, had won Esmeralda's heart. Victor Hugo could have created a better world, changed history, and invented the first antihero."

-don Jesus M. Ramirez

I once believed my life story was similar to that of Quasimodo, the main character in Victor Hugo's *The Hunchback of Notre-Dame*. My father was the evil archdeacon of Notre Dame, Claude Frollo, and my siblings were members of the crowd who mocked and reveled in my torment. It was only after I refused to relive old memories that I was able to be free of his oppression. My escape from Texas demanded much more than merely leaving. In truth, such environments exist everywhere, and Epitaph is no exception. Hatred looms over this region like an evil presence, infecting and influencing people beyond their ability to recognize. Racist rednecks, confederate flags, and hanging ropes are still found in nearby towns. Therefore, it was not the absence of conflict, but my ability to recognize and distance myself from it that brought me freedom.

True liberation came when I finally let go of anger and accepted society's indifference. More importantly, it came when I stopped wanting to punish my father for stealing my childhood. No bells sounded, nor did trumpets of triumph blow the day he died. In fact, the ease of his passing only validated the effectiveness of this discipline. Via years of struggle, by the time of his death I had achieved a degree of *detachment*, and unburdened myself of mountains of emotional baggage. I had anticipated his death for years, and it served only as a moment of comfort to know that all tyrants will die. I escaped Texas to get away from those who deliberately harmed me. Although I have no idea where I got the courage to do so, I know my never adopting the concept of Christian forgiveness was partly responsible. Freedom is not free, and I paid a heavy price for my independence. Some practitioners of the Toltec discipline believe that Warriors have been reincarnated, and are unknowingly guided via the knowledge they obtained in previously lives. Other than a tremendous curiosity and a love for foreign languages, I have no recollection of any past lives. Years of *inner silence* opened me to the powers of the Universe, and I was aware long before I could understand what I was experiencing or why. It's no wonder then how I understood why my father disliked me. He knew I *saw* him as the monster he was, and his response was to beat me with indifference. His death is reminiscent of Hitler, who despite being responsible for the murder of millions supposedly shot himself in his right temple before being captured. Although what exactly took place in Berlin on April 30, 1945 is shrouded in mystery, what's certain is that he was never held accountable, and neither was my father. As I gathered energy I was able to *see*, and what I *saw* were not kind self-discoveries. The realizations shattered any remaining fantasies I might have had. This harshness is difficult to conceive and required decades to acknowledge. It was only after these horrible realizations that I was able to *see* my oppressors as victims of the same brutality. While this in no way condones their behavior, it frees me of the anger and hate I once felt towards them. Even so, the battle continues, as there are times when weakness creeps up on me, stirring negative emotions. It has taken years to write about my experiences without anger or sadness. You cannot make someone care no matter how much you need them. One of the many stumbling blocks was the question of how someone who supposedly believed in God could abuse children. I discovered this was just another version of "why me?" that kept me enslaved. There is no why. People are who they are and things are as they've always been. Angels will not come to rescue you. I survived because I imposed discipline upon myself and chose joy. There are no happy storybook endings. Give up the idea that things will ever be the way they're supposed to be. I no longer identify with Quasimodo, and although I have endured cruelty, I no longer feel sorry for myself. I am fortunate I did not have an Esmeralda to show me kindness, as I was forced to suffer until I discovered the Warrior's path. My struggles were the keys to my freedom.

My father's death brought about dozens of new problems. A Warrior must deal with such issues in an impersonal manner and let them go, which takes tremendous discipline. I've accepted that he had powerful energy, which protected him and allowed him to receive more than he'd earned. This validates that the Universe only acknowledges power and is not concerned with good or bad. It bestows attention upon those who store and gather energy and makes no distinction of how it is gathered. The Universe is indifferent towards suffering and sacrifice, and has no equivalent. Only those who have experienced its presence can understand, and even then, words lack the ability to accurately describe it. There are no comparisons or adequate analogies.

I deliberately chose to not be present at my father's passing, as well as not attend his funeral. I would not willingly place myself at a stranger's death simply as an act of kindness. Aside from our biological connection, we had no emotional ties and had not spoken for years. I sensed him prior to his passing when his energy was seeking mine. Death makes all things equal and emphasizes how meaningless everything else really is. Once it touches you, nothing and no one else matters. Bad and good are equal. Evil and good are subjective depending on perspective, culture, and etc. I once felt angry and trampled upon, but now it no longer matters. It was impossible to reconcile or amend, and forgiveness was meaningless.

The aloneness of a Warrior once again swept me away as if I'd been struck by a giant tsunami. I spoke with a doctor who was absolutely incompetent, but a traditionally educated and licensed psychologist. She was a petite Asian American woman who was no more than 28-years-old. She was as helpful as a blind traffic cop at an intersection, and her main concern was that I was not ill enough to receive treatment under the medical mental health model. In other words, I needed to be suicidal and needing medications in order to receive assistance. Otherwise, as she put it, "We'd only go on a fishing expedition." The inaptness of mental health specialists was validated, as they only serve as a distraction. I chuckled at my own folly, as I'd known what was going to occur before I arrived. There is nothing an average person can do to help anyone, including themselves. After our encounter I drove to the bank, and then headed to Barnes & Noble Book Store where I received a call from my nephew. To his credit he spoke briefly about school and his marriage before telling me my father had died at 4:30PM, Texas time. I had been talking about him to a student of mine the very moment he died, and realized our spiritual connection had never been broken. I'd sensed him thinking about me many times and had been communicating spiritually, as I'd always known. He was a powerful individual who might have accomplished tremendous things, had he not given in to his every weakness. I later learned he'd been in intensive care for over a month. He'd refused to eat or take medications and was being fed and medicated through an IV. Apparently he pulled it out and stated that he wanted to die. On the day he passed, my sisters, who were caring for him, had gone out to eat. When they returned they were told that he died in his sleep. He might have pulled out the IV that was giving him the medication which kept his heart beating. Man's last and most powerful enemy, old age, claimed another victim. No one may ever really know what happened that day at Spohn Hospital in Corpus Christi, Texas. He may have pulled out the IVs, or perhaps his heart simply stopped. He died the second best death possible, in his sleep. Everyone's predictions of him suffering for his horrible sins never occurred. I wanted him punished for all the harm he'd caused, but in the end, it didn't matter. He'd been punished by his sin, not for his sins.

Anger over my father's estate created conflict, and as anticipated my siblings began hurling accusations at each other. It's difficult to describe how ugly things got. The conflict got downright nasty. One of the many accusations is that Bumper deliberately changed my father's medications in order to make him die sooner. Another is that Hijacker found him unconscious, covered in his own feces. Apparently he then stole $10,000 from a sack hidden in our father's underwear. I refer to this incident as the "Scrotum-gate scandal," and it remains an unresolved family legend. Another accusation is that Bumper stole nine thousand dollars, but he claims it was a loan he'd gotten in order to buy a used electric scooter. In another story, he borrowed the money to build something in his backyard, but when he learned that Punk had received $30,000 from our father over the years, Bumper refused to repay the money. He also filed a report for a stolen vehicle when Hijacker took our father's old pickup truck, said to be worth $15,000. Legal action has been threatened and both are foaming at the mouth, with their respective wives fanning the flames.

I am out of sight and out of mind, and don't expect to be on the list of beneficiaries if and when the estate is settled. I am not surprised at the mind-boggling harshness of reality, and I am in awe of the elegance of the Toltec discipline. My lack of self-importance, which stems from the knowledge of my own death, makes me indifferent to their bickering. I am able to listen to these stories without judgment or taking sides. I find none of their behavior better or worse than the other, as it is all equally average. I've validated another of my own lessons which I teach my students. Never expect to receive more than you've given. I feel amazingly free and may choose never to see my siblings again, or I may see them tomorrow. The years upon this path have *detached* me from all their bickering, and I have no ax to grind for old injuries. The reality of my own death seems even closer than ever, and at times like an old friend.

As I go about my life disguised as an average person, I am content. I am in awe of the elegance and power of the Toltec discipline. Its wisdom guides me and I find that living as a Warrior is its own reward. I congratulate all who are determined to do the same. Never forget that 96ers are your greatest challenge. Average people cannot see beyond their projections and are driven by greed. The challenge of a Warrior living amongst armies of fools is to interact with them, no matter how frustrating or pointless it may seem. Keep in mind that as long as you maintain decorum, appropriate behavior, and use correct vocabulary, you can participate at any level of society you desire. I suggest reading, studying, and sharing with others whenever possible. This is not done for the purpose of seeking approval, nor the intention of helping others, but to test what you think you know and claim to believe. Know that it is entirely up to you, and all the work will have to be done alone. Don't waste time seeking a teacher or attending seminars which cater to the masses. Keep notes, develop your own study aides, and become your own teacher. Seek assistance whenever possible from the Toltec Institute, but always remember that on this journey the only way to learn is by *doing*. You may read this material, but you'll never know it until you implement it in your life. You may be aware of your impending death, but you'll never have freedom until you witness it. You may believe this a worthwhile journey, but you'll never know it unless you stay upon the path. Don't make the classic 96er mistake and expect payment, riches, power, or fame for adopting this discipline. Take a lesson from today's self-proclaimed teachers as they attempt to help their children along. These individuals either wrongfully believe they can bequeath knowledge to them, or are deliberately defrauding all of their followers by appointing them false titles. Unfortunately, no one can inherit wisdom, and these self-named masters are actually doing their children harm by placing them on a pedestal. They do so while plastering their photographs all over everything they sell and endorse, which does not reflect a Warrior's discipline. Those who seek fame fail to recognize the power of anonymity. Distance yourself from those whose life does not reflect their statements. A Warrior's disguise is their greatest asset in the struggle to gain freedom. This discipline is so difficult because of its awesome simplicity.

Texas escapee,

don Jesus M. Ramirez

Epilogue
Born under a Wondering Star

"There's always another valley, another river, another mountain. Now the wind blows through me and takes me there."

–don Jesus M. Ramirez

Some people are said to be born with a silver spoon in their mouths, while others with a plastic spoon in theirs. I was born sad and unwanted. I developed a taste for adventure that began with my search for the white pony. No longer do I suffer from the wanderlust which once possessed my soul. I have journeyed across the earth and explored its mysteries, finding many teachers along the way. Via their examples they've helped me learn to manage self-importance, a Warrior's greatest enemy. Their pomposity and self-indulgence has helped me erase my past, connecting me to my folly and teaching me to laugh at the mistakes of my life. I once believed the call to adventure was a beckoning from God, which not all were blessed with. The call to roam arrived in the form of a cloud in the shape of a dancing pony. Its figure was as clear as the smile of God's promise and gave me an urge to see what was on the other side of the mountain. This desire gripped me with an urgency which I addressed the only way I knew how. At the age of nine I was found wandering miles away from home. I was discovered by a farmer who was not impressed with my accomplishment. He called the police to notify them of my presence on his property. I had traveled over twenty miles by climbing on the back of a truck carrying cotton to the gin. My father took a belt to me and promised to do it again. I discovered the fear of his belt was not enough to prevent me from seeking further adventures, and I surrendered to wanderlust. I once believed that not only was I born with a call to adventure, but also given the gift of attracting challenges. You know what they say, "What doesn't kill you, makes you stronger." Perhaps Batman's archenemy, The Joker, would say, "Whatever doesn't kill you, simply makes you... stranger." My ability to get into dicey situations usually left me alone. Any would-be friends soon learned that the reality of adventure isn't as much fun as it sounds. I was filled with a sensation that displaced loneliness and fear. I learned that although I might be alone, I was not lonely, as there was always the hope of a friendly face, a helping hand, and a kind word from a stranger. Hope is a wonderful thing for a child.

My earliest memories were of living in a tent, camping out beneath the stars. My parents were poor and their only blessing was an abundance of unwanted children. As a teenager I surfed the waves of the Gulf Coast of México in Corpus Christi. This may sound absurd to California surfers who have six foot breakers to enjoy year-round. However, on the Gulf Coast of México, the only time we got decent breakers was during hurricane season, and those who surfed never missed an opportunity to ride a twenty foot wave. The small detail and additional concern was that the hurricanes also brought about surprises. The winds stirred up the waters and sharks, along with every other kind of fish, were herded towards the shore. The presence of eighteen foot great hammerhead sharks was common in hurricane season. During one of my surfing adventures a huge hammerhead shark came up on my right side as I rode a wave. Its giant head rose and pushed me and my board out of the water. I was lucky. If it had wanted to take a bite out of me, I probably wouldn't be here to tell the tale. Either that or I'd be writing it with one arm. The guy surfing next to me wasn't so lucky. The great shark came back around and knocked him off his surfboard as it took a bite out of it. I stared in awe as he swam like a madman towards the beach. Poseidon surely saved him that day. He gave up surfing and I never saw him again.

  Several years ago I had been suffering from traveling fever. I decided to head to San Antonio, Texas, and visit several professional boxing gyms. I love the sweet science, and often travel to different cities to visit the gyms. I write their story and watch the fighters train. I study boxing the same way lawyers study law. I love boxing. It's the best sport in the world. Having fought many times, I know something about what fighting requires. My adventures have taught me many lessons, and the need for a variety of skills. I was traveling from Kingsville to San Antonio, which is about 150 mile trip. Zeus, Hera, or maybe even Jesus must have decided I needed another challenge, as a tornado hit the small town and flooded it. Everything from furniture to automobiles had been caught up and washed away by the raging winds. The dark storm clouds painted the sky as I waved to my friends who stood on the other side of the ravine I had just crossed, heading back to San Antonio. I was off to meet with Tony Ayala Senior, father of the famous Tony Ayala Junior, former middle weight boxing champion of the world. I was driving north on Highway 35 doing about 55 miles an hour, while idiots were passing me doing 80. I was following a big rig, hoping he could plow into whatever was in front of us and I wouldn't be hurt by the impact. The small rental car I was in would have folded like tin if I'd hit something. I thought I was doing great, when suddenly I began hearing heavy thuds striking the roof of the car. I imagined birds had gone mad in the storm and were committing ritual suicide. The thuds increased and I noticed blood and entrails on my windshield. Between splashing from the puddles and the sheets of rain, I saw that large frogs were being caught in the wheels of the semi-truck, which sent them spiraling up into the air. They were landing on the windshield of my car, leaving a trail of intestines behind, which were then messily blown away or washed off by the pounding rain. Saying a short prayer, I backed off and slowed down. The storm grew worse and thunder sounded like rolling artillery. I could see lightning light up the black sky as the rain increased and I decided to speed up. As I attempted to pass the giant truck it hit a huge puddle, causing its massive tires to splash water into the lane I was taking. My little rental car hit the wave of water and began to hydroplane. The illusion of any control quickly faded as I watched the world spin all around me. It was amazing. I completed three or four spins when I noticed the following cars were trying to avoid hitting me by driving off the road. The cars were swerving and dodging every which way as my car kept spinning and splashing sheets of water in every direction. *The Three Stooges* or *Keystone Cops* couldn't have done a better job. It's too bad there wasn't a movie camera filming, as it would have made for great cinematography. It was frighteningly hilarious. My car finally lost enough momentum for me to regain control. I slowed down, came out of the spin, pointed my nose towards San Antonio, and hit the gas. I dared not look back. Besides, there wasn't much I could do for those who were now stuck in the mud on the side of the road. I kept on moving and made my appointment. The storm slowly passed and gradually the skies cleared.

    Helen Keller once said, "Life is either a daring adventure or nothing." I am not bragging when I say my life has been a tremendous, yet sometimes painful adventure. I have journeyed all around the world. I have visited many wonderful places, along with some which were not so nice. I have climbed mountains and crossed valleys, deserts, rivers, and oceans. Writing the tale of my escape from Texas has helped me answer many questions, and continues to assist in my Warrior's inventory. I continue my quest for freedom and will never call myself a master, guru, or shaman, nor will I ever adopt any other such title. I am a Warrior — a student of the Toltec discipline. As such, I will never bow to anyone, nor will I allow others to bow to me. There is simply too much to learn to claim mastery of anything. Everyone, even those of us who choose discipline, structure, and establish boundaries will have doubts. This is our human side. The part of us which remains tied to the world binds us to our weaknesses, and is the reason for this struggle, which will never end. In the course of my journey the lessons of the Toltec discipline have clearly demonstrated power, effectiveness, practicality, and necessity for anyone seeking spiritual freedom on this plane. As well as for anyone disillusioned with today's watered-down versions of religion, or those sickened by our political, criminal justice, educational, medical, and mental health systems. Those who have always wanted to belong to something bigger than themselves, but have never found anything worthy of their mettle, are now called to action. Those seeking to grow, expand their minds, and unburden themselves of yesterday's pain, must answer the challenge. Are you ready to change? Do you no longer wish to be who you are? Are you tired of living the mundane existence of the average person? You'll have many opponents to such a decision. However, keep in mind that of all your challengers, no one and nothing is offering anything more than the same shallow, meaningless life you've always known. They'll point out the many complex concepts and criticize, but again, not be able to offer solutions. These are the average fools who take up your time and waste your energy.

I see my challenge as the implementation of a program in which Seekers who wish to continue on the Warrior's path can find help in unraveling its mysteries. I invite interested individuals to contact me through Toltec Institute. Be forewarned, I have no patience for liars, cowards, frauds, or fools. I seek honest, hardworking, disciplined individuals. My program is available to anyone who is willing to dedicate themselves, do the work, stay the course, and forge ahead. Newcomers are urged to remember that nothing worth doing is easy. I strongly advise taking a serious look at yourself before seeking guidance. Everyone is encouraged to live their lives to the fullest, fight their fears, and challenge what they believe. Each Seeker must determine whether to accept reality as they perceive it or adopt another's. There are millions of 96ers who deliberately live in denial of their paranormal experiences. There are millions more who because of their lack of energy have never, and will never experience the wonderment of this precious existence. No one is required or requested to adopt another's worldview or perspective. As in death, we are all alone. Each Seeker must make their own way, as there is no single manner in which to approach knowledge. Seekers are reminded that every endeavor should be approached with caution, fully aware of the consequences and prepared to manage the possibilities. No promises are made, guaranteed, implied, or offered. I encourage you to sing louder, dance more, love, run, and play. Stop being shy and surrender to the idea that you are going to die. You have no time to waste being timid. Whether you attempt to free your spirit or not, you're going to die regardless. Those who enter these dark waters will have come to know themselves before they die. Those who don't, will die ignorant of the power they've allowed to slip through their grasp. Death is stalking all of us. This cannot be overstated. We have no guarantees.

There is no assurance that tomorrow will come, and if it does, that it will be the same as today.

I'll be expecting you.

Texas escapee,

don Jesus M. Ramirez

Essential Concepts and Vocabulary

"No one will ever know you as well as you should know yourself. Until this challenge is accomplished, peace will forever be elusive and personal power a mystery."

-don Jesus M. Ramirez

Newly arriving Seekers should expect to spend as much as two or more years getting to know themselves well enough to start. A commonly overlooked rule of the Universe is that everyone must start where they are. You must begin wherever you find yourself, no matter where that is. You could be homeless and living on the streets, a prisoner in a cell, a multimillionaire in a mansion on top of a hill, or just another ordinary, timid, and scared individual. No matter, self-importance is the best and worst part of us. It is what drives us towards excellence, yet simultaneously causes the average man's destruction. The overwhelming impact self-importance has on our lives demands that this concept be addressed repeatedly throughout this work. This is a point of significance, as repetition is intentional. My objective is to illustrate the many forms in which self-importance attacks, as well as how it manipulates us to act against own higher knowledge. Those upon this journey must have an understanding of its impact before starting. To defeat self-importance one must follow directions without self-pity, as if removing a cancer. This is essential and must not be overlooked. Do not jump ahead without understanding this concept.

Countless self-proclaimed masters of the Toltec discipline

have wrongfully minimized the concept of self-importance, making it appear as though it were just a bump in the road on the path towards knowledge. Conveying the near impossible task of defeating self-importance in such a manner makes this discipline appear accessible to the masses. This is a perfect example of watering-down a discipline beyond resemblance of truth in order to make it more marketable. This is a betrayal and deliberate misrepresentation based on the desire to make a dollar. Without conquering self-importance, advancement towards power is impossible. I have met alleged Buddhist masters and leaders of religious cults who claim spiritual enlightenment, yet have no understanding of this concept. I make this a point of consequence for those who believe themselves innately advanced and beyond the average person. I have taken great care to convey this concept using many different illustrations, which will be helpful to genuine Seekers willing to set aside their egos and study them. My comprehension of this enemy came at the cost of many years of steadfast dedication, as I had no help in gaining an understanding. Consequently, it took me much longer than it will take you, because you will have a guide. It would have been impossible had I not become fanatical about it. Even so, it required years of experimentation, failure, and experience to draw from.

    Self-importance is one of the most difficult concepts to grasp, as well as one of the greatest obstacles to identify in our lives. It has always been and continues to be an extremely difficult lesson to convey to prospective students, as it goes against the grain of the average person. The near impossible task of defeating this enemy challenges what society has consistently drummed into them. Experiencing the resistance to change, along with continuous refusal to examine this aspect of their character, has caused many promising Seekers to surrender. I have watched many would-be Warriors leave in confusion, only to stumble and crash into themselves as a result of indulgence in self-importance. I do not expect many to grasp how destructive this enemy is, nor will I hold it against you when you don't. I expect you to fail. I expect you to throw this book across the room in revulsion, as it would not be average if you didn't. However, I hope that as time and life repeatedly beats you down, you, and all of those who left, will return. A wonderful aspect of this discipline is that no one is punished for being average. Averageness is the curse of being born. Keep in mind that a commonly overlooked universal rule is that no one changes because they want to. People change because they have to. As a Seeker or Pathfinder, you are fortunate, as I am also on this path. I understand how difficult it is to rein in behavior which you were told demonstrates confidence. I know how difficult it is to live like a Warrior amongst millions of lost, violent, lying, cheating, untrustworthy average people. These mindless drones will antagonize and frustrate you with their self-centered behavior. This applies tenfold to those of you who are married, have children, or are attempting to change while surrounded by a herd of average people.

Relationships are impossible with average people. This will be by far and without exception the best relationship book you will ever read. Why, you ask? Because this book teaches you how to manage your partner, while at the same time managing yourself. It teaches you to overlook most behaviors, and yet does not hold you responsible for anyone but yourself. It will teach you to *see* people as energy and determine whether you should or shouldn't interact with them. It teaches how to recognize deception and gives you the strength to cut anyone or anything from your life in an instant. You'll be amazed to discover the power you've always had, but never knew how to use. None of this is guaranteed, and no one will do it in a short while. The journey never ends, and will take the rest of your life.

The need for affection, relatives, and occupation are some of the many obstacles a Seeker faces upon their path towards knowledge. You will stumble, fall, suffer, and agonize many times throughout your life. You will be betrayed, disappointed, and lied to, and you'll make many poor decisions, as we all do. Yet, you will also see how these same events will destroy others, but not you. This discipline will give you the tools and strength of heart to continue to struggle, which is all that life will ever be. I have had to battle the same demons you'll face. I have had to learn to silence my *internal dialogue* and control my reactions. I had to train myself to respond to the message, and not the messenger or their words. I have trained myself to recognize and *read* human emotion, via learning to recognize my own. Another commonly unknown universal rule is that only those who are constantly at war against their weaknesses find peace.

I have no master other than myself. I claim no supernatural powers or knowledge. Although I have acquired much education in the academic sense, there are no titles, certificates, or degrees that matter. I do not claim to have known or met any alleged famous shaman or teacher. Anyone who bases their supposed knowledge on such claims or believes such things matter disqualifies themselves. Such an individual has not conquered their self-importance and does not understand the meaning of *detachment*, both of which are essential to this discipline. Such individuals are driven by a need for recognition, and I would not trust their quality or interpretations. There is no need to name those whom I am describing. It does however bring to mind those who have started their own churches and given themselves a title. It's amusing, pitiful, and amazing that they can find such large flocks of sheep to fleece so easily. I am as equally amused by gurus who bequeath their flocks of sheep to their children. There can be no better example of average behavior than a person wanting to make their child successful, instead of requiring them to achieve success for themselves. Why not just call them divine and be done with it. It is ridicules. I hold myself to strict universal standards because I am in this for my own benefit. Death is stalking me. I have felt it brush past me and experienced its presence. These are not just words on page for me. I choose to gather and store energy in order to fight for my own life and keep death at a distance for as long as possible. I am not in competition for recognition or public endorsement. I am not motivated by greed or pride. Death has shown me how truly worthless the trophies of average men are. As I lay dying, death showed me how meaningless everything and everyone is. Titles, money in the bank, cars, women, and positions of power mean nothing when you are dying. It is the loneliest experience one will ever know. The challenge is to face death sincerely, with the knowledge that you have lived like a Warrior and fought the best fight you could.

Another commonly unknown universal rule is that regardless of position, appearance, or social station, comparing yourself to another will only lead to strife. This is an extremely difficult concept. By not comparing yourself to other people, you are never less or more than anyone. This stores and saves an amazing amount of energy. I have provided many illustrations and relevant examples in hopes that genuine Seekers will begin to understand. There is so much to learn, but for now I will focus on man's greatest enemy; self-importance. Please note that my use of the words "man, him, himself, his, and etc." is in reference to "mankind," and not the male gender/sex. Students of this discipline already know that women make dangerous and lethal adversaries, as well as great allies. Great caution should be taken if you have made a female enemy. You are advised to remember another universal rule; no one forgets nothing.

Before we begin the journey into ourselves, it is necessary that essential concepts and vocabulary be identified, explained, and defined. Firstly, I would like to give you a picture of who "those" average people who drive you crazy are. The average man is a gigantic vulgar conglomeration of ideas and behaviors, which create an unbelievably difficult problem for themselves and the world. These contradicting and mutually exclusive ideas and behaviors are what average people consider to be special and unique about themselves. This is one of the many lies and uncorrectable mistakes the average parent makes when socializing their child. All children within our society have been lied to from birth, being told they were wonderful and unique, but in reality they are as common as rocks, and just as uninteresting. The average man's view of the world, along with his opinions of himself, is twisted. His reality is based on lies and half-truths. His views and interactions with the world are nothing more than an expression of self-promoting desires and delusions. He spends his entire life wanting more, as it has become his nature to do so. He is driven by these cravings and the feelings that he believes their fruition will bring. This self-centeredness manufactures a completely delusional self-concept that demands it be catered to, nurtured, comforted, and stroked like a mother would a neurotic baby. The need for the average man to have his narcissism fed is based on a desperate neverending need for validation. His self-deception and desires feed and validate his prejudices. This is what average people call, normal. The average man wants what he wants and will use religion, the law, violence, and any other advantage or accessible resource to gain it. He makes no apology for his vanity, pride, or greed. This applies to land, property, titles, money, power, or other people. The Southern plantation slave masters proved that greed, fed by fraudulent claims of divine rights, can lead a nation to war.

According to an independent study, the primary reason why small businesses fail is due to employee theft and fraud. The consensus is that the average employee will either create or take advantage of an opportunity to steal.

- Twenty percent of employees deliberately plan to steal from their employers, and will create an opportunity to do so.

- Forty percent of employees will occasionally give into temptation to steal if the opportunity arises.

- Twelve percent of employees will commit fraud regardless of circumstance.

- Twenty-four percent of employees will commit fraud if they have the need, opportunity, and believe they can rationalize their behavior.

Statistics concerning the behavior of individuals employed in larger companies is said to be remarkably similar. The primary difference is that smaller businesses are incapable of withstanding the financial losses accompanied with such behavior. Although the intention of this study was to investigate the source of small business failure, it succeeded in exposing the nature of the average person, as the general population and that of the workforce are one and the same. According to this study, 96 percent of the workforce are compromised and fall into one of the 4 categories listed above. It is for this reason that I have coined the term "96er," which is just another name for average people. This same study also unintentionally revealed that only four percent of people will not steal or commit fraud, regardless of need, opportunity, temptation, circumstance, ability to rationalize, and etc. I refer to these individuals as "Four Percentors."

Average people, or 96ers, are unashamedly unethical in every aspect of their lives. It is indeed the trademark of a 96er to be randomly cruel, kind, loving, or hateful. They justify and rationalize every act and every thought, no matter how bizarre, because it's what they want, or worse, how they feel at the time. In their minds there is no need for explanation or reason, other than their own personal desire. Their narrow-mindedness, prejudices, and ignorance is easily justified and rationalized. An average person can justify stealing from their family as easily as they can rationalize cheating on their spouse. Furthermore, average people can do so, so effectively, as to completely wipe away guilt and remorse. They are ethical vacuums without a moral barometer. They have taken the shamelessly hedonistic marketing catchphrase, "What happens in Vegas, stays in Vegas," to the extreme. Such hedonism rapidly leads to self-destruction. The truth, as everyone knows, is that there are consequences for such behaviors. In addition to this is the universal rule that no one forgets nothing. This is especially true with law enforcement.

The recent reports of young American soldiers killing innocent Iraqi men, women, and children demonstrate and validate how under the right circumstances, average people can justify and rationalize any action. The average person staggers and stuns the world with acts of premeditated cruelty. It is mindboggling for many to understand how allegedly "good" young American soldiers, become dehumanized in such a short time, as to commit these hideous crimes while serving their country. The average person manufactures within themselves limitless inconsistencies and contradictions, and then rationalizes and justifies them. No matter what the problem or how unethical their solution, their self-deception is equally as bizarre. The average man, fueled by self-importance, is a walking and talking contradiction. He operates and is governed by emotions in his endless search and hunger for validation.

These unpleasant and disgusting tendencies are not limited to the poor uneducated masses, but are equally as noticeable amongst the so-called "enlightened" population. Race, ethnicity, social and economic status, job title, position, religious background, education level, gender, family connections, and etc., have no relevance in any regards to the quality or inferiority of a person's character. In addition, they have no positive effect on the average man's ability to deceive himself.

Man's destructive self-importance, which is constantly reinforced, is a Warrior's greatest enemy. This is so because it exists within himself. It will attack him in so many ways that it's impossible to identify them all. A Seeker will be bombarded and machine-gunned relentlessly by his own weaknesses (biases, insecurities, stereotypes, and etc.), which I refer to as "personal demons." Simultaneously he will be attacked by average people, who use what they consider to be "common sense," to rationalize and justify their behavior. The new and untrained Seeker will want to give as good as he got, earn respect, and get some payback. The urge to, do as the Romans do, when in Rome, will be difficult to resist, yet that is the challenge. Indeed, a new Seeker will have to battle himself, while battling the average person. This will be a difficult period, as readjustment without constant reinforcement is nearly impossible. The truth is that the only real way to learn this discipline is to live it. In order to live it, one must have an example and constant reinforcement of this discipline's many facets. A Seeker needs his teacher's energy in order to grasp and see the discipline applied in normal life situations. There are no shortcuts and those who truly wish to live as Warriors need continuous reinforcement. This extreme difficulty is why those who elect to undertake such a challenge are called Warriors. As Warriors they must go to war against the socialization that has kept them bound, and continues to bind the rest of the world. The challenge seems nearly impossible, as those who dare to accept it are also products of this twisted society. As such they must constantly battle the brainwashing and propaganda they endured, as well as the ever-present pressure to assimilate. One of the most seemingly insurmountable obstacles one on this path must face is that of unresolved childhood issues. The heart wrenching and painful discoveries hidden within the souls of many Seekers are often devastating. Another unknown universal rule is that acceptance is much more important than understanding. Therefore, the challenge for all new Seekers is to identify these unresolved childhood issues and document events in as much detail as possible. They must include every detail, including time, place, what they felt, what they saw, and etc. One of the most important aspects of this task will be to recall those involved, noting what role they played, who helped, who refused to help, and etc. It is paramount that a Seeker does this knowing that they do not need to understand, but only document. You should not attempt this unless you are under the guidance of a genuine Warrior. Social workers, counselors, therapists, and psychiatrists are frauds. Stay away from these average people if at all possible. They hide behind alleged qualifications earned via intellectualization in academia, rather than real-life experience. This cannot be overstated and must not be attempted unless you have a solid support system. I suggest you avail yourself of groups such as Hospice, Alcoholics Anonymous (AA), Narcotics Anonymous (NA), Veterans Affairs (VA), and other survivors and support groups, including those of elderly and widowed individuals, and etc.

As a new Seeker, interacting with 96ers will undoubtedly be your greatest challenge. For this reason I have dedicated much of this work to their fundamental management and defeat. I suggest thinking of the average person as being mentally deficient or mentally handicapped, as mentally and emotionally inept is an accurate description. In addition to this, interacting with them from this perspective will assist in eliminating any expectations you might have had of them. Never share personal experiences, mistakes, or flaws of character with 96ers. If you must talk to someone, travel out of town, find a social gathering place, and speak with a stranger. Never reveal your indiscretions, accidents, or fantasies with anyone who is part of your daily existence. All 96ers are your competitors and willing executioners.

All average people hate being challenged, questioned, or contradicted. They demand everyone support their pompous and delusional concepts, no matter how false. They seek clear and easy answers to any question, no matter how complex the issue. They want simple instructions which they can agree with, but also does not challenge their concept of reality. They hate to be embarrassed or shown up, and always see themselves as being good, while seeing others as being bad. They demand immediate justice and punishment when it comes to others, but kindness and understanding when it comes to themselves or their loved ones. Average parents will condone murder, theft, assault, molestation, or rape by their children, but will not tolerate any infraction of rules by anyone else. They desire fame and public recognition, but refuse to offer congratulations, even when it's obviously due. They crave power, authority, and lordship over the masses, while longing to be flattered and have their asses kissed to the point of religious idolatry.

Self-importance is the best and worst part of us. It is what drives us towards excellence, yet simultaneously causes the average man's destruction. The average man who is seen as successful has learned to use these weaknesses to manipulate, control, and direct others. These are the so-called leaders of society, and they have learned via older manipulators how to use the average man's weaknesses against him. These individuals have developed the use of language, and adopted the right image in order to position themselves in authority. However, they are essentially and fundamentally the same creature they despise. They are extremely dangerous and personify self-importance. These individuals will not be found at antiwar demonstrations or working towards social justice. Not only do they not have such feelings, but they are aware that behaving in such a manner would not serve them. It would be impossible to manipulate the rich masses if they gave the impression of having different values and beliefs. These powerful 96ers hide behind masks of respectability and call themselves "conservatives."

A new Seeker must accept that interacting honestly with average people is hopeless, impossible, and pointless, yet that is whom he must share the world with. This is why the Toltec discipline and the Warrior's path is applicable, empowering, and enriching. Exploring your own self-importance will take years, countless battles, victories, and defeats. It is why I call myself and anyone upon this path, a Warrior.

Self-importance

Self-importance comes at you in many shapes and disguised in many forms. Let's examine this complex challenge, starting with a definition. Keep in mind that self-importance is the best and worst of us. It is what drives us towards excellence, yet simultaneously causes the average man's destruction. It is also the main cause of energy drainage, and the very heart of a 96er. This concept is not easy to understand, nor is the subtleness of its destructive potential. As in all disciplines, the journey is what makes the experience so valuable and inspiring. You will have to unravel many challenging ideas to answer your own questions, just as I did. Those of you who read this material will have an edge, but only if you apply the discipline. These concepts are extremely difficult to grasp. There are no shortcuts, and you must learn them via steadfast discipline while engaging in a never-ending struggle.

I suggest every Seeker begin by gaining an understanding of *detachment*, *forbearance*, *timing*, *inner silence*, and *will*. Without these basic and essential tools you will never discover how to defeat self-importance. You must be in touch with the reality of your impending death, knowing that you have no time to waste indulging in excesses or deprivation of pleasures. I urge every Seeker to volunteer at Hospice and visit VA hospitals via their ongoing volunteer programs. This must be done consistently for at least a year. However, Seekers must be aware that dealing with someone else's death is in no way comparable to dealing with your own. These experiences simply assist in the development of understanding and learning *detachment*. There is no other way to attain an understanding of death, other than to face your own and temporarily win. Those who have, know the horrible and tremendous impact which such an experience has upon one's development. This is why learning *detachment* is essential. This cannot be overstated.

Detachment is a difficult concept for new Seekers to understand, as they often confuse it with an average person's disconnect and calloused indifference, learned via brutalization. To develop an understanding of this concept I would suggest considering the act of judging others, which is a major component in energy drainage. If you make a critical judgment of a person or situation, you are not *detached*. If you feel insulted or angered when someone makes fun of you, you are suffering from injured pride, and expect others to see you as you see yourself. You are not *detached* and are "expecting," thus setting yourself up for disappointment. You should have nothing to defend; no pride, no ego, no nation, no creed, and no one other than yourself. There should be no one important enough to make you feel insulted or complimented. As long as no one physically harms you or someone you love, you have nothing to defend. If this happens, then you are now on a completely different level, and should defend yourself enthusiastically. Yes, there are many exceptions, and as in all things regarding this discipline, there are no black and white answers. You can decide how far to take it from there. Remember, you must survive on this plane, and if you harm, cripple, or kill someone, there will be consequences. No matter what you do, you must do it to your advantage. It must serve you. It cannot come from anger or a need for revenge. Study the laws of self-defense. This must be considered carefully. Also, note that when I say, "someone you love" I am referring to a husband defending his wife, or a parent their child, and etc. This does not apply to loudmouth average fools of any gender or relation who instigate altercations, regardless of whether or not they claim the title of "friend."

If you are going to do anything outside of the law, you must do it alone, and be prepared to live with it for the rest of your life in secret. You must also be fully prepared to live with the consequences. It won't be easy. Prisons are filled with allegedly "good" individuals, who lost it during a moment of anger and killed or crippled someone. If you are involved in a physical altercation, you must never lose your judgment, and always manage your emotions. It will be the clear thinker who wins the battles, and sometimes the war. Remember, Warriors do not always win. Do not expect justice. Cops are dangerous average people with a lot of authority. Never give a cop a personal reason to see you jailed.

If you find yourself feeling sorry for someone, you are indulging in self-importance, and are not *detached*. This behavior is a reflection of your desire for others to feel sorry for you, or to be like you. While an average man sees someone and feels sorry for their position or circumstance, a Warrior only *sees* a person who is engaged in the consequences of their decisions, and therefore does not feel sorry for them. If you feel sorry for someone because they appear ignorant, you are indulging in self-importance. This is a reflection of your desire for an individual who you see as being ignorant to be more like you. You are setting yourself up as the example or standard of how everyone should be. A Warrior will discover the many forms of self-importance as he comes across the subtle and varied manners in which this enemy presents itself. It is a never-ending struggle which never gives respite.

One of the many benefits of this discipline is the ability to *read* others. The ability to do so, and do so correctly, will make you feel powerful. As much as feeling powerful helps, it can also hurt you if you permit yourself to be deceived by it.

After examining some common aspects of self-importance, it

is not difficult to see how defeating it is a near impossible challenge. The many disguises and forms in which it presents itself in our lives are overwhelming. Keep in mind that although absolutes are much easier to understand, this is not how life presents itself. The test is in monitoring yourself. Defeating self-importance is not a game, and you must become deadly serious about doing so. Developing a guardian who will help, watch over, and protect you is essential. You must become your own guardian and best friend. Of all the people in the world, you must learn to love yourself the most, but never allow yourself to indulge in self-destructive, egotistical thinking or behavior. Great care must be taken in the development of your guardian, less it becomes a guard. There are essential differences between the two that a Seeker must grasp and fully understand. This is another difficult concept, and will require great study.

The challenge of defeating self-importance is never-ending and will be very difficult. It is for this reason that I have incorporated the use of the "seven deadly sins," or the "cardinal sins." These seven sins have been used since early Christian times by religious leaders to educate and assist people in monitoring and managing their behavior. I have adopted their use for the same reasons. However, I place no religious value in any of them. Sin is merely another word for failing to hit the mark or perform to your own standards. The objective is to save energy via avoiding the consequences of self-destructive behaviors. I have no belief in a religious God, and I don't believe there is a paradise where I will be safe, protected, and never suffer. After many years of experience, I have discovered that the seven deadly sins serve as an excellent foundation, with which a Seeker can grasp hold of self-importance. They assist in a basic categorization of the innumerable forms in which self-importance presents itself. Readers are advised that although I place no religious value in any of these "sins," society and the law have similar ideas of morality, crime, and punishment. You should remember that no one forgets nothing, and no one forgives anything. If you've wronged someone, you should expect consequences. Don't expect forgiveness, and don't forget those you've wronged. I can assure you that they will not forget you. Once the fight begins, it won't matter who threw the first punch or fired the first shot. Violence is a normal part of existence in the United States. We are a hostile and bigoted country. I will not paint romanticized pictures for you, nor will I attempt to comfort you by adding to your delusions. If you've harmed, wronged, or betrayed another human being, you must remain alert for the rest of your life, or theirs. There is no such thing as real forgiveness amongst average people. If you are a parent who has molested, abused, or neglected your child, be prepared to face them as they grow stronger, older, and bolder. The effects of child abuse last forever. The effects of bad parenting never stop hurting a person and continue for the rest of their lives. It will not be pleasant. I suggest everyone read the book *Toxic Parents* by Susan Forward. It's filled with great information and illustrations. It is not a nice book, but it may help you manage your demons.

Seven Deadly Sins

Seekers are encouraged to examine the following sins for ways to choose less energy draining responses to situations. The objective is to store and maintain energy so as to better face the powers of the Universe.

- Pride
- Greed
- Envy
- Wrath
- Lust
- Gluttony
- Sloth

Pride

Definition:

1. A high or inordinate opinion of one's own dignity, importance, merit, or superiority, whether as cherished in the mind or as displayed in bearing, conduct, etc.

2. The state or feeling of being proud.

3. A becoming or dignified sense of what is due to oneself or one's position or character; self-respect; self-esteem.

4. Pleasure or satisfaction taken in something done by or belonging to oneself or believed to reflect credit upon oneself.

5. Something that causes a person or persons to be proud.

Synonyms: Arrogance, conceit, haughtiness, loftiness, pomposity, pretension, superciliousness, vanity, dignity, ego, honor, pleasure, satisfaction, self-confidence, self-respect, egoism, egotism, gratification, pridefulness, self-love, self-regard, self-satisfaction, self-sufficiency, self-worth, amour-propre, ego trip, self-admiration, self-glorification, self-trust.

Antonyms: Depression, gloom, melancholy, misery, pain, sadness, sorrow, trouble, unhappiness, woe, disgrace, humility, modesty, shyness, timidity, meekness, reserve.

Pride comes disguised in many forms. It is the reason why 96ers react to insults and perceived threats. Average people are very sensitive about many things, but no one knows for sure what those things will be at any given moment. They themselves do not know how they will react to anything, as they always react according to how they feel at the moment. They live their lives led by their emotions. You must *read* whomever you are speaking with, as well as everyone around them. Whenever you come across arrogant loudmouths, remember that they are not really proud, just stupid. Avoid stupid people of all ethnicities, genders, ages, and social and economic levels. If you must interact, do so without drinking. Don't go any place they might wish to show off, as they may decide to use you as their scapegoat.

Early Christian leaders have identified humility as being the opposite of pride. I discard religious views on most matters. Organized religion is a business designed to keep average people obedient and fill the pockets of church leaders, while simultaneously perpetuating government and society. In prewar Germany religion was used to motivate women into having more children, so as to fill military ranks. I've known many priests, pastors, ministers, and etc., and none have impressed me. A Warrior could only be humble with and amongst other Warriors. Having to operate on this plane, it would not serve him to appear humble amongst average people, as they would interpret his humility as weakness, and respond with insult or assault. In the world of average men it is better to appear competent, mysterious, and potentially dangerous. The only instance in which it would serve a Warrior to appear humble is if he were practicing *stalking*, and wished to present himself as such. A Warrior must be able to camouflage himself and become whoever he wishes. The key is to behave or act in a humble manner. Doing so is nothing as nonsensical as sincerely feeling humble. It's a Warrior's strategy to do what serves him, when it serves him. The key element in his strategy is *detachment* from what 96ers think or say. A *detached* Warrior has the potential to be an extremely dangerous adversary. As a Seeker working to attain understanding of a Warrior's strategies, you should always keep in mind the manipulative nature of 96ers. Those in authority have a great dexterity for manipulating others via fine words, such as honor and duty. Do not allow yourself to be fooled. Old men send young men to war in order to get richer and guarantee that their children won't have to fight the wars they've started and perpetuated. It's the history of every nation. Most politicians have never fired a shot in defense of themselves or anyone else. These individuals are perfect examples of average people.

I believe the opposite of pride is loneliness, emptiness, hopelessness, despair, and mourning. A lack of self-esteem is a multifaceted issue, which is why it's almost impossible to help someone find it. I believe the best way to teach someone self-esteem is to give them responsibility. Only through learning how to manage an assigned task and being accountable for it will they learn self-esteem. There must also be an element of danger and serious consequences for failing. Otherwise the experience will be meaningless. The essence of self-esteem is autonomy, which can only be learned via responsibility.

Despite what the average person would like to believe, the only way to learn anything is through action. There are thousands of recently graduated psychiatrists, psychologists, therapists, counselors, social workers, and etc., who believe their education fully qualifies them to offer advice to their clients. In truth, the most difficult challenge many have ever faced themselves was leaving home and getting daddy to pay for their education. I've known many such individuals who consider themselves professionals, when in reality they are simply frauds taking money under false pretenses. They repeat what others have told them is true, and most of those people have learned what they claim to know via reading about it in a book. They never experienced it themselves, nor do they know their alleged truth to be real. Their words are mere transference of misinformation, which no one ever bothered to verify. Such behavior is dishonest, fraudulent, and a violation of universal laws. Higher education generates thousands of deluded average people, pretending to be something they're not. Therapists, counselors, social workers, and alleged mental health experts of all sorts should rarely be trusted. Priests and nuns who counsel about sexual matters should be laughed at.

Greed

Definition:

1. Excessive or rapacious desire, especially for wealth or possessions.

Synonyms: Avarice, grasping, grudging, illiberal, mercenary, miserly, parsimonious, selfish, devouring, gluttonous, ravenous, stingy, excess, gluttony, hunger, longing, selfishness, acquisitiveness, avidity, covetousness, craving, cupidity, eagerness, edacity, esurience, indulgence, intemperance, piggishness, rapacity, ravenousness, voracity.

Antonyms: Apathy, charitable, generosity, munificent, philanthropy, sharing, full, satisfied, dislike, distaste, indifference, benevolence.

I find greed to be the major motivator with all 96ers, which makes it the easiest tool to use against them. Greed can be used to move mountains amongst average people. It can be used to start wars, make peace, build bridges, and establish elaborate schemes which could serve a Warrior greatly. The key is to remember that a Warrior must be able to live amongst 96ers, but never be one of them. A Warrior in the process of executing a plan must be able to exhibit all the symptoms of a greedy individual, without feeling them. He is able to do so because he knows that in the end it doesn't matter. He knows the Universe will provide him with prosperity if that is what he desires. The difference is that he will never be a slave to it, or to what it brings. *Detachment* is the key to his freedom and peace of mind. As mentioned before, the concept of *detachment* requires great effort to understand and implement. This is where having a teacher helps. If a Warrior chooses, he can involve himself in projects of any nature. It must be done with complete awareness and acceptance of the consequences. He must have an ace up his sleeve and an alternative plan in the event one is necessary. He must also be wary of betrayal, knowing that greed is a 96er's greatest weakness, as well as justification for horrible actions. New Seekers are reminded that betrayal always comes from within the group.

Early Christian leaders have identified charity as being the opposite of greed. I disagree. For a Warrior, giving things away has nothing to do with being charitable. It is once again based upon pleasure, indifference, or deliberate manipulation of a situation or a person. When a Warrior gives something, he does so for completely different reasons than an average person. I often direct my students to give things away to strangers, knowing they'll never see them again nor receive anything in exchange. This helps new Seekers learn to squash their self-importance and develop *detachment*. I suggest approaching this exercise deliberately with the intention of giving away your greed. This teaches new Seekers to place less value on money, and focus on the knowledge of how easily 96ers can be manipulated. It also feeds into a 96er's fantasies of magic and the goodness of people. Seekers are reminded to be wary of generous 96ers. Money in this society comes with a lot of strings. Once you discover what a 96er wants, you've got a direct line into their mind. Next to greed, pride is a 96er's greatest enemy. Remember the adage from the Sixties, "Cash, grass, or ass, nobody rides for free." Throughout history sex has often been used as currency, typically by women. Seekers are reminded to be wary of women who ply them with sexual favors. I repeatedly warn my male students that women do not offer sex without strings. Even those who don't want marriage will ask for something. Society has conditioned women to view sex differently than men. I warn my female students that if they bed an average man, he will typically consider them to be his property. This never has pleasant results.

Envy

Definition:

1. A feeling of discontent or covetousness with regard to another's advantages, success, possessions, etc.

2. The feeling of antagonism towards someone because of some good which they enjoy but which one does not have oneself.

3. An object of envious feeling.

Synonyms: Hatred, ill will, malice, prejudice, resentment, rivalry, backbiting, coveting, covetousness, enviousness, grudge, grudging, lusting, malevolence, maliciousness, malignity, opposition, spite, evil eye, green-eyed monster, grudgingness, invidiousness, jaundiced, resentfulness.

Antonyms: Friendliness, like, liking, love, loving, comfort, confidence, contentedness, good will, kindness, pleasure, indifference.

The envy of an average person is intermingled with pride and greed. It is a black potion of veil low frequency emotion that provides the justification for many of the world's evils. It attacks 96ers like water carries wetness. It is almost impossible to distinguish one of these weaknesses from other average behavior.

Early Christian leaders have identified love as being the opposite of envy. I don't agree with this analogy. Nor do I agree with the common belief that hate is the opposite of love. I don't believe love is the opposite of anything. It is unique in its qualities and just as difficult to find. Within the context of this common belief I find indifference to be a more suitable opposite to love. Any person who has experienced indifference can attest to the difficulty of both facing and accepting it. Think of all those good Southern descendant of European immigrant (DOEI) Christians throughout history, who stood by watching while thousands of people of color were beaten, jailed, and murdered. It was their indifference that condemned thousands to suffer and die under the yoke of racism, poverty, and government oppression. This example should serve as a warning to all genuine Seekers. Religious beliefs have never overpowered bigotry, nor have they instilled physical courage.

     I believe the opposite of envy is sincere joy for someone else's success or happiness. Such joy can only be experienced by a Warrior who has steadfastly followed this path for at least five to six years. This is the approximate time required to develop the necessary *detachment* from your own weaknesses. During this stage a Seeker also bridges their disconnection and sheds the layers of calloused indifference created via a lifetime of brutalization. Envy has many layers, but its basic form is easy to identify in your behavior. If you are not genuinely happy for another's success because you feel you deserve it, or because you feel you're better, more gifted, or superior in anyway, then you are enslaved by envy. None of these concepts are black and white, nor are they easy to identify. Each of these very common weaknesses requires tremendous concentration and fanatical attention.

Wrath

Definition:

1. Strong, stern, or fierce anger; deeply resentful indignation; ire.

2. Vengeance or punishment as the consequence of anger.

Synonyms: Acrimony, asperity, conniption, dander, displeasure, exasperation, flare-up, fury, hate, hatefulness, huff, indignation, ire, irritation, madness, offense, passion, rage, resentment, rise, stew, storm, temper, vengeance.

Antonyms: Calm, calmness, delight, ease, glee, happiness, kindness, liking, love, peace, pleasure.

Great care should be given to this emotion. However, it is important to note that not all anger is destructive. Anger can serve to assist you in times of crisis. A Warrior can learn to use it to help shut off his *internal dialogue* and hide his energy. When a Warrior learns to manage his anger, it becomes fury, and *focused* fury is a powerful and very useful weapon against the *unknowable* entities that cross our path unexpectedly. Anger becomes a weakness and is self-destructive when we engage it in response to feelings of indignation, self-righteousness, pride, greed, or envy.

    Early Christian leaders have identified patience as being the opposite of wrath. I disagree with this analogy intensely. I believe the opposite of wrath is indifference. If a Warrior feels indifference when faced with the *unknowable*, then he is ready to manage himself in such a manner as to be able to survive the confrontation. When he can experience indifference intermixed with controlled fury, then he may not only survive, but win. Japanese martial artists refer to this state of mind as Mushin, which translates to "no mind." It is achieved during combat when a Warrior is only in the moment, not thinking about reacting or about what to do next. The actions of his opponent dictate and direct his responses, so no thought is required. I teach my students to respond from a position of no thought, in which there is no distance in time from the moment one sees an opening to the point one takes a counter shot. Much concentration must be given to questions regarding this concept. Years and many tests may be required to master this challenge.

Lust

Definition:

1. Intense sexual desire or appetite without idealized or spiritual feelings.

2. Uncontrolled or illicit sexual desire or appetite; lecherousness.

3. A passionate or overmastering desire or craving.

4. A lust for power of pleasure.

5. Ardent enthusiasm; zest; relish.

Synonyms: Craving, desire, excitement, fervor, greed, hunger, libido, longing, yearning, sensuality, thirst, animalism, aphrodisia, appetence, avidity, carnality, concupiscence, covetousness, cupidity, eroticism, itch, lasciviousness, lechery, lewdness, licentiousness, prurience, salaciousness, salacity, sensualism, urge, wantonness, weakness.

Antonyms: Apathy, dislike, distaste, hate, hatred, chastity, purity, restraint, aversion, disenchantment, disgust, loathing.

I have a problem classifying lust as a weakness in the context of average people. Thoughts of sexual conquests are fed into our minds on a continuous basis via our eyes. These images are then transferred into how women dress and display their bodies. I cannot find fault in a young man wanting to bed every young girl that via her manner of dress and behavior is suggesting a possible liaison. I have no religious ax to grind, and I do not believe sex is sinful or wrong. However, there are certain boundaries and practical questions we must consider. Before I embark on this discussion I want to remind readers that I do not have "value judgment" on women or men who have multiple sex partners. Powerful men and women throughout history have considered bedding multiple partners a part of being in power. But, as I said, there are boundaries. I teach my students not to lie to potential partners in order to facilitate sexual relations. I instruct them to be honest. Yet at the same time, I also instruct them to offer an alternative personal history and disconnect from their past. To an average person or newly arrived Seeker this may seem contradictory. A Warrior however, knows that this is strategy and deliberate action with the intention of expending the least amount of energy. Always keep in mind that the overall objective is to gather and store energy. I advise my students that to lie to someone who has genuine feelings towards them, while they do not reciprocate those feelings, is wrong. It is also unnecessary in today's society. For example, most young people who desire sex will not hesitate or give morality a second thought. Most of those who do hesitate only do so out of fear of the potential consequences. I also advise my students to be direct about what they do and do not want. If a person is not prepared to enter a relationship, then I suggest they say so. If they do not want to have an exclusive relationship, then I suggest they be upfront about this. If by doing so, the individual who they are pursuing refuses to engage them sexually, then so be it. At least that person will have the opportunity to move on, knowing their situation. If they choose to stay, which I believe most will, they will do so with a clear understanding of what is real. Regardless of behavior or action, a genuine student of this discipline would neither suffer remorse or guilt. Therefore, these suggestions are not based upon morality, but strategy with the intention of expending the least amount of energy. It is not strategic to create enemies via sexual conquests under false pretenses. My students are obligated to remember that everyone is responsible for their conduct. Precautions should be taken to avoid transmitting sexual illnesses.

Serial womanizers, or "players," are untrustworthy. I would never trust anyone who habitually lies to women in order to bed them. Nor would I be willing to continue an association with such an individual on any level. My reason for doing so is simple; I could not trust them to be honest with me, and I do not suffer cowards, liars, or fools. The world of a Warrior must be compact, disciplined, and clear of emotional baggage. Every individual already has plenty of baggage to deal with, without bringing more into their lives by lying to their sex partner.

Another important point in regards to this subject is that women become energetically connected to the men they bed. I will not go into detail at this time, as it is lengthy. However, let it suffice to say that a female interested in bedding a potential partner must ensure the person is worthy. In all likelihood, they will be connected to that person for the rest of their lives. I am not suggesting women should be celibate or remain virgins. I am however suggesting caution and a high level of selectivity about whom they choose to bed. I know it has become more sociably acceptable to have multiple partners. This will change, just as other customs have throughout history. It is also a matter of quality verses quantity. Sexual relations with someone whom you have genuine feelings for is a spiritually uplifting experience, whereas random and casual sex becomes something to hide. The objective is to not add unnecessary baggage to your life. This can potentially become very troublesome in the future. If her past is well-known, a woman will be stuck with the history of her behavior, as will her husband. Women should realize that the average man's ego cannot withstand such a blow. Female Seekers are forewarned. If you've had multiple partners and your husband knows about these experiences, problems will occur. This is one of the best arguments for erasing your past. Do not make your husband your social worker or counselor, it won't work. Keep your sexual history secret and out of areas of discussion. As an illustration, I made a rule with my wife to never share details, names, places, and etc., about our prior relationships. I simply stated that I did not want to know how many lovers she had before I met her. Any time this topic comes up I always repeat the same thing, "I don't want to know. That was before I met you, and it has nothing to do with our relationship." This eliminates hours of arguing and saves tons of potentially wasted energy. Today, after over 25 years of marriage, it has become one of the good habits we've developed. When she behaves in a jealous manner or wants to know one of my ex-girlfriend's names, I say in a lighthearted manner, "I've been married so long I can't remember anyone else's name but yours." It always eases the tension and gets her to smile, because she knows I'm kidding. Seekers who haven't been in relationships for as long need only change the words to utilize this tactic. For example, "The first time I saw you, I fell so in love I forgot everyone's name but yours." The objective is to keep the peace and save energy. In an average relationship, one of the couple must surrender their ego in order to keep the marriage from blowing up. As much as everyone says they want honesty, they cannot handle it. This often happens with women who were popular in their youth. Jealously becomes a major and never-ending problem in relationships. I advise everyone who wishes to be happily married to move away from their hometown into another state. This is especially significant if you partied a lot in your youth and had multiple sex partners. No man wants a woman who has slept with men they know. It creates endless problems of jealously and may be the cause of a breakup. During the settlement of the West it was common practice for lonely men to marry "working girls." Many lonely men married women who worked in brothels and saloons. However, those were very different times and circumstances. Today, this leads to angry and jealous outbursts of violence. Another point to consider is that a woman will not want her children to know her past. Average people make terrible parents. They talk about everyone they know, and will either tell their children directly, or their children will overhear them. The next thing you know it will be going around in school, and then your kids will hear about it. It will be the cause of many very embarrassing and humiliating problems. It's best to think long-term and be very selective about whom you bed. Anyone who has been the subject of gossip will understand how damaging and painful it is. Many people are in jail or in the ground because someone repeated something they heard about someone they didn't know, and then did so at the wrong time and place.

There have been thousands of people who've been undone as a result of their involvement in inappropriate or illegal sexual liaisons. We've seen church ministers, politicians, celebrities, doctors, lawyers, and etc., caught with someone other than their spouse. I will not point fingers or pass judgment, as doing so would serve no purpose. I will only say that those who follow this path, regardless of gender or sexual preference, will attract many possible suitors. Individuals with an excess of energy are very alluring, and as such, you will have many opportunities to engage in new relationships, as well as play outside of existing ones. If you decide to cheat I advise caution, discretion, and complete secrecy. Never have an accomplice cover or lie for you, and always let your partner know that you are cheating and the consequences would be severe if exposed. I would suggest restraint rather than a foolproof plan.

For female Seekers I suggest finding a male counselor/adviser, not another woman. Yes, it's true that you'll want to feel safe, secure, and be able to relate to your counselor. However, you must ask yourself whether you want a friend or someone who will be honest with you. Do you want someone to cosign your misery, problems, and experiences, or would you prefer someone who can actually enlighten you and help you understand men? Every woman in the entire world has been conditioned to respond to men via their upbringing and experiences with their father. All women are conditioned to nurture, revere, and subject themselves to men. This is not an attack, just a description. All women, depending on their upbringing and religious background, have baggage regarding men to some degree or another. A woman who has been married will not be as able to assist you with your relationship as a man who has been married. Yes, it's true that it will be uncomfortable and difficult to find someone to talk with, which is why you can contact me. However, it is important to keep in mind that talking about sex, relationships, mistakes, and etc., should be difficult. It should be a growing experience. Keep in mind that no one changes because they want to. They change because they have to. Average people don't ever really change. They just run out of gas. If you are uncomfortable, then you are in the right place. However, for your protection, establish boundaries and stay *grounded*. Students should be wary of transferring their emotions to their counselor. Sexual transgressions are serious violations of ethics. Serious consequences can be expected when the Universe seeks its balance.

Early Christian leaders have listed chastity as being the opposite of lust. I believe an absence of sexual desire is as negative as an absence of any other natural instinct. Such matters are too complex to give simple suggestions or directions. Much will have to be considered, as well as many points and situations examined. I would suggest continued study and analysis.

Gluttony

Definition:

1. Excessive eating and drinking.

2. To endure or perform a task of a specific nature.

Synonyms: Craving, demand, fondness, greed, hunger, overeat, overfeed, overstock, oversupply, flood, gorge, cram, stuff, inclination, longing, lust, passion, penchant, propensity, stomach, taste, thirst, weakness, willingness, yearning, zeal, zest, appetence, appetency, itch, liking, proclivity, ravenousness, relish, urge, voracity.

Antonyms: Apathy, disinclination, dislike, hate, hatred, indifference, lethargy, antipathy, aversion, abstain, curb, disgust, distaste, loathing, repulsion, revulsion.

Individuals who excessively overeat have emotional issues. They have become habituated to behaving in certain manners, and do so without thinking. A Warrior does not feel the need to overeat or horde anything. He knows the Universe will reward him with more food, opportunity, and etc. A Warrior is generous towards those within his circle. There is no sense of desperation — no need to cling or squeeze the life and love out of anything or anyone. A Warrior touches the world gently, with care and the assurance that there is plenty more to enjoy. He applies this confidence to everything in his relationships, or his eating for that matter. He monitors and manages his desires, knowing the real joys of life come in small packages and quantities.

Early Christian leaders have identified temperance as being

the opposite of gluttony. For the average person, moderation of an indulgence may suffice as an inverse. A Warrior however, is absent of the need to horde or overindulge. He knows his personal power will provide him with all he desires and more. The endless yearning to have more is an integral, innate aspect of 96ers. This characteristic is one of the many horrors that poison them. They are infected with pride, greed, envy, wrath, and lust. These weaknesses become so entangled with gluttony, they are impossible to separate. The endless indulgence of the average person gives way to enumerable problems. In their compulsive quest for more, they indulge in comparisons, which only lead to more destructive behavior. It is a never-ending cycle of misery. Much to the world's chagrin, this inevitably leads to spiritual decay, which spreads like a lethal virus. This includes criminal and anti-social behaviors, ranging from gossip to murder. According to research, the major cause of crime occurs when people compare what they want to what others have. Outwardly this appears to be a battle between the haves and have nots. In reality, it's the manifestation of the unceasing, yet normal indulgences of average people. Those who believe they deserve what others have, simply because they've worked all their lives to achieve a 96er's concept of success, have created our culture of criminality. A Warrior who has experienced recapitulation no longer envies anyone, and acknowledges that everyone lives the results of where they invest their energy. For instance, if a farmer desires corn, he cannot plant cotton seeds. As a Warrior, if you desire material riches, by all means go after it. There is no universal law against wealth, only in how you obtain it. While it is true that unfair laws, social injustices, wars, and other manmade disasters play a part, a Warrior never knocks down obstacles, but instead goes around them. Racism plays a major role in how people develop, where they live, and how they live. In our society, above all other random events in our lives, the color we are born is the most significant. This, along with a desire to gain wealth without struggle, creates monsters who die young and harm many while they live. As it is with most illnesses of the spirit, it begins with self-importance. It is not self-destructive to want to live better. However, it is self-destructive to believe that others don't deserve what you desire as much as you. While it's not wrong to want to win, it is disadvantageous to believe you deserve to, simply because you want to. In the end, you only get what you've earned.

Sloth

Definition:

1. Habitual disinclination to exertion; indolence; laziness.

2. Spiritual apathy.

3. Failure to pursue virtue.

Synonyms: Idleness, inactivity, indolence, inertia, laxness, lethargy, listlessness, slackness, slothfulness, slowness, sluggishness, do-nothingness, lackadaisicalness, languidness, supineness.

Antonyms: Activity, busyness, energy, life, liveliness, vigor.

A Seeker will never succeed if they possess the characteristics associated with this weakness. A Warrior must work nonstop to achieve even a small expertise in any aspect of the lessons upon this path. He must study, read, examine, travel, and challenge his body and his mind relentlessly. He must experience and fail, then get up and do it again. There are no shortcuts and no translators or helpers. Unless you are fortunate enough to have found a teacher, you will be on your own. There will be no one to guide you. You may have to give up your old thinking patterns and agree that you need someone like me in your life. I wish I'd had a mentor like myself to help me along the way. My life would have been very different. Without a mentor, guardian, or guide, you will use this book and the books of others, but ultimately it will be up to you to either continue or surrender. I would never consider a lazy person for a potential position within my program. Anyone who does not have the strength of discipline to have discovered this knowledge is half-dead already. I will not consider anyone who portrays the slightest degree of laziness or cowardice. My experience is that lazy people are scared to try. Their sensitive nature has made them incapable of withstanding the realities of their surroundings. They have surrendered. I would advise anyone who has surrendered to consider the fact that all of us have been pushed against the wall many times. Struggling is the nature of our existence, and so is being alone. Yes, this is harsh, but no harsher than the millions of lazy individuals who burden their parents for the rest of their lives, with their inadequate conduct and below standard behavior. I am not a Christian. I do not believe anyone deserves forgiveness or a second chance. A Warrior is always pragmatic about his choices. He uses simple logic with immediate results. On a combat patrol inside enemy territory, a leader would eliminate anyone who jeopardized or endangered his men. The Spartans went as far as discarding infants who were born deformed or sickly. It was not done with malice or evil intent, but for the protection and perpetuation of their society. Today, movies are made of their culture and they are considered heroes. During the Battle of Thermopylae, "The Hot Gates," a student of the Toltec discipline would have fought a guerrilla war, attacking the Persian's supply lines, not throw lives away in some foolish last stand. As a Warrior, I suggest letting another fool die for his country. You live for yourself. Let the wannabe heroes and medal winners die if they choose. I will live for me and my freedom, and continue on the path with heart. I speak from hindsight after serving in the United States Army for over 23 years.

Early Christian leaders have identified diligence as being the opposite of sloth. Of all the opposites provided, I would have to say that I agree with this one the most. The use of the word diligence, which is defined as constant and earnest effort to accomplish what is undertaken, assists new Seekers with attaining an understanding. However, this does not come close to describing the true ruthlessness and discipline of a Warrior. Years of fanatical dedication to this discipline is required to gain such an understanding. For this purpose, and for the sake of assisting new Seekers with comprehension, this example will suffice as an opposite. Wealth dictates which doors are opened and which are closed. Sloth is an equal opportunity success killer. As poor, but ambitious individuals, watch the parade of wealthy kids obtain what they cannot, it may appear as though trying is useless. Average people raise their children to believe that no matter what they do, things will always be the same. It is then no wonder so many choose crime instead of an education. Learning a trade or skill is valuable in any culture. Wealthy people may have further to fall before they hit rock-bottom, but they will eventually hit harder. Poor people have little room for indulgence and must quickly acquire discipline or die. Although there are no easy answers, the competition is not that tough. Warriors know that 96ers operate on less than fifty percent or their capacity. This is especially true for children of wealthy parents. These individuals have little or no discipline, have never faced adversity, and lack physical and spiritual courage. A Warrior, regardless of ethnic background, has learned to squash his self-importance, and knows it is not necessary to be first. He knows it's not always the fastest runner who wins the race. A Warrior knows that material possession is not a sign of quality or intelligence. Things never give a person value, just as a lack of them does not infer inferiority. Real intelligence can be better measured in how one makes decisions, as well as how much discipline one demonstrates while doing so. Our educational system is based on intellectual analysis, repeated dogma, and memorization. Good grades in class are not a sign of superiority or superior intelligence, but rather training and practice. Most people could do equally as well in class, if they'd received the same training and attention. To succeed in our educational system one must have staying power. One must have the willingness to endure and push through the challenges, distractions, and temptations of life. Wealth alone does not bring happiness or guarantee a long life. Without wisdom and a spiritual foundation, riches will always bring about destruction. On a darker side, laziness becomes a habit, which then becomes a pattern, which leads to a tragic ending. Anyone who desires the strength and wisdom of a Warrior must ask themselves whether they possess the fortitude to stay the course. Unbeknownst to 96ers, once an individual makes contact with power, there is no turning back. Power will not release or forget those who have challenged it. This is not mere dramatization, but an accurate description based on firsthand experience. I would advise most people to remain blissful in their ignorance. Knowledge, like wisdom, is accompanied by sadness and disillusionment. On this path, what you don't do, matters as much as how you spend your time. Everything in life, no matter how seemingly insignificant, matters. This is especially true for a Warrior seeking power. Those who surrender to sloth have failed to conquer their self-importance, and have overlooked the fact that death never rests. As lazy individuals die, they are riddled with regrets and remorse, knowing they have wasted their lives doing nothing. The happy drunk and local drug addict are perfect examples of average people. They've indulged in their weakness until it was all they knew, and now it is all they are. Warriors know there will never be enough time to do all the things they've wanted to do, and their time on this earth will be altogether too short. Although there are better ways to spend their lives, both the slothful and the Warrior will eventually die, making them equal. In the end, how you spend your life matters little, but everyone must decide for themselves.

Note to Reader

In addition to conventional grammatical use, italics are commonly used throughout this work to emphasize the distinction between a word's traditional description and its reference in terms of the Toltec discipline. Understanding this is of paramount significance to attaining comprehension of the concepts discussed and explained throughout this work. Please note that this is an independent publishing endeavor. I did not wish to subject myself to big publishing companies, who for profit would censor and restrict my work. This book is specifically written to assist Pathfinders, Seekers, and Warriors. As such, rather than conforming to industry standards, it has been designed in a workbook fashion. Line spacing has intentionally been made slightly larger, therefore providing readers with the option of keeping notes on any page. Additional space for note taking can be found at the back of the book. You may find errors in spelling, punctuation, grammar, formatting, and etc. I make no apology. Anyone concerned with such things in light of the awesomeness of the Toltec discipline, has many other problems which need addressing before they're ready to tackle sorcery.

The following are definitions of words and acronyms commonly used throughout this work. Please note that this is a basic list of basic descriptions, added for the benefit of the reader's comprehension. Complex concepts will not be expanded upon in this section, nor confined to such simplistic descriptions.

Pathfinder: A Pathfinder is an individual who is searching for the Warrior's path. They have become aware of the emptiness which their average existence has created in their lives. Although this inner void has led them on a search for a better way to live, they do not know what the freedom they desire will cost, or how to go about attaining it. Many Pathfinders are newly introduced to the Toltec discipline and have begun reading related books, searching for answers and a path to follow.

Seeker: A Seeker is an individual who is on the Warrior's path. However, they have not yet learned to silence their *internal dialogue*, *see*, or move energy. A Seeker's challenge is to become a Warrior via following the path they have found. This is done by living like a Warrior; deliberate application of the Toltec discipline on a daily basis. A Seeker must train himself to replace his average person's reactions to life's situations with a Warrior's response. Through deliberate, disciplined *focus* he will eventually learn to manipulate power, silence his *internal dialogue*, *see*, and move energy.

Warrior: A Seeker becomes a Warrior when his deliberate actions and responses are no longer a habit, but a part of who he is.

It is important to note that these words are used in an effort to explain complex and abstract information. There are no clear boundaries, as an individual's development is always in a continuous state of flux. Anyone can have a setback at any moment, just as anyone can touch the stars, if only for an instant.

96er: Another word for average person.

Four Percentor: One of the four percent of people who work to defeat their weaknesses.

Sorcery: The deliberate manipulation of awareness and deliberate implementation of discipline.

Tweak: S*hifting* the *assemblage point*, raising the ability to perceive. Influencing a person and/or situation via energy.

Average people, as well as Four Percentors, come in all shapes and sizes. Race, ethnicity, education, occupation, status, money, gender, age, and etc., does not matter. Behavior is all that matters. Warriors *see* everyone in terms of energy, and know that death makes all things equal. This makes the idea of any person believing their race grants them a level of superiority completely ridiculous. How can one biological creature be superior to another, if they are both going to die? In spite of this truth pseudoscience, racist government legislation, religious propaganda, and the ignorant masses have continuously perpetuated delusional ideals of ethnic superiority. I do not believe a description of someone's ethnicity should degrade them, nor should it compliment them. However, in the United States being called "White" is considered favorable in contrast to "Mexican," or "Black," and etc. My refusal to accept the inferior title assigned to me by those who demand I address them in a manner they see as superior, led to the impartial creation of a new method of categorization. Please note that this method is very general, and does not account for all the complexities associated with race and ethnicity. I simply refuse to endorse a system which unashamedly perpetuates delusional ideals of ethnic superiority.

DOEI [do-ee]: Descendant of European immigrant

NTOMA [nuh-toh-muh]: Native Tejano of Mexican ancestry

NCOMA [nuh-coh-muh]: Native Californian of Mexican ancestry

AMOAFA [uh-moh-fuh]: American of African ancestry

AMOASA [uh-moh-suh]: American of Asian ancestry

Texas escapee,
-don Jesus M. Ramirez

TOLTEC INSTITUTE
INTERNATIONAL INSTITUTE OF TOLTEC STUDIES

Toltec Institute was born via the determination of a band of Seekers of knowledge, united in their steadfast commitment to the discipline of the ancient Toltec Warrior. Comprised of members from various regions across the globe, they initially met in secret, both in person and via the advantages of contemporary technology. Their objectives were to discuss, understand, and develop strategies for implementing the discipline of a modern Toltec Warrior. Undermined by self-promoting, self-proclaimed spiritual leaders, gurus, and masters, these determined individuals struggled to find direction. This search continued until Toltec Institute members discovered *Sorcerer's Secrets, Book 1: Translated Secrets of Carlos Castaneda* by don Jesus M. Ramirez. This amazingly powerful book has swept away the competition with superior explanations of complex concepts, authentically translating secrets of ancient Toltec wisdom for modern application. Seekers of all levels and backgrounds can now benefit from following a previously nonexistent roadmap to spiritual freedom.

Toltec Institute was founded by its current president, don Roberto San Miguel, a student of many spiritual disciplines. Originally of México City, México, don Roberto now resides in London, England, and has written on many topics of interest to New Age enthusiasts. Although he has visited and lived in many areas known for their spiritual energy, such as Venezuela, South Africa, India, Pakistan, the deserts of México, and the American Southwest, he lives the life of a simple man. Following the discipline of the modern Toltec Warrior, don Roberto works unceasingly at defeating his weaknesses, and refuses to be photographed or have his image reproduced. In true Toltec fashion, don Roberto, like don Jesus, believes that to be a Warrior is the highest title or rank any man can aspire. As such he refuses to be called a master, guru, or leader, and rejects those who would claim such titles. He humbly considers himself a student, like any other, and continues to struggle to stay on the path of knowledge.

Of the hundreds of books that were reviewed, don Roberto, along with a dozen other Seekers, selected *Sorcerer's Secrets, Book 1: Translated Secrets of Carlos Castaneda* to be Toltec Institute's official manual. In exchange for permission of use, Toltec Institute has become acting administrator to don Jesus and his works. All letters, requests, questions, opinions, analysis, rebuttals, challenges, and reviews of the material within this highly controversial book can be sent to Toltec Institute via the email or physical address listed below. Direct contact with don Jesus or don Roberto is unavailable. All mailed material will be rerouted to the addressee. With the exception of information of an illegal or illicit nature, all material received will be kept confidential. All mailed material will become the property of Toltec Institute or the addressed recipient, and may be used as per our discretion. Replies are not guaranteed. Each letter is reviewed individually and independently of all others. Please note that due to the high volume of emails Toltec Institute receives, hard mailed letters to the physical address are given priority.

We welcome you to participate.

Toltec Institute Director,

-Roberto San Miguel

The Toltec Institute
PO Box 6552
San Jose, CA 95150

www.toltecinstitute.com
info@toltecinstitute.com

Notes

Notes

Notes

Notes

Notes

Notes

Notes

Notes

Notes

www.ingramcontent.com/pod-product-compliance
Lightning Source LLC
Chambersburg PA
CBHW022001160426
43197CB00007B/219